THE CIVIL WAR IN AMERICAN CULTURE

BAAS Paperbacks

Series Editors: Simon Newman, Sir Denis Brogan Chair in American Studies at the University of Glasgow; and Carol R. Smith, Senior Lecturer in English and American Studies at the University of Winchester.

Published in association with the British Association for American Studies, this exciting series has become an indispensable collection in American Studies. Each volume tackles an important area and is written by an accepted academic expert within the discipline. Books selected for the series are clearly written introductions designed to offer students definitive short surveys of key topics in the field.

The Civil War in American Culture

WILL KAUFMAN

EDINBURGH UNIVERSITY PRESS

© Will Kaufman, 2006

Edinburgh University Press Ltd
22 George Square, Edinburgh

Typeset in Fournier by
Koinonia, Manchester, and
printed and bound in Great Britain by
Antony Rowe Ltd, Chippenham, Wilts

A CIP Record for this book is available from the British Library

ISBN-10 0 7486 1935 6 (paperback)
ISBN-13 978 0 7486 1935 1 (paperback)

The right of Will Kaufman to be identified as author
of this work has been asserted in accordance with
the Copyright, Designs and Patents Act 1988.

A portion of Chapter 6 has appeared in the *Women's History Review*.

Will Kaufman is supported by

 Arts & Humanities
Research Council

The AHRC funds postgraduate training and research in the arts and
humanities, from archaeology and English literature to design and
dance. The quality and range of research supported not only provides
social and cultural benefits but also contributes to the economic success
of the UK. For further information on the AHRC,
please see our website: www.ahrc.ac.uk

Published with the support of the Edinburgh University
Scholarly Publishing Initiatives Fund

Contents

Figures

Acknowledgements

I owe a great debt of thanks to many people. For placing their confidence in this project in its embryonic stage, I am particularly indebted to Janet Beer, Dick Ellis, Alan Karras, Alasdair Kean, Heidi Slettedahl Macpherson and Helen Taylor.

I am equally grateful to those colleagues and friends who read my work, helped me to clarify my ideas and/or pointed me to valuable sources and resources: Bosse Blomqvist, Jude Davies, Diana Duvall, Jeanne-Marie Kenny, Stephen Kenny, Jan Lundgren, Clive Meachen, Alan Rice, Terry Rodenberg, Janice Wardle and Robert Yates.

To Joy Stephenson and the trustees of the Payne Fund for International Scholars at Central Missouri State University, I owe my thanks for the hospitality and funding that enabled me to conduct research at the university's invaluable James C. Kirkpatrick Library.

Mike Bussey, J. D. Spencer, Paul and Jill Hilditch and other members of the 43rd North Carolina Infantry invited me into the world of Civil War re-enactment on a fine but rainy summer's day in Ackworth, Yorkshire. They and their colleagues in the American Civil War Society (UK) shared their campfires, hardtack and coffee with me as they answered all my questions with patience and good will.

To a great American songwriter and performer, John McCutcheon, I am grateful for permission to reproduce the words of his song, 'The Abraham Lincoln Brigade', with royalty fees generously waived. All John asks in return is that I direct interested readers to his website, where they can learn about the contexts of his songs and his activities in pursuit of global peace and justice. I happily do this: John's website is, appropriately, www.folkmusic.com.

To a great American film-maker, Kevin Willmott, I am grateful for the precious trust of an advance screening copy of the film, *CSA: The Confederate States of America*. I can think of no other film that has explored the cultural legacy of the Civil War with such incisiveness. I must also thank the film's director of photography, Matt Jacobson, for contributing his photograph of Mr Willmott.

Once again, Jeanne-Marie Kenny, a fine Southern photographer, was well placed to capture a store of provocative images reflecting the public debate over the display of the Confederate battle flag, and I am most grateful to her for sharing them with me. Derek Drummond not only provided me with excellent photographs but was also responsible for the downloading, uploading, scanning, collation and what-all-else that enabled the illustrations to appear in this book – many thanks, Derek!

Nicky Ramsey, the commissioning editor at Edinburgh University Press, was always there to respond graciously to an intensifying barrage of questions and requests from me. My greatest thanks go to Carol Smith and Simon Newman, editors of the BAAS Paperbacks Series, who encouraged me to develop the project and offered considerable moral support through the writing and rewriting stages. Carol's trenchant review of the manuscript not only made for a much better book, but also marked a superhuman effort on her part, as my submission coincided exactly with the birth of her beautiful daughter, Rosa.

My year's sabbatical was willingly facilitated by my colleagues in the Department of Humanities at the University of Central Lancashire, and was partly funded through a generous Research Leave Grant from the Arts and Humanities Research Council (AHRC). Without the AHRC, a major funding source for research and postgraduate training in the arts and humanities, British scholarship in these areas could not thrive, and this book could not have been written. The AHRC website is www.ahrc.ac.uk.

Finally, to my family – my wife, Sarah, and our sons, Reuben and Theo: this book is dedicated with love to you. I can't promise that I'll never mention the words 'deadline' and 'Civil War' again, but I owe you a break.

Introduction

I take the risk of introducing this study by admitting that at the age of ten years old I wrote my first and only novel, a story about a werewolf who wins the American Civil War for the Union. By day he is a common Federal soldier. By night, when the moon is full, he charges through the Confederate positions and tears them to shreds. Fortunately the manuscript was lost long ago, but since then I have had occasion to reflect upon the impulses that led to such a bizarre fusion of history and cultural expression (such as it was) – in this case, Civil War history with popular horror.

Other, more accomplished, writers have acted on a similar impulse: Harry Turtledove's 1992 sci-fi novel, *The Guns of the South*, has a band of time-travelling Afrikaners from the year 2013, equipped with AK-47s, winning the Civil War for Robert E. Lee. Abraham Lincoln has been beamed aboard the starship *Enterprise* and into the company of Marilyn Monroe and the Simpsons, while Ann McMillan's Civil War mysteries – to date, *Dead March* (1998), *Angel Trumpet* (1999), *Civil Blood* (2001) and *Chickahominy Fever* (2003) – present the suspenseful dramas of a medical sleuth team who owe as much to television's *E.R.* and *Quincy, M.E.* as to Sherlock Holmes and Dr Watson. The Civil War dovetails with Homeric epic and romance in Charles Frazier's *Cold Mountain* (1997) and Anthony Minghella's film of the novel (2003), while, in examples too numerous to list, the boundary between the genres of the war film and the western is often imperceptible when it comes to the Civil War.

The struggle between the Blue and the Gray continues to be played out in popular monthly magazines and on computers and PlayStations both in and outside of the United States. It has travelled around the globe and has been understood and accepted as an event of great cultural significance, whether in film, literature or battlefield re-enactment. The cultural legacies of the Civil War have been expressed in debates over women's sphere of action, the public display of the Confederate flag, the iconography of Southern rock and country music and the design of products, labels and advertising. Its central characters have been appropriated, fetishised and demonised, its two-dimensional images recycled in 3-D and the results of its battles gleefully overturned in a host of alternative scenarios. The Civil War is moveable property across the boundaries of time, space, cultural form and genre.

As a cultural property, the Civil War is also jealously guarded, and for understandable reasons: as Stuart Hall reminds us, cultural practices are the activities 'through which men and women make history' (Hall, 1980: 63) – implicitly, their own versions of history – while, in James Clifford's words, 'culture' is always 'contested, temporal and emergent' (Clifford and Marcus, 1986: 19). One recent example of the implied high stakes in these two definitions of culture is the well-publicised lawsuit in 2001 against the Houghton Mifflin Company by the estate of Margaret Mitchell, which failed to block the publication of Alice Randall's *The Wind Done Gone* (2001), a parody that re-writes *Gone with the Wind* from the perspective of Scarlett O'Hara's mulatto half-sister. A letter in support of Randall by twenty eminent writers and scholars argues her case on the grounds of cultural ownership that goes well beyond the legal concerns of literary copyright:

> The discussion of the painful legacy of slavery is ongoing among American citizens across the nation. Because of the extraordinary popularity of *Gone with the Wind* and its unique mythic status, Mitchell's novel has become a prime source of knowledge about plantation life for much of mainstream America. Now is the time for the American public to hear another perspective on this legend (Houghton Mifflin, 2004: n. p.).

The call for 'another perspective' on the Civil War and its associated issues has been ongoing. This book focuses on various ways in which that call has been answered in modern and contemporary culture. Moreover, it responds to the call by foregrounding race and openly challenging those who deny the centrality of race and slavery in the Civil War and in the numerous cultural expressions and practices it has spawned.

While this is predominantly a book about the Civil War *since* the Civil War, it recognises that, in cultural as well as historical terms, that war was not a spontaneous event. Consequently, the first chapter,

'Antebellum Groundwork', explores the role of antebellum culture in the developing sectional crisis that exploded into full-blown war in 1861. It sets out to establish the relation between the cultural landscapes of the North and South and the politics of sectionalism and race by exploring the readership and usage of antebellum fiction, travel narratives, oratory and journalism. It then focuses on the complex cultural form of blackface minstrelsy and its racial caricatures, as well as the contestation of this act of white appropriation by African-Americans, particularly through journalism and the slave narrative. The concluding discussion assesses the impact of *Uncle Tom's Cabin* upon popular culture and the sectional divide.

Chapter 2, 'Reunion and Resistance', turns to the immediate aftermath of the Confederate defeat, when nostalgia for the Old South and the plantation order characterised not only the Uncle Remus tales of Joel Chandler Harris and their later re-workings by Walt Disney in *Song of the South* (1946), but also the more vicious expressions of Thomas Dixon's novels (1902–07), D. W. Griffith's *The Birth of a Nation* (1915) and Mitchell's *Gone with the Wind* (1936). All of these texts are seen as attempts to demonise the prospect of black empowerment brought about through Reconstruction. The manifesto of the Nashville Agrarians is then considered as an intellectualised expression of Old South nostalgia in the 1930s.

Chapter 3, 'Martyrdom and Memory', explores the construction of the Civil War's martyr figures as one of the earliest and most far-reaching cultural tasks for a host of contesting voices from across the sectional and racial divides. Two case studies – John Brown from the North and Stonewall Jackson from the South – are used to interrogate the prodigious cultural energy that has been put towards both the elevation and the deflation of Civil War martyrs. The representations of John Brown – whether though the addresses of Thoreau, the poetry of Melville, Benét and others, the films of Michael Curtiz and Paul Bogart, or the fiction of George MacDonald Fraser and Russell Banks – will be shown to raise important questions over the uses and abuses of martyrdom as a cultural trope. In the case of Stonewall Jackson, the discussion centres on the cultural preparations for martyrdom that began in his lifetime and were either utilised or contested after his death. Northern and Southern poetic treatments of Jackson, biography, public memorial and film are all scrutinised with particular regard to the racial implications of any identification with the man and his cause.

The Civil War's greatest martyr figure and the cultural uses to which he has been put is the subject of Chapter 4, 'Abe Lincoln's Mixed Reviews'. Lincoln's use as a parodic figure in film and television is considered as a cultural expression in keeping with the tremendous tug-of-war over his reputation that has persisted between his defenders and detractors. His use in political culture – introduced in the context of the September 11th attacks and the second Iraq war – is explored further with reference to the years of the New Deal and the Second World War through the biographies of Carl Sandburg, the drama and film of Robert E. Sherwood and John Ford, and the music of Aaron Copland. Finally, the assessment of Lincoln as 'the white man's president', voiced by Frederick Douglass in an 1876 elegy, launches an exploration of the critique carried on by contemporary black cultural producers such as the novelist Ishmael Reed, the film-maker Kevin Willmott and the playwright Suzan-Lori Parks.

The contemporary vindication of the South's 'Lost Cause' is the subject of Chapter 5, 'Rebels, Inc.', which explores Confederate apologia as a white supremacist enterprise of corporate scale and sophistication, impacting upon cyberspace, the musical arena, civic space and the marketplace. From long-established organisations such as the Sons of Confederate Veterans and the United Daughters of the Confederacy to the recently founded League of the South, the call for white Confederate pride finds its parallel expression in the words and imagery of Southern music, notably Southern rock and country. The ongoing crisis over the display of the Confederate flag that reached a peak in the late 1990s and early 2000s in Georgia and South Carolina is a further manifestation of this momentous attempt to ward off the spectre of white Southern defeat. All these expressions are examined along with their commercial counterpart, the Confederate and rebel imagery in merchandising that has persisted since the late nineteenth century – suggesting in the aggregate that, in the minds of many, the Civil War is not yet over.

Chapter 6, 'The Regendered Civil War', views the war as a site of both progressive and reactionary cultural input in terms of gender equity and women's ownership of public history. In considering women's writing as a response to the antebellum 'cult of true womanhood', the chapter explores the Civil War diary of Eliza Wetherby Otis and the oratory of Sojourner Truth in conversation with Harriet Wilson's *Our Nig* (1859) and Harriet Jacobs's *Incidents in the Life of a Slave Girl* (1861). These and other texts all work towards destabilising received definitions of womanhood in both the North and the South. Thus, the martial connotations of Louisa May Alcott's *Little Women* (1868) are echoed in the purported 'diary' of Mary Chesnut (1905) and Elizabeth Keckley's memoir, *Behind the Scenes, Or Thirty Years a Slave and Four Years in the White House* (1868). The narratives of the Civil War's distaff soldiers – women in male disguise – are then examined, with particular focus on Sarah Emma Edmonds (Union) and Loreta Velazquez (Confederate). Such challenges to patriarchy on the page are mirrored in the successful legal challenge brought by the historian Lauren Cook Burgess against the Antietam Battlefield Park in 1993 following her discovery in male disguise and her unlawful expulsion from a battle re-enactment.

The subject of Civil War re-enactment is only one area further explored in Chapter 7, 'The Virtual Civil War', which begins with an analysis of the war's visual images, in particular the photographic manipulations – or 'stagecraft', as Alan Trachtenberg calls it – of Mathew Brady and his associates. The chapter charts an apparent progression along the road from visual to virtual participation in the Civil War, dwelling on such milestones as the 'illusion of depth' created by the stereopticon and the problems of historical empathy raised by Ken Burns's documentary series, *The Civil War* (1990). The discussion concludes with an interrogation of the vicarious possibilities for 'total immersion' offered by Civil War computer games and the re-enactment culture.

In Chapter 8, 'The Transnational Civil War', the journalism of Karl Marx is explored as the first of three case studies establishing the war as an event of great transnational significance. The Irish-American connection to the war, particularly with regard to race relations, is examined through attention to Martin Scorcese's *Gangs of New York* (2002) and the song-writing of Steve Earle, which re-works the fictional representations of Michael Shaara's novel, *The Killer Angels* (1974). Finally, the chapter explores overtones of the American Civil War in cultural representations of the Spanish Civil War and the 'Lost Cause' of the Abraham Lincoln Brigade, particularly in the writings of John Dos Passos, Ernest Hemingway, Langston Hughes and Martha Gellhorn.

The concluding chapter – 'History is My Starting Point' – considers the problems surrounding the attempt to seize hold of Civil War history through connecting with its living associates, as witnessed in the celebrity of the last surviving widows of Civil War veterans and slaves as late as 2004. Central to the discussion are Allan Gurganus's novel, *Oldest*

Living Confederate Widow Tells All (1989) and Ernest J. Gaines's *The Autobiography of Miss Jane Pittman* (1971), both of which elaborate upon problems of historical reliability associated with the WPA slave narratives collected in the 1930s. The 'What If?' industry spawned by Southern defeat is examined through the analysis of MacKinlay Kantor's *If the South Had Won the Civil War* (1960), Turtledove's *The Guns of the South* (1992), various speculations about Stonewall Jackson's survival, and the major African-American response to date, Kevin Willmott's faux documentary, *CSA: The Confederate States of America* (2003). Southern defeat as a route to catharsis and personal healing is considered in terms of Barry Hannah's fiction – *Airships* (1978) and *Ray* (1980) – and Ross McElwee's film, *Sherman's March* (1991), both of which, in conjunction with Gurganus's novel, explore the meanings of the word, 'Appomattox'.

That word is considered by many to signify the end of the Civil War. However, as this book sets out to demonstrate, in terms of American culture, 'Appomattox' is hardly the final word. If anything, it marks the beginning of an immensely productive cultural history. Consequently, any scholar hoping to explore the cultural representations of the Civil War must initially be faced with massive territory to cover, and must arrive at a workable process of organisation, selection and exclusion. More importantly, any critical investigation should strive towards a new positioning and encourage its readers to do the same. Thus, some may query (for example) the near-absence of William Faulkner's fiction in this study, the complete absence of Stephen Crane's *The Red Badge of Courage* and minimal attention to the film of *Gone with the Wind*. However, with the realisation that such examples have been amply covered elsewhere and no doubt shall continue to attract critical examination, I have taken the risk of excluding them to devote more space to sources and examples that have as yet received little attention. I must also acknowledge the great debt I owe to the preceding work of David Blight, Jim Cullen, Stephen Cushman, Tony Horwitz and Elizabeth Young, all of whom have explored the culture of the Civil War with an insightfulness that I could only hope to approach.

CHAPTER I

Antebellum Groundwork

The role of culture in war can, of course, be overemphasised. Mark Twain, in *Life on the Mississippi* (1883), satirically blamed the romantic novelist, Sir Walter Scott, who 'had so large a hand in making Southern character, as it existed before the war, that he is in great measure responsible for the war' (Twain, 1883: 469). Scott's novels, Twain argued, engendered and perpetuated a cultural regime in the antebellum South characterised by corrupt, 'jejune' codes of romance, religion, chivalry, patriarchy and class distinction – all of which condemned the white South to start, fight and lose the American Civil War. As Peter Stoneley warns, 'Twain overstates his case with his stock-in-trade bravura diatribe' (Stoneley, 2004: 395).

However, Twain's point is that culture is not innocent, and is politically potent. Cultural texts, as the representations of a group, exert immense pressure on the perception of that group, both by its own members and by others. Through cultural texts, the American South – as Richard Gray explains – 'has always represented itself historically as different, deviant, and (usually) in danger; and it has been marked, for good or ill, by its own sense, at any given time, of what it was different and deviating *from* and what it was in danger of' (Gray, 2004: 19). Gray emphasises the South's own part in perpetuating the sense of its difference from the rest of the United States. This assertion of Southern difference is the primary subject of this chapter, for it is necessary to examine the ways in which antebellum culture sought to assert Southern difference in terms of social and racial identity, gender, class, labour practices and what the South's white defenders habitually called its 'way of life'. However, it must be remembered that Northern cultural practice also contributed to this sense of difference. A range of cultural institutions, Northern and Southern, played their part in the antebellum sectional divide, in particular the print sector (novels, travel literature and political journalism) and white popular culture (music and the minstrel stage). The racial distinction here is important, for white dominance of literary and popular culture led black cultural practitioners, both Southern and Northern, to engage vigorously across all cultural arenas to combat the racial defamation that characterised so much of antebellum culture. Beginning with literature, we turn first to one of the most popular fictional genres: the plantation novel.

The Plantation Cult

Walter Scott was not responsible for the American Civil War, but his antebellum popularity is instructive. We can only assume that, since Scott's writings were popular across both the North and South, what matter are the ways in which antebellum culture ensured that his romanticised feudal values would be more peculiarly identified with the South than with the North. In an early study of popular American literary taste, James D. Hart notes that Southern audiences were particularly devoted to dramatic adaptations of Scott's novels and longer poems (Hart, 1963: 75). James Chandler points to earlier work identifying antebellum trends in naming Southern babies after Scott's characters, modelling Southern state houses on the architecture described in his romances, and adopting his diction in Southern writing and speech (Chandler, 1994: 245).

Scott's reception, at least in part, grew out of a larger cultural movement bound up in the need to justify the South's peculiar labour practices – dominated by chattel slavery – and the perpetuation of its plantation economy. As Andrew Hook notes, 'the South did not invent itself in its final form until the 1830s, when the slavery issue began to dominate the American political stage' (Hook, 2004: 421). However, the cultural origins of this project – the invention of the South – pre-date both Walter Scott and the 1830s, marking the early consolidation of separate regional identities for North and South. The 'invented' South was conjured up early in the 'Utopian longings' of European colonisers who in the sixteenth and seventeenth centuries presented the seaboard South – Virginia and the Carolinas – as 'Edenic, a garden, a virgin land' (Roberts, 1996: 90). Gray points to the colonial pamphleteers who, in the service of the London Virginia Company, effectively 'wrote the South' into existence in order to attract investors and colonisers to a cross between Eden and Arcadia (Gray, 1997: 6). Further North, the Plymouth Colony and, later, Massachusetts Bay had their pamphleteers, too. However, they could never invoke the pastoral imagery of the subtropical Virginia climate. If anything, their largely Puritan convictions ensured a more austere and proto-urban version of the New World. Massachusetts, as John Winthrop wrote in his *Model of Christian Charity* (1630), was not a garden (Edenic or otherwise), but rather a city – 'a City upon a Hill' – more devoted to the planting of a rocky-faced Christ than tobacco or cotton. William Taylor observes how the early impression of a 'divided culture' between the two regions took root. The one was characterised by Northern, Anglo-Saxon Roundheads, and the other by Southern, Norman Cavaliers. The one was 'democratic' and 'commercial' while the other was 'aristocratic' and 'agrarian'. These perceived differences flourished in spite of the fact that, topography and climate notwithstanding, 'essential similarity rather than ... divergence' marked the historical development of North and South together (Taylor, 1963: 15–16).

By the mid-eighteenth century, Virginia planters such as Thomas Jefferson and John Taylor had succeeded in constructing a code out of agriculture and land-owning that explicitly raised the moral worth of a yeoman farmer or planter over that of a city dweller, thus drawing 'primitive portraits of the Southerner and Yankee' (Gray, 1997: 27). By the 1830s, a variety of Southern social factors combined to 'foster the trappings' of a plantation cult relying upon 'climate, seasonal idleness, isolation, traces of the old frontier violence, [and] black men who gave their owners such a flattering sense of power and the most abject white man someone to look down on' (Stewart, 1965: 99).

Although the influence of the plantation cult was all out of keeping with the small number of planters who 'set the tone of Southern society' (Ibid.: 98–9), it was a cultural project with great implications, not least for the women of the South, both white and black. As Taylor argues, the 'Southern gentleman' – the planter who must appear, unlike the Northern capitalist, 'aloof from money-making' – was at pains to assert his 'manhood': 'The Southern answer to this question lay in the cult of chivalry – in having the Cavalier kneel down before the altar of femininity and familial benevolence' (Taylor, 1963: 148). However, such a cult was, in reality, hardly benevolent: 'Any tendency on the part of any of the members of the [plantation] system to assert themselves against the master threatened the whole, and therefore slavery itself. It was no accident that the most articulate spokesmen for slavery were also eloquent exponents of the subordinate role of women' (Scott, 1970: 17). Anne Firor Scott notes, in particular, the patriarchal rhetoric of the apologist for both chivalry and slavery, George Fitzhugh of Virginia. Of the Southern lady operating within the strictures of the chivalric code, Fitzhugh says, 'So long as she is nervous, fickle, capricious, delicate, diffident and dependent, man will worship and adore her.' If she transgresses, however, her fate is in fact the same as any slave's: 'The right to protection involves the obligation to obey ... If she be obedient she stands little danger of maltreatment' (quoted in Ibid.: 17). This is clearly a sinister warning.

Such intimations of violence lay far beneath the surface of the popular 'plantation novels' that appeared from the pens of Southern writers engaged in the mobilisation of popular culture 'to affirm the Southern way of life in general and the proslavery point of view in particular' (Cullen, 1995: 15). With Walter Scott's romances as the habitual models, such novels as George Tucker's *The Valley of the Shenandoah* (1824), John Pendleton Kennedy's *Swallow Barn* (1832), William Alexander Caruthers's *The Kentuckian in New York* (1834) and *The Cavaliers of Virginia* (1835), and Nathaniel Beverley Tucker's *George Balcombe* and *The Partisan Leader* (both 1836) perpetuated views of plantation life that, with increasing stridency, defended Southern honour and tradition against all Northern abolitionist attacks, both real and imagined. Within their pages, slaves are happy and loyal to their owners, and women, far from being tyrannised, grow from sheltered ladies into powerful matriarchs – mistresses who, with their wise judgements and watchful eyes, become both the spiritual and practical centre of the plantation system.

It is important to acknowledge that Northern writers did much to consolidate these regional literary types and patterns. James Fenimore Cooper's first major novel, *The Spy* (1821), and James Kirke Paulding's *Westward Ho!* (1832) and *The Puritan and His Daughter* (1849) consolidate the stereotypes of Yankee and planter. Nor is all such sectional writing wholly antagonistic. However, even a hint of abolitionist criticism in Northern novels such as Sarah Josepha Hale's *Northwood, Or, Life North and South* (1827) could provoke a brand of Southern invective that increased as the political and territorial rivalries between the Slave States and Free States intensified towards the mid-century. By then, according to Hook, 'intolerance of criticism' had become 'the most striking feature of the cultural life of the Old South' (Hook, 2004: 421). Consequently, by 1856, as he charged Northerners for the impending 'destruction of this once Grand Confederacy', the adoptive Mississippi novelist, William Gilmore Simms, set aside the chivalrous models of Walter Scott for more incendiary, nakedly sectional rhetoric during readings across the North (Simms quoted in Aaron, 1973: 230).

Thus, a host of antebellum writers must share the bulk of the responsibility for perpetuating the impression of a divided culture – not only novelists and pamphleteers, but journalists and travel writers as well; not only Northerners or Southerners, but also Europeans. As Helen Taylor observes, beginning with the earliest visitors to the nineteenth-century South, whether William Cullen Bryant and Walt Whitman from the North, or Frances Trollope and William Thackeray from Britain, perceiving and describing the 'difference' of the South required 'different kinds of perception and judgment than those in the rest of the United States' (Taylor, 2001: 10). However, it was not only travellers to the South who perpetuated the impressions of difference. Visitors to the North, whether from the South or from Europe, also contributed to the cultural divide, often based on highly selective experiences. Hence the influential descriptions by Frances Trollope in *Domestic Manners of the Americans* (1832) – applauded in the South and angrily denied in the North – of New Englanders as 'sly, grinding, selfish, and tricking' (Trollope, 1949: 302). Trollope's strategy of putting such damning impressions into the mouths of boasting New Englanders themselves no doubt helped to enhance their plausibility among Southern readers, and helped to perpetuate a stereotype that increased the sense of sectional difference.

When antebellum Southerners themselves travelled northwards, their experiences were just as likely to be selective. Bruce Collins notes that 'the vast majority of Southerners who travelled to the North visited one or more of the three great cities – New York, Philadelphia and Boston – or one of a small number of spa resorts' (Collins, 1981: 28). With little experience of the Northern pastoral landscape, Southern observers drew crude urban stereotypes based on Northern profiteering and industrialism, with no acknowledgment of the bustling activity in Southern cities and factories. Thus, as the sectional divide intensified in the mid-nineteenth century, the South Carolina pastoralist William J. Grayson penned one of the most saccharine paeans to plantation slavery, 'The Hireling and the Slave' (1856), elevating the lot of the slave over that of a Northern factory 'hireling', and mendaciously claiming that in the South 'no city discords break the silence' (Grayson, 1907: 56).

Still, Grayson was right in asserting the one undeniable factor in the mid-nineteenth century that, for the most part, distinguished the North from the South, in spite of all other similarities: the existence of chattel slavery. In actuality, this distinction was relatively recent: 'By 1800, some 36,505 Northern Negroes still remained in bondage, most of them in New York and New Jersey' (Litwack, 1961: 3). Officially, abolition did not reach Abraham Lincoln's Illinois until 1818, and New York until 1827. By mid-century, the Northern states were the centre of the abolitionist movement, with their own recent slaveholding history almost forgotten by all except the Southerners now alone in the critical spotlight.

Thus, from this point until the outbreak of the Civil War, no sector of the reading public was spared from engaging with slavery and abolition. Avery Craven describes the plethora of abolitionist hymn books pouring out of Boston and New York, along with farmer's almanacs padded with 'abolitionist propaganda' (Craven, 1957: 145). In one year alone (1837–38) the American Anti-Slavery Society churned out '7,877 bound volumes, 47,256 tracts and pamphlets, 4,100 circulars, and 10,490 prints. Its quarterly *Anti-Slavery Magazine* had an annual circulation of 9,000; the *Slave's Friend*, for children, had 131,050; the monthly *Human Rights*, 189,400, and the weekly *Emancipator*, 217,000' (Ibid.: 145). The Northern newspaper sector was at the forefront of the slavery/abolition debate, led by William Lloyd Garrison's Boston abolitionist banner, *The Liberator*, which threw down the gauntlet on New Year's Day, 1831: '*I do not wish to think or speak or write with moderation*... I am in earnest – I will not equivocate – I will not excuse – I will not retreat a single inch, AND I WILL BE HEARD' (reprinted in Garrison, 1885: 225). Daily and weekly broadsheets such as Horace Greeley's *New York Tribune* (launched 1841) habitually editorialised on the atrocities of slavery, their articles picked up and reprinted in Southern papers that scornfully denied the charges. Major Northern newspapers throughout the ante-bellum period sent their correspondents below the Mason–Dixon line to describe the poisonous impact of slavery on the Southern economy. Some of their writings reappeared as bound volumes, such as Frederick Law Olmsted's letters for the *New York Times*, collected as *A Journey in the Seaboard Slave States* (1856). Greeley's *Tribune* also sent reporters to describe 'The Southerners at Home', while the Cincinnati *Gazette* regularly printed its 'Letters from the South'. In all of these, as Eric Foner notes, the argument and the burden of evidence 'was always the same – the southern economy was backward and stagnant, and slavery was to blame' (Foner, 1970: 40–1).

Southern newspapers doggedly fought back against the abolitionist diatribes with visceral and elaborate defences of slavery on economic, religious, moral and ethnographic grounds. Aware that American publishing was both economically and editorially dominated by Boston and New York, Southern entrepreneurs launched such periodicals as *The Southern Literary Messenger* (1834–64) and *The Southern Review* (1828–32) to carry the defence of slavery and Southern difference to the world. Within their pages, naturalists and pseudo-scientists such as Richard Colfax, J. J. Flournoy and the notorious Dr Josiah Nott propounded theories of innate African inferiority and – as Nott argued in particular – the separate species of whites and blacks. The process of antagonistic cross-fertilisation only succeeded in raising sectional tempers, as, for instance, through *The New York Tribune*'s reprinting of an editorial from Georgia's *Muscogee Herald* in 1856: 'Free Society! we sicken at the name. What is it but a conglomeration of greasy mechanics, filthy operatives, small-fisted farmers, and moon-struck theorists ... hardly fit for association with a Southern gentleman's body servant' (quoted in McPherson, 1988: 197). Likewise was the oratory of abolitionists and Southern 'fire-eaters' recorded, printed and distributed both ways across the Mason–Dixon line. Southern slaveholders saw themselves described as 'mad bulls' or 'a knot of snakes' by both white and black Northerners who, on the eve of the Civil War, could not set foot in the South with their safety assured (Smith, 2001: 174). Northern readers, for their part, could read the Alabama congressman William Lowndes Yancey's equation of geographical and moral difference in which Northerners from 'the region of frost' were 'cool, calculating, enterprising, selfish, and grasping', while Southerners – 'ever smiling' in the warmth of the sun – were 'ardent, brave and magnanimous, more disposed to give than to accumulate, to enjoy ease rather than to labor' (Yancey quoted in Taylor, 1963: 7). The print culture thus played a central role in the perpetuation of sectional difference, but it was not alone in exacerbating either the sectional or the racial divides that ran through the American cultural landscape before the Civil War.

'Blacking Up'

Antebellum culture was profoundly influenced by popular public entertainments, particularly the stage and music. Consequently, one of the most provocative contributors to the cultural landscape was the practice of blackface minstrelsy, which after 1830 became the country's

Figure 1 *Plantation Melodies*, minstrel song sheet, c. 1847 (Library of Congress, Prints and Photographs Division, LC-USZ62-109812).

most popular form of entertainment. Put succinctly by Eric Lott, it was 'an established nineteenth-century theatrical practice, principally of the urban North, in which white men caricatured blacks for sport and profit' (Lott, 1993: 3). African-Americans, as an entire group, were thus publicly appropriated by Northern whites who were 'blacked up' to mimic them on the stage. This is the first of many ironies surrounding this degrading practice of theatrical caricature: although it is over-whelmingly characterised by sentimental scenes of 'happy darkies' on the old plantation, blackface minstrelsy grew primarily out of a Northern fixation on both the Southern plantation culture and the bodily presence of the African-American. As Jim Cullen argues, minstrelsy marked a 'political coalition' between aristocratic Southern agrarians – slave-holders – and Northern urban workers who 'shared an interest in white supremacy' (Cullen, 1995: 15).

The minstrel show was part of a broader theatrical tradition that reflected the sectional, racial and class tensions of the antebellum period, and was dominated by a handful of influential figures – nearly all of them white composers and performers – whose names remain staples in American dramatic and musical history, spawning generations of imitators in the United States and Europe. Of the first-generation minstrel men, the figure whose popularity outpaced all others was the acknow-ledged father of American minstrelsy, Thomas Dartmouth 'Daddy' Rice, also called 'Jim Crow Rice'. Rice, a white New Yorker, gained both Northern and Southern acclaim for his 'darky act' in the early 1830s, even as the terror from the Nat Turner and Denmark Vesey slave rebellions was still fresh amongst whites of both regions. Rice brought to life a singing and dancing caricature of an old crippled slave, Jim Crow, whose name inspired the segregation practices of the post-war South, and who, for the delight of a public engulfed daily in the heated rhetoric of abolition and slavery, capered about the stage, singing 'Weel about and turn about and do jis so, / Eb'ry time I weel about I jump Jim Crow' (Anon., 1882: 209). Other white Northern progenitors of the minstrel show included Daniel Decatur Emmett, who claimed the contested authorship of 'Dixie' (see Sacks, 1993) and who first appeared in 1843 with his 'Virginia Minstrels', otherwise known as the 'Ethiopian Deline-ators'. A name such as the latter was an arch reference to a minstrel troupe's fundamental mission of not only re-drawing the physiognomy but also denying the sexuality of the African-American male and, through cross-dressing, the female. This white cultural project asserted itself in a period when the fear of miscegenation fuelled much pro-slavery rhetoric in the South and racially separatist rhetoric in the North.

Other conventions furthered minstrelsy's dehumanising mission. The 'Christie Minstrels', an all-white troupe named after their leader, Edwin P. Christie, formalised two of the most notoriously demeaning carica-tures of the minstrel tradition: the cross-bantering tambourine player, 'Mr Tambo', and his counterpart, the castanet-playing 'Mr Bones'. Their clever punning and word-play did not necessarily amount to racial defamation, but their appearance certainly did, with their artificial colouring of burnt cork, their rolling eyes and other physical exagger-ations, as instructed in a contemporary stage manual: 'Apply a broad streak of carmine to the lips, carrying it well beyond the corners of the mouth ... Put on the wig, wipe the palms of the hands clean, and the makeup is completed' (quoted in Townsend, 1996: 124).

A further important feature in the minstrel tradition was the senti-mentalising of the slave's daily life in the plantation South, an approach dominated by two of minstrelsy's most important contributors, the composers William Shakespeare Hays and – at the pinnacle of American popularity – Stephen Collins Foster. Both of these white Northerners evinced a fascination for the slave cabin that did much to anchor the image of the 'happy darky' in American popular culture, springing from minstrelsy to infect literature and film well into the twentieth century. William C. Malone's back-handed compliment – 'Foster's conception of the South represented a victory of the imagination because he had little firsthand acquaintance with the region' – could be applied to the great stock of Northern minstrel men, most of whom appear to have been Pennsylvanians and New Yorkers (Malone, 1979: 19–20). Fusing race, slavery and an imagined Southern topography with the cult of sentimentality that characterised much of Victorian American literature and parlour song, composers like Hays (with his 'Little Old Log Cabin in the Lane'), James Bland (a black Northerner responsible for 'Carry Me Back to Old Virginny') and Foster ('My Old Kentucky Home'/'Old Folks at Home') anchored the presumably freed American slave in a treacle of nostalgia for life on the old plantation, where the master was always kind and where there was more play than work. Hence the lines of Foster's 'Away Down South', collected in his *Songs of the Sable Harmonists* (1848):

We'll put for de souf – Ah! dat's the place,
For the steeple chase and de bully hoss race –
Poker, brag, eucher, seven up and loo,
Den chime in Niggas, won't you come along too.
    (*chorus*)
No use talken when de Nigga wants to go,
Whar de corn-top blossom and de canebrake grow
                    (Foster, 1848: 2–3).

Not surprisingly, the period from 1846 to 1854 – in Lott's words, 'the moment of minstrelsy's greatest popularity' – saw some of the most bitter political crises in advance of the Civil War: 'labor struggles in New York and other major cities, the Wilmot Proviso debates over the extension of slavery, the Seneca Falls women's rights convention, the Astor Place theatre riot, the Fugitive Slave Law and its aftermath, the Kansas-Nebraska Act' (Lott, 1993: 9). The concurrent minstrel vogue was 'no accident', according to Robert Toll:

> Precisely because people could always just laugh off the performance, because viewers did not have to take the show seriously, minstrelsy served as a 'safe' vehicle through which its primarily Northern, urban audiences could work out their feelings about even their most sensitive and volatile issues (Toll, 1974: 65).

Toll is correct in his assessment of minstrelsy as a comedic safety valve. However, it is debatable whether minstrelsy effected a 'working out' of white preoccupations with blackness rather than a repression of them (just as the humanity of the caricatured African-Americans was itself repressed through the minstrel conventions). After all, although a small minority of black artists, such as the popular Henry Lane (under the name of 'Master Juba'), did perform on the minstrel stage and took to challenging white caricaturists at their own game, the mass of minstrels were white men engaged in 'blacking up'. Confronted with 'this wilful stylization and modification of the natural face and hands', as the African-American author Ralph Ellison described it, a white audience could indeed enjoy 'the fascination of blackness', but not unless it repressed the 'awareness of its moral identification with its own acts and with the human ambiguities pushed behind the mask' (Ellison, 1967: 49). While Ellison, for one, claimed that the white identity of the performer was not important – what mattered was the dehumanising impact of the caricature itself – the humour scholar Constance Rourke believed that the performer's white identity was crucial, since a white masked as a black masked as an outlandish buffoon furthered the distance between the audience and the human subject so grossly caricatured. As part of a 'highly conscious self-projection', this double mask acted as a mitigating front because it suggested that an entire enslaved race might actually be as impotent as a clownish white man with burnt cork on his face (Rourke, 1931: 87).

For this reason, Frederick Douglass was the most scathing in his denunciation of blackface minstrels, calling them in an 1848 review 'the filthy scum of white society, who have stolen from us a complexion denied to them by nature, in which to make money, and to pander to the corrupt taste of their white fellow citizens' (quoted in Lott, 1993: 15). Even when the performers were themselves black, as were the members of Geritt's Original Ethiopian Serenaders, Douglass urged them to 'cease to exaggerate the exaggerations of our enemies; and represent the colored man rather as he is, than as Ethiopian Minstrels usually represent him to be' (quoted in Blackett, 1999: 200).

Finally, one of the greatest ironies surrounding blackface minstrelsy was its function in effecting a union between North and South at a time when, in all other respects, the Union was rapidly disintegrating. Southern audiences seized on this largely Northern tradition and made it their own, since it sentimentalised a social regime that increasingly required more vociferous defence. Malone notes that, although Northern minstrel songs 'were immediately appealing to audiences everywhere, they found a natural, and seemingly permanent, home in the rural South', along with the 'styles, dances, jokes, and even the corking of the face [that] became almost permanent facets of southern folk and popular culture' (Malone, 1979: 23). Thus, for both the North and the South, blackface minstrelsy functioned as 'a socially approved context of institutional control [that] continually acknowledged and absorbed black culture even while defending white America against it' (Lott, 1993: 40). However, if minstrelsy was indeed an agent of union, it was a union fraught with tension and paradox.

African-American Challenges to White Minstrelsy

As the pervasive and, in most ways, pernicious influence of blackface minstrelsy indicates, one of the greatest struggles of the antebellum black community was self-definition in the face of white supremacist culture.

Perhaps better than any other cultural form, minstrelsy illustrates the oft-quoted claim of Toni Morrison in *Beloved*, that 'definitions belong to the definers – not the defined' (Morrison, 1988: 190). On the eve of the Civil War, minstrelsy had done its work so well that Frederick Douglass was obliged to devote extensive discussion in his *Narrative* (1845) to the popular stereotype of plantation slave songs: 'I have often been utterly astonished, since I came to the north, to find persons who could speak of the singing, among slaves, as evidence of their contentment and happiness' (Douglass, 1845: 14–15). In the first years of the twentieth century, W. E. B. Du Bois was still at pains to correct the misapprehensions fostered by the antebellum blackface minstrels, including in *The Souls of Black Folk* (1903) a long chapter on what he termed 'the Sorrow Songs', analysing the history and signification of spirituals and black folk songs, and eulogising African-American groups like the Fisk Jubilee Singers for their battles against 'the contemporary "coon songs"', 'caricature' and the 'debased melodies which vulgar ears scarce know from the real' (Du Bois, 1903: 253, 257).

One great problem was that the 'Ethiopian Delineations' of the minstrel men infected other arenas of antebellum culture, including literature. Witness Edgar Allan Poe's comprehensive adaptation of minstrelsy in 'The Gold Bug' (1843), in which the buffoonery of the faithful old slave, Jupiter, who cannot tell his left from his right, would easily fit him for the part of Tambo or Bones: 'Yes, I knows dat – knows all about dat – 'tis my left hand what I chops de wood wid' (Poe, 1993: 86). In contrast, Herman Melville, in 'Benito Cereno' (1855) and *The Confidence-Man* (1857), was all but unique among white antebellum writers in using deceptively sinister minstrel figures to challenge one of the prime assumptions of minstrelsy: the impossibility 'that a negro, however reduced to his stumps by fortune, could be ever thrown off the legs of a laughing philosophy' (Melville, 1984: 902). Nonetheless, Melville's uniqueness is obvious testimony to the general proliferation of minstrelsy in antebellum literature.

Thus, the struggle against imposed definitions or 'delineations' is one reason why the pseudonymous columnist 'Dion' in *Frederick Douglass' Paper* would lament in 1853 that the writings of black Americans were 'mainly contained within the narrow limits of pamphlets or the columns of newspapers, ephemeral caskets, whose destruction entails the destruction of the gems which they contain' ('Dion', 1853: n. p.). The 'ephemeral caskets' to which 'Dion' refers include one of the least-known bodies of African-American writing, what Henry Louis Gates, Jr calls 'a veritable dark continent of journalism' (Foreword, in Danky and Hady, 1999: viii). Thus, against the power of the minstrel on stage and in fiction, and against the invective of pro-slavery journalists (as well as the paternalism of white abolitionists), 'Dion' reiterates the call of his fellow African-Americans, John Russwurm and Samuel Cornish. On March 16, 1827, these pioneers of black journalism had released the first issue of their *Freedom's Journal* with the banner: 'We wish to plead our own cause. Too long have others spoken for us' (Russwurm and Cornish, 1827: 1). As the earliest African-American newspaper, *Freedom's Journal* was the first of forty-two black-run titles that appeared between 1827 and the outbreak of the Civil War, a repository of critical commentary on labour and slavery, the arts, racist lynching, and national and international affairs that challenged all assumptions of white supremacy. Although *Freedom's Journal* only ran for two years, it was particularly important for its sponsorship of essayists such as David Walker, whose *An Appeal in Four Articles* (1830) threw down the gauntlet to a host of defamatory commonplaces. Against the charge of automatic black lust for white women, Walker wrote: 'I would not give a pinch of snuff to be married to any white person I saw in all the days of my life' (Walker, 1830: 11). On the need for white abolitionist sponsorship: 'Let no one of us suppose that the refutations which have been written by our white friends are enough – they are whites – we are blacks' (Ibid.: 17). On the need for black quietude and non-violence: 'Will not these very coloured people whom they now treat worse than brutes, yet under God, humble them low down enough?' (Ibid.: 86).

Freedom's Journal was followed by a series of other African-American periodicals sharing the similar combination of brief life and resounding argument. A number of them stand out for the clarity of their mission against white supremacist institutions. Cornish's *Weekly Advocate*, soon re-titled the *Colored American* and published in New York from 1837 to 1841, demanded immediate emancipation, the renunciation of all colonisation schemes, and the investiture of black Americans' rights as citizens (Dann, 1971: 181). One of the most celebrated African-American newspapers of the antebellum period – Douglass's *North Star*, launched in 1847 and jointly edited with Martin Delaney – declared as its object 'a printing-press and paper, permanently established, under the complete control and direction of the immediate victims of slavery and oppression' (in Foner, 1950: I, 280). Out of Ontario, Canada, came Mary Ann Shadd

Cary and Samuel Ward's *Provincial Freeman* (1854–57), which set out to fuse anti-slavery agitation with the defence of a strong British presence in North America as a bulwark against the Fugitive Slave Act and the imperial designs of pro-slavery expansionists (Rhodes, 1998: 70 ff.). One of the last major African-American periodicals before the Civil War was *Frederick Douglass' Paper* and its various titular incarnations, sprung from the ashes of the *North Star* in 1851 and the declared adversary of the church and the government as the twin pillars of American slavery. Douglass's paper ceased printing in 1859, the year that Thomas Hamilton launched the *Anglo-African Magazine* in New York. Although that journal did not survive its second volume, it offered some of the most important prose of Frances Ellen Watkins Harper, including 'The Two Offers', generally acknowledged as the first short story to be published by a black American woman.

These and other periodicals, with small distribution amongst the Northern free black and abolitionist communities, rarely if ever enjoyed the benefit of circulation in the South – even through the mechanism of 'pick-up' and reprinting in snatches by Southern papers. Yet the antebellum black press stands as a monument to African-American print culture at a time when prohibitions against black literacy were heavily enforced in the South, and when Northern journalism was dominated by competing factions of white abolitionists and anti-abolition accommodationists such as the New York *Herald*.

Elsewhere in the print sector, black voices stood out against the prevailing dominance of the white literary establishment. Having published her first volume of poetry, *Forest Leaves* (1841), as a sixteen-year-old, Frances E. W. Harper returned with *Poems on Miscellaneous Subjects* (1854), largely to challenge the dialect parodies and situational buffooneries of minstrelsy. Other African-Americans wrote against the popularity of the minstrel stage and the sympathetic renderings of slavery and Southern slaveholders that informed such successful dramatic productions as Dion Boucicault's *The Octoroon* (1859), which enjoyed enormous popularity on both sides of the Atlantic on the eve of the Civil War and afterwards.

One of the most prominent black writers to engage with white-dominated antebellum culture was William Wells Brown, who made his mark across a range of genres: the slave narrative (*Narrative of William Wells Brown, a Fugitive Slave*, 1847), the novel (*Clotel; or, The President's Daughter*, 1853, generally acknowledged as the first by an African-

American) and drama (*The Escape; or, A Leap for Freedom*, 1858). As a fugitive from slavery in London, Brown openly acknowledged the range of white power structures he had to negotiate if he were to be heard at all. *Clotel*, depicting the tragic end of Thomas Jefferson's mulatto daughter, relied as much for its source material upon 'American abolitionist journals' as upon the oral tales he had heard from other escaped slaves (Brown, 1853: 244). Moreover, Brown shared an added burden with fugitives such as Frederick Douglass and William and Ellen Craft, who were all obliged to make their voices heard from abroad, for reasons that went beyond the immediate dangers of the Fugitive Slave Act. The 'main object' of *Clotel*, he said, was to target 'British public opinion' and to 'aid in bringing British influence to bear upon American slavery' (Brown, 1853: v) – for in America, *Clotel* was unpublished and would remain so until the Civil War was nearly over.

A similar fate was shared by the Creole dramatist and poet from Louisiana, Victor Sejour, who, finding few outlets for his work in America, found in France a willing audience for his poems, stories – including 'The Mulatto' (1837), arguably the first major African-American short story – and such dramas as *The Fortune-Teller* (1859) and *The Jew of Seville* (1844). It is telling that both of these plays waited until 2000 for their first translations into English (Sejour, 2000 and 2000a).

In spite of all such structural or systemic disadvantages in American culture – the popularity of the plantation novel and the minstrel show, the dominance of the white-owned press, and the violent suppression of literacy among the mass of American slaves – African-Americans succeeding in establishing an entire literary genre, the slave narrative, which had a profound impact upon antebellum American life and culture. In his introduction to the 'classic' slave narratives of Olaudah Equiano, Mary Prince, Frederick Douglass and Harriet Jacobs, Gates identifies the 'process of imitation and repetition' by which escaped slaves who either dictated or wrote their autobiographies built upon the narrative conventions of their predecessors, constructing 'a communal utterance, a collective tale, rather than merely an individual's autobiography' (Gates, 1987: x). Of the roughly six thousand narratives estimated by Marion Wilson Starling to have been written or narrated by former slaves, over one hundred book-length manuscripts were published before the Civil War (Starling, 1988: 1–2; 222).

Even within this immense black literary genre, however, writers and narrators were often obliged to resist or submit to white control, particularly when their texts were sponsored by abolitionist editors and publishers who habitually required the inclusion of stock subjects and scenes – the slaveholder's lust, brutality at the whipping post, familial separation – within a Christianised or evangelical frame of reference. In such cases, as Cynthia Hamilton describes it, the antebellum slave narrative was 'fraught with tension as the black voice sang variations on a tune given structural shape by white abolitionists' (Hamilton, 1999: 74). John Blassingame, one of the pioneer scholars of slave testimony, argues: 'An editor's education, religious beliefs, literary skill, attitudes toward slavery and occupation all reflected how he recorded the account of the slave's life' (Blassingame, 1975: 474). Thus, narratives such as that dictated by Solomon Northup (1853) to his New York editor, David Wilson, appear to be controlled by the diction of the amanuensis – effectively the ghost-writer – which at times approaches the quality of a religious sermon if not a sentimental novel. Hence Northup's conclusion:

Chastened and subdued in sprit by the sufferings I have borne, and thankful to that good Being through whose mercy I have been restored to happiness and liberty, I hope henceforward to lead an upright though lowly life, and rest at last in the church yard where my father sleeps (Northup, 1853: 321).

At the other extreme, and fortunately less frequently, a dictated narrative might employ heavy-handed attempts at African-American dialect that, on the page, bear embarrassing similarities to the minstrel stage, for all the editor's good intentions. Hence a snatch of dialogue from Kate Pickard's rendition of the Peter Still narrative (1856): '"I reckon", said Levin, "mammy's gone to church. The preachin' must be mighty long! O! I's so hongry! I's gwine to meetin' to see if she's thar"' (Pickard, 1856: 25–6). Paul Gilmore has argued that, to some degree, even narratives that were unquestionably written by the ex-slaves themselves might be knowingly infected with the germ of minstrelsy. In particular, Gilmore points to William Wells Brown's deliberate utilisation of minstrel dialect and imagery in his writings: 'Whether in narratives, lectures or fiction, professional fugitives were called upon to prove their authenticity by providing, as Frederick Douglass recalled his white supporters putting it, "a *little* plantation manner of speech"' (Gilmore,1997: 744).

If a former slave had actually written the text, the claim 'written by himself' or 'by herself' would usually follow the title; but even a narrative so undisputed in its origin as that by Frederick Douglass carries

authenticating prefaces by the white abolitionists William Lloyd
Garrison and Wendell Phillips. Moreover, some appended claims of
authenticity are ambiguous, as in the title, *The Life of Josiah Henson,
Formerly a Slave, Now an Inhabitant of Canada, Narrated by Himself*
(1849) – which does not quite succeed in obscuring the shaping hand of
Henson's white Bostonian ghost-writer, Samuel Eliot.

Nonetheless, as Ishmael Reed (see Chapter 4) implies in his parodic
re-working of the slave narrative, *Flight to Canada* (1976), the slave
narrative genre indeed worked its way into the literary consciousness of
antebellum America where, largely through its absorption into one novel
– Harriet Beecher Stowe's *Uncle Tom's Cabin* (1852) – it helped lay the
groundwork for the Civil War:

> *Old Harriet. Naughty Harriet ...*
> *She popularised the American novel and introduced it to Europe.*
> Uncle Tom's Cabin ... *The story she 'borrowed' from Josiah Henson ...*
> *She'd read Josiah Henson's book. That Harriet was alert.* The Life of
> Josiah Henson, Formerly a Slave. *Seventy-seven pages long. It was
> short, but it was his. It was all he had. His story* (Reed, 1998: 8).

The extent of the reliance of America's first worldwide best-seller on
Josiah Henson's narrative is still a matter of debate (see Stowe, 1853;
Henson, 1876). There is no doubt, however, that, immediately upon the
appearance of Stowe's novel, African-American writers were galvanised
to combat its stereotypes – including Frederick Douglass, whose only
work of fiction, *The Heroic Slave* (1853), was among the most immediate,
resurrecting Madison Washington, the historical leader of a slave rebellion,
to act as a counterpoint to Stowe's meek and passive eponymous hero.
Douglass's Washington declares at the outset, '*Liberty* I will have, or die
in the attempt to gain it' (Douglass, 1853: 178) – an entirely alien
resolution for Uncle Tom, who, some might argue, dies in order to
remain enslaved. Still, there is much more to Stowe's novel than its hero.

Uncle Tom and his 'Tomitudes'

Whether or not *Uncle Tom's Cabin* was – as Abraham Lincoln reportedly
teased its author – the book that started the Civil War (Fields, 1898:
269), it is probably no exaggeration to concur with Jim Cullen's
assessment of it as 'the major work of popular culture in the nineteenth
century' (Cullen, 1995: 69). Appearing first as a serial in the anti-slavery
periodical, *The National Era*, from June 1851 to April 1852, in book form

it sold 300,000 copies in the US in its first year. This was 'comparable to at least three million today … the best seller of all time in proportion to population' (McPherson, 1988: 88–9).

In popular culture terms, the novel's importance lies in its function as a cauldron into which were poured the major forms of antebellum expression in the service of abolitionist propaganda. From the plantation novel came the 'decayed old houses, kind masters and mistresses, [and] docile and affectionate household "servants"' (Taylor, 1963: 308). Abolitionist oratory and evangelical rhetoric inspired many narrative intrusions, while the inclusion of Southern newspaper notices drama-tised the horrors of the auction block and the Fugitive Slave Law. Popular pseudo-anthropology informed Stowe's blanket stereotypes of 'the negro mind', which she depicted as 'naturally patient, timid, and unenterprising' or 'childlike' (Stowe, 1852: 78, 165, 275). From the senti-mental novel came the break-up of families, the suicide of a forsaken slave mother and her child, and the melodramatic death of Little Eva, while the novel of seduction inspired the tragedy of the betrayed quadroon, Cassy. The slave narrative, of course – whether or not it came specifically through Henson – provided Stowe with escape plots and scenarios of brutality. Finally, from the minstrel stage itself, Stowe plucked the 'delineations' of Topsy and Uncle Tom – the latter, as Lott argues, bearing 'resemblance to the many sentimental slaves of Stephen Foster's complacent "Plantation Melodies": Old Uncle Ned, Old Black Joe, and so on' (Lott, 1993: 33).

As a cultural phenomenon, *Uncle Tom's Cabin* is not only important for the political debate that it forced into popular consciousness in America and Europe, but also for the many cultural texts and practices that it spawned. In its wake came a mini-industry of 'anti-Tom' novels denying Stowe's depictions of cruelty, under such crudely parodic titles as Mary Henderson Eastman's *Aunt Phillis's Cabin; or, Southern Life as It Is* (1852) and John W. Page's *Uncle Robin, in His Cabin in Virginia, and Tom Without One in Boston* (1853). In these defiant pro-slavery texts, the object was to give the slave 'fictional equity with the planter' (Taylor, 1963: 307). Jeffrey Richards has noted that, 'as the nineteenth-century stage was the equivalent to today's television movie industry', *Uncle Tom's Cabin* attracted 'opportunistic playwrights and managers who thought to make a profit from Stowe's popularity' in a pre-uniform copyright era when 'no one needed to ask the author's permission or pay royalties' (Richards, 1997: 369). Thus came the outpouring of dramas headed by George Aiken's six-act production the year of the novel's release, and followed into the 1930s by literally hundreds of derivative melodramas, burlesques, parodies and 'Tom Shows' that reinforced Stowe's characters as household figures even for those who had not read the book. Stowe herself picked up on the theatrical potential, drafting a series of readings for the mixed-race actress, Mary E. Webb, in 1855.

Motion pictures followed the drama at the turn of the century, with Edwin S. Porter releasing a ten-minute reel in 1903 – a month before the appearance of his landmark, *The Great Train Robbery* – and inaugurating an industry of Uncle Tom films that dominated the silent screen until 1927. The novel infiltrated a host of other nineteenth- and twentieth-century popular culture domains. In addition to stage productions, songs and poems, children's adaptations and films, the US and Europe saw a further proliferation of what critics have called 'Uncle Tomitudes' (after the title of an anonymous 1853 review in *Putnam's Monthly*), that is, commercial spin-off productions based on scenes and characters from the book. This astounding output includes jigsaw puzzles, decks of cards, paper dolls and cut-outs, dice games, decorative plates, pitchers, Staffordshire mugs, decorated spoons and jars, mantlepiece screens, and countless advertisements for products such as 'Uncle Tom's Root Beer', 'Topsies and Evas' dessert candies, 'Uncle Tom and Little Eva' Ink-o-Graph fountain pens, 'Topsy Tobacco' and 'Uncle Tom Health Food' (Hirsch, 1978: 303–30; Railton, 2004).

The interplay between *Uncle Tom's Cabin*, its source material and the variety of cultural forms and practices that it spawned feeds into a broader and more complex matrix in which authorship, race, the contestation of stereotypes, textuality and public debate all interlock. The cultural heat that was absorbed into the novel, and heightened and generated from it, blasted through the tinderbox of American sectionalism in which also swirled the sparks from other acts and events – the Fugitive Slave Law (1850), the Kansas-Nebraska Act (1854), the Dred Scott case (1856–57), the guerrilla wars of 'Bleeding Kansas' (1856), Harper's Ferry (1859) and the election of Lincoln (1861).

Thus, Harriet Beecher Stowe, like Walter Scott before her, cannot assume sole responsibility for igniting the Civil War – Lincoln and Mark Twain notwithstanding. But both authors, and the audiences who received, emulated, and challenged them, performed much of the groundwork that prepared the cultural battlefields of the war and – most important, for our purposes – its aftermath.

CHAPTER 2

Reunion and Resistance

The project to lament the passing of the old Southern plantation order was well under way before the first shots of the Civil War were fired. However, in many ways the war – for all its profound impact upon the US Constitution and the socio-political order – succeeded in perpetuating, rather than arresting, the values of the old South as they were absorbed into cultural practice. There are identifiable reasons for this, as Mark Twain implies in *Life on the Mississippi* (1883): 'In the South, the war is what A.D. is elsewhere: they date from it' (Twain, 1883: 454). This quote has resonance for white Southerners who have wished to invoke the trauma of invasion and defeat, and for whom the Confederate surrender at Appomattox in 1865 marked the onset of a brutal modern history (beginning with Reconstruction) and the end of a golden age. The aim of this chapter is to explore the ways in which post-bellum American culture adopted, reflected, perpetuated and otherwise utilised the values of the Old South in the wake of Confederate defeat and Reconstruction. Through examining key texts in literature (Joel Chandler Harris, Thomas Dixon, Margaret Mitchell), film (D. W. Griffith, Walt Disney) and polemic (the Nashville Agrarians), we can mark the beginning and the adolescent stages of a project of Southern vindication that continues to this day. Inevitably, it was and remains a highly divisive, racially provocative project.

As they had done before the war, the post-bellum defenders of the plantation order looked first to the (now former) slaves to validate their claims, recycling the antebellum comparisons between the supposedly content, loyal slaves in the South and the miserable factory operatives or 'hirelings' in the North. However, what was different was the fact of Reconstruction, and Reconstruction brought – ever so briefly – a degree of empowerment to Southern blacks that had been unmatched in their history. The Reconstruction amendments to the Constitution outlawed American slavery for ever and conferred upon former slaves the rights of citizenship, voting (for men) and equal protection under the law. Black political mobilisation and a vocal black leadership at state level drove the Republican agenda in the South, where African-Americans served in the state legislatures, in municipal offices and on juries, as well as in the US Congress in Washington.

As argued in Chapter 1, during the antebellum period, the fear provoked by the mere prospect of black empowerment had been one of the driving forces of white American culture. Hence the barely controlled racial hysteria and caricatures of the antebellum minstrel stage that were prompted, in no small measure, by the fear of slave rebellions and obsessions over black sexual potency. Thus, when black empowerment became a reality after the war, the defenders of the old South had substantial cultural work to perform, and the former slaves were their most frequently used tools. As David Blight observes, 'the image of the loyal slave may be one of the most hackneyed clichés in American history, but no understanding of the place of race in Civil War memory is possible without confronting its ubiquitous uses' (Blight, 2001: 284).

One of many examples located by Drew Gilpen Faust reveals how this figure had been employed before the war's end to respond to both the threat and the actuality of emancipation. In a Southern magazine poem, 'Philanthropy Rebuked: A True Story', a would-be liberator from the North is rejected by a loyal, old slave:

> Now, Massa, dis is berry fine, dese words
> you've spoke to me,
> No doubt you mean it kindly, but old Dinah
> won't be free.
> I 'spect your home's a happy one – I hope it
> may be so –
> But I's better in de cotton field dan 'mong
> your hills ob snow.
> Ole Massa's berry good to me – and though I am
> his slave,
> He treats me like I's kin to him – and I would
> rather have
> A home in Massa's cabin, and eat his black
> bread too,
> Dan leave ole Massa's children and go and
> lib wid you.
>   (in Faust, 1988: 63–4)

Figure 2 Confederate Memorial, Higginsville, Missouri, 2004 (Will Kaufman).

Such myths as the benign, familial, sexless quality of the slave-master relationship, the primacy of the master's children in the affections of the slave, and the slave's natural attachment to the South in preference to the North – all displayed in this poem – pre-date the Civil War. As we have seen, they were already consolidated by the 1830s in the plantation novels and the pro-slavery rhetoric responding to an increasingly aggressive abolition movement.

Even at the dawn of the twenty-first century, the myths persist to the extent that – in just one example – the contemporary black artist, Kara Walker, has devoted a substantial part of her career to subverting them. Walker's celebrated silhouettes distort or signify upon stereotypical antebellum images (loyal slaves, wet-nurse mammies, plantation belles) in order to foreground the violence, sexual and otherwise, that underlay the plantation system (see Berry, et al., 2003). Far from revealing a benign relationship between slaves and their masters, Walker confesses that her work lays bare images that she herself is 'shocked to encounter in the dark alleys of [her] imagination' (Walker, 1998: 49). Walker's objective is clearly to rewrite the benign plantation myth and present it as terrifying and grotesque. However, as Leon Litwack points out, even the bloody watershed of the Civil War, which demolished American slavery itself, could not demolish these benign myths:

> The war taught the owner who claimed to 'know' his Negroes best that he knew them least of all, and that he had mistaken their docility for contentment, their deference and accommodation for submission … Many years later, white southerners preferred to ignore this 'moment of truth', opting for stories of black duty and loyalty (Litwack, 1996: 131).

Such stories have become landmarks in American culture as well as political battlefields in their own right. Among them are those that combined in an instructive partnership between a long-deceased white Georgia writer and one of Hollywood's most influential studio moguls. The combined stories of Joel Chandler Harris and Walt Disney have been among the most powerful transmitters of the plantation myths to which Litwack refers, and that Walker still strives to subvert.

Songs of the South

Catherine Clinton calls Walt Disney's *Song of the South* (1946) 'the last gasp of Hollywood's love affair with plantation settings' (Clinton, 1995:

135). This live-action and animation musical – which grossed $13 million and was enormously popular through its original run and re-releases (Campbell, 1983: 10) – is now a staple item on websites defending or selling banned and discredited films. It is no longer listed in the Disney retail catalogue, although it enjoys a healthy circulation on eBay. In cultural terms, *Song of the South* was not merely 'a corruptive piece of Old South propaganda put together to make money' (Bogle, 1994: 136). Rather, it was the sad culmination of an extensive project to rewrite and sweeten both antebellum and Reconstruction history, based on the more complex 'Uncle Remus' stories of Joel Chandler Harris, who had himself relied on the anonymous voices and tales in the African-American oral tradition.

It must be said that Harris's adoption of the African-American voice was accomplished with more authenticity than was habitually done in the minstrel routines, which Harris called 'intolerable representations' (Harris, 2000: 3). His vocal adoption also raises questions of cultural proprietorship or ownership that have continued to influence critical debate. This point is made by (among others) Allan Gurganus in his novel, *Oldest Living Confederate Widow Tells All* (1989; see Conclusion), in which the narrator, Lucy Marsden, says of Harris: 'Strange that a white man should get famous for first writing down these freed-slave animal tales. But no, not strange at all. Look at young Mr. Elvis, God rest his soul' (Gurganus, 1990: 300). Most importantly, the relation between Harris and Walt Disney suggests both a perpetuation and commer-cialisation of Reconstruction-era nostalgia that extended well beyond the geographical confines of the South.

Disney's *Song of the South* adopts the tale-telling structure devised by Harris in *Uncle Remus: His Songs and Sayings* (1880) and its numerous sequels appearing between 1883 and 1910: a young white boy is swept every night into the world of Brer Rabbit, Brer Fox and Brer Bear by the nightly tales of the devoted, aged retainer, Uncle Remus. This structure, according to Darwin Turner, manifests Harris's antebellum 'utopia', his 'dream of a world in which "old-time" slaves, particularly African slaves, worshipped their aristocratic Anglo-Saxon masters'. The white child is 'entertained, comforted, and advised by a devoted black nurse or a slave playmate who is more faithful than a pet hound. As an adult, he is attended by servants who, like dutiful genies, live only for his pleasure while he, like an indulgent father, protects them and supervises their growth' (Turner, 1981: 114).

In his introduction to the first volume, Harris removes all doubt about Uncle Remus's affection for his days in bondage, and asserts his own belief in an organic process of reunion disturbed, if anything, by the Reconstruction initiatives:

> If the reader not familiar with plantation life will imagine that the myth-stories of Uncle Remus are told night after night to a little boy by an old negro who appears to be venerable enough to have lived during the period which he describes – who has nothing but pleasant memories of the discipline of slavery – and who has all the prejudices of caste and pride of family that were the natural results of the system; if the reader can imagine all this, he will find little difficulty in appreciating and sympathizing with the air of affectionate superiority which Uncle Remus assumes as he proceeds to unfold the mysteries of plantation lore to a little child who is the product of that practical reconstruction which has been going on to some extent since the war in spite of the politicians (Harris, 2000: 8).

Disney carries Harris's wish-fulfilment into the film as Uncle Remus, about to launch into his signature tune, 'Zip a Dee Doo Dah', sadly shakes his head and says, 'In dem days everything was satisfaction … It was bettuh all around.' As for Brer Rabbit, who had fled from his 'own briar patch, the place where [he] was raised', Uncle Remus concludes: 'He left his old troubles behind, all right. But he was in for a mess of new troubles.' In the musical background, the field-hands quote the Boll Weevil of the folk song: 'Let the rain fall down, let the cold wind blow, I'm gonna stay right here' (Foster, 1946). The film thus echoes not only Harris but also the accomodationist philosophy of Booker T. Washington's Atlanta Compromise (1895), which urged the South's blacks, 'Cast down your bucket where you are', while mollifying the whites: 'In all things that are purely social we can be as separate as the fingers, yet one as the hand in all things essential to mutual progress' (Washington, 1901: 219, 221–2). It must be said that Washington's conservative pragmatism cloaked a more progressive, if not radical, agenda than that put forward by Harris in his appeal to black stasis. Certainly, Washington cannot have shared Harris's antebellum nostalgia. But the point is that they both accomplish the same cultural work, if not with the same intentions, and it is this work that Disney carries on in the film.*

* I am grateful to Carol Smith for articulating the distinctions between Washington and Harris in this context.

Disney also clearly perpetuates Harris's own ambivalence over the fate of the South at large at the close of Reconstruction. In his editorials for the Atlanta *Constitution* in the 1870s and 1880s, Harris had argued for the region's economic development and re-integration into the Union – a fundamental objective in the agenda of what its proponents called the 'New South'. Paul Gaston summarises this agenda as the 'harmonious reconciliation of sectional differences, racial peace, and a new economic and social order based on industry and scientific, diversified agriculture – all of which would lead, eventually, to the South's dominance in the reunited nation' (Gaston, 1970: 7). However, as Blight notes, Harris was opposed to the New South's 'greed and industrialism' and 'seemed to favor progress of a sort, but preferred that it remain agricultural and pastoral' (Blight, 2001: 228). As he wrote his cautious editorials, Harris began to publish stories based on the slave tales he had heard as a young apprentice working on a Georgia plantation at the start the war. The nostalgia for the doomed plantation that drives the Uncle Remus tales clearly acts as a brake on whatever enthusiasm Harris may have felt for the New South's economic developments.

That ambivalence finds its way into *Song of the South* in the form of a family crisis surrounding the little white boy, Johnny. The boy's mother and grandmother are symbols of the old plantation matriarchy, while his father, an Atlanta journalist, alienates them with his New South advocacy of 'cotton mills and railways'. Early in the film, Johnny's father abandons the plantation for the city, leaving Uncle Remus to provide the emotional and moral sustenance for Johnny and his new, poor white friend, Ginny. Near the end, after Johnny is almost killed by a bull (and all the black servants gather to moan in vigil outside the Big House where he lies unconscious), his father returns to the plantation, turning his back on the New South with the vow: 'I'm staying right here where I belong.' In the concluding reprise of 'Zip a Dee Doo Dah', the three personified constituencies of a happy South – the white aristocrat (Johnny), the poor white (Ginny), and the willingly subservient black (Uncle Remus) – skip down the road together in a gesture of harmony. While the live action that frames the animated Brer Rabbit tales is understood to be post-Reconstruction, its visual imagery is indistinguishable from the antebellum period. The Civil War itself is wholly erased, the wise Old South instructs the New, and – as the NAACP argued in its critique of the film – the 'impression of an idyllic master-slave relationship' succeeds as 'a distortion of the fact' (in Bogle, 1994: 136).

It must be said, however, that the distortions of Harris and Disney are positively benign when compared with those in the texts to which we must now turn, given their influential place in the history of American literature and cinema. The novels of Thomas Dixon, D. W. Griffith's *The Birth of a Nation* (1915) and Margaret Mitchell's novel, *Gone with the Wind* (1936), are all part of a cultural continuum – shared by Harris and Disney – in which the implied blessings of slavery are, for Southern blacks and whites alike, matched by the implied evils of emancipation and Reconstruction.

Reconstructing Reconstruction

One brief moment in *Song of the South* particularly fixes its connection to these other mutually related texts. When Johnny and his parents first arrive at the ancestral plantation, they approach the Big House through a run-down section of former slave cabins. In the fields, the black workers erupt into a joyful rendition of the song, 'Uncle Remus Said', which includes the refrain, 'That's how the leopard got his spots.' Importantly, this is not a link back to Harris, but rather to two other influential sources. First, it links to the racism of Rudyard Kipling's tale, 'How the Leopard Got His Spots', published in his *Just So Stories* for children (1902). Kipling had drawn on the Bible for both his title and his plot – Jeremiah 13:23: 'Can the Ethiopian change his skin, or the leopard his spots?' Second, and through Kipling, the Disney moment links to the work of one of America's most notorious racist authors, Thomas Dixon, who drew on Kipling for the title, subtitle and implied moral of his novel, *The Leopard's Spots: A Romance of the White Man's Burden, 1865–1900* (1902). The inspiration of this novel to Disney – whether deliberate or unconscious – must remove all consideration of *Song of the South* as harmless entertainment.

Dixon, a minor Democratic politician from North Carolina, had quit party politics for the Baptist church, which he in turn abandoned for what he called the 'wider pulpit' of literature (May, 1983: 80). Incensed by the enduring popularity of *Uncle Tom's Cabin* and its many successful dramatisations through the turn of the century, Dixon responded with his 'Reconstruction Trilogy'. *The Leopard's Spots* was followed by *The Clansman: An Historical Romance of the Ku Klux Klan* (1905) and *The Traitor: A Story of the Fall of the Invisible Empire* (1907). As Dixon wrote, his object was 'to teach the North ... what it has never known – the awful suffering of the white man during the dreadful Reconstruction period ...

[and] to demonstrate to the world that the white man must and shall be supreme' (in Litwack, 1995: 138).

Beginning with *The Leopard's Spots*, which takes characters from *Uncle Tom's Cabin* and situates them in a Southern white supremacist's nightmare – a South ruled by black legislators – Dixon called for a return to an 'aristocracy founded on brains, culture and blood' to revive a South which 'but for the Black curse ... could be today a garden of the world' (in Lang, 1994: 9). As Lary May points out, Dixon's obsessive writing was the extreme expression of Southern Democratic party ideology, which demonised Reconstruction as 'a corrupt regime' imposed on Dixie by the Radical Republicans: 'Using the freed slaves' voting power, they disenfranchised the white citizens and unleashed a reign of terror' (May, 1983: 80–1). Dixon casts it thus in *The Leopard's Spots*: 'Congress became to the desolate South what Attila, the "*Scourge of God*", was to civilised Europe' (Dixon, 1902: 101).

In fact, the domination of Reconstruction governments by blacks was a myth, however culturally and politically potent. William Faulkner perpetuates this myth in *Intruder in the Dust* (1948), representing the former white master as one who 'was not merely beaten to his knees but trampled for ten years on his face in the dust to make him swallow it' (Faulkner, 1996: 155). Litwack notes, however, that 'even where blacks comprised a majority of the voters, the number of black officeholders was never commensurate with their electoral strength. Only in South Carolina did black legislators outnumber whites (eighty-eight to sixty-seven), but in no state did blacks control the executive mansion' (Litwack, 1995: 138). Arguably, this could be beside the point if one accepts that, in terms of equity, a theoretical black domination of Reconstruction government would be no more of an outrage than the white domination that actually preceded and succeeded it.

Nevertheless, Dixon's fanatical renderings of sexually predatory black men, white virgins in peril, faithful and submissive 'good darkies' and heroic Klansmen lay the foundations for two of the twentieth century's most influential popular culture works. Dixon – whom the black activist and editor William Monroe Trotter called an 'unasylumed maniac' – might have drifted into obscurity were it not for his rescue by two white Southern champions, the film-maker, David Wark Griffith, and the novelist, Margaret Mitchell (Trotter quoted in Lang, 1994: 9). As Jim Cullen notes, Griffith 'more than any other man brought the Civil War into the twentieth century' with his epic, *The Birth of a Nation*, based on Dixon's novels, while Mitchell's *Gone with the Wind* 'owed a great deal to Dixon' (Cullen, 1995: 17, 23).

At one point, Mitchell's narrator interprets the complexities of Reconstruction as follows:

> Aided by the unscrupulous adventurers who operated the Freedmen's Bureau and urged on by a fervor of Northern hatred almost religious in its fanaticism, the former field hands found themselves suddenly elevated to the seats of the mighty. There they conducted themselves as creatures of small intelligence might naturally be expected to do. Like monkeys or small children turned loose among treasured objects whose value is beyond their comprehension, they ran wild – either from perverse pleasure in destruction or simply because of their ignorance (Mitchell, 1993: 645).

Although certainly not plagiarised, this is hardly an original utterance: it is found, among other precedents, in the pages of Dixon's novels. Mitchell's fey Southern hero, Ashley Wilkes, fights out of remembrance of 'how the moonlight slants across the white columns' of the Twelve Oaks plantation, and 'the old days, the old ways I love so much' (Ibid.: 210). He, too, is echoing Dixon and other peddlers of the moonlight and magnolia, the 'garden' destroyed by the 'Black curse'. In 1936, in response to a letter of praise from Dixon, Mitchell replied: 'I was practically raised on your books, and love them very much. For many years I have had you on my conscience, and I suppose I might as well confess it now' (in Aitken, 1965: 9).

D. W. Griffith also had Dixon on his conscience. As the son of a Confederate veteran, the Kentucky-born Griffith held an 'idealised view of the South, founded upon his family mythology and a romantic literary and historical tradition' (Armour, 1981: 20). As an established director and producer of one-reelers for Biograph Films, Griffith was present at the dawn of the cinema age; his encounter with Dixon's *The Leopard's Spots* and *The Clansman* led to the world's first cinema epic. *The Birth of a Nation* ran for over three hours and twelve reels, pioneering such techniques as 'the close-up, cross cutting, rapid-fire editing, the iris, the split-screen shot, and realistic and impressionistic lighting'; it altered 'the entire course and concept of American moviemaking' (Bogle, 1994: 10). Its spectacular success transformed cinema-going into a respectable bourgeois pastime. In its wake, 'movie palaces' and 'temples of silent drama' were built across America, surpassing 'legitimate theaters in plush ostentation' (Silverman, 1981: 27). With *The Birth of a Nation*, 'the motion picture as art, propaganda, and entertainment came of age' (Litwack, 1995: 135).

Concurrently with the film's release, Griffith predicted in an article for the magazine, *The Editor*:

> The time will come, and in less than ten years ... when the children in the public schools will be taught practically everything by moving pictures. Certainly they will never be obliged to read history again ... There will be no opinions expressed. You will merely be present at the making of history. All the work of writing, revising, collating, and reproducing will have been carefully attended to by a corps of recognised experts, and you will have received a vivid and complete expression (in Geldud, 1971: 34).

With the apparent belief that he was producing a work of transparent history in the guise of drama, Griffith combined the plots of *The Leopard's Spots* and *The Clansman* with excerpts from the former academic – and now president – Woodrow Wilson's *A History of the American People* (1902), an association Wilson later had cause to regret.

The action revolves around two families, the Northern Stonemans and the Southern Camerons, who begin the film amidst mutual attachments of friendship and romantic interest between the young family members. The Civil War comes to disrupt the harmonic order of the Cameron plantation, while in the North, the elder Stoneman – a powerful Radical Republican senator based crudely on Thaddeus Stevens – succumbs to the temptations of his mulatto mistress, who drives him into a corrupt rule of the defeated, prostrate South. Whites are disenfranchised while drunken blacks (white actors in minstrel blackface) mob the streets, terrorise their former masters and gorge themselves on fried chicken in the hallowed halls of the Southern legislatures that they now control, passing laws promoting inter-racial marriage. The predatory black 'buck' figure, Gus, attempts to rape Cameron's youngest daughter, who throws herself off a cliff. In the spirit of outraged Southern honour and revenge, her brothers form the Ku Klux Klan, who ride to the rescue to the strains of Wagner. They virtually liberate the white South, which symbolically reunites with the white North through the marriage of Stoneman's daughter and Cameron's son. As Griffith's Copyright Office synopsis proudly concludes, 'At the next election the negroes dare not vote and the threat of a black empire is dissolved' (quoted in Lang, 1994: 11).

The silent film is supported with a host of intertitles, such as:

The bringing of the African to America planted the first seed of disunion.

In the slave quarters. The two-hour interval given for dinner, out of their working day from six to six [on screen, happy slaves are shown dancing to banjo music].

Excerpts from Woodrow Wilson's 'History of the American People' … 'In the villages the negroes were the office holders, men who knew none of the uses of authority, except its insolences'.

'The white men were roused by a mere instinct of self-preservation … until at last there had sprung into existence a great Ku Klux Klan, a veritable empire of the South, to protect the Southern country'. WOODROW WILSON.

'Brethren, this flag bears the red stain of the life of a Southern woman, a priceless sacrifice on the altar of an outraged civilization' [as the hooded Camerons inaugurate the Ku Klux Klan].

The former enemies of North and South are united again in common defence of their Aryan birthright.

(all in Griffith, 1915)

In total, as Richard Dyer notes, '*The Birth of a Nation* shows the forging of a national identity, in which geographical division (North versus South) is transcended through a realisation of a common white racial identity, but one defined in southern terms' (Dyer, 1996: 165).

At its New York première, *The Birth of a Nation* was advertised by a company of white-robed and hooded actors on horseback; in many cities screenings resulted in street violence, as posters and advertisements – particularly in the South – promised a film that 'will make you hate'. Bogle suggests that such promotional campaigns 'may have been effective, for in 1915 lynchings in the United States reached their highest peak since 1908' (Bogle, 1994: 15). Other cultural historians have questioned the extent to which *The Birth of a Nation* was in itself responsible for the great Klan revivals of the early 1920s but, as Blight points out, it surely 'reinvigorated direct-action resistance and inaugurated a new era of dissent in popular culture' (Blight, 2001: 397). One signal event in that campaign of resistance was the black film-maker Emmett J. Scott's twelve-reel, three-hour rejoinder, *The Birth of a Race* (1918), which in the end could not compete with the promotion machine at Griffith's disposal and which is still unavailable for commercial distribution (Snead, 1988: 17–18). However, challenges by the NAACP and other civil rights organisations ensured that, after the Second World War, *The Birth of a Nation* met with sustained, organised protest at virtually every screening. As late as 1992, when the Library of Congress placed the film on the National Film Registry, it was with the apologetic defence of its historical and technological significance and a denial that it deserved 'some kind of national honor' (Litwack, 1995: 141). In any event, *The Birth of a Nation* remains a monument in its own right – not only to cinematic ingenuity, but also to race-hatred, historical amnesia and highly selective remembrance.

Damn Yankee Communists

If post-Reconstruction nostalgia finds its most technically creative expression in *The Birth of a Nation* and its most commercially profitable expression in the book and film of *Gone with the Wind*, its most intellectualised expression is found in the writings of the Nashville Agrarians, a group of white Southern poets, novelists and essayists who in 1930 combined their voices into the manifesto, *I'll Take My Stand*, published under the collective authorship of 'Twelve Southerners'. Dominated by Allen Tate, John Crowe Ransom, Donald Davidson and Robert Penn Warren, the Agrarians sprung into action against what they perceived as Northern cultural and intellectual arrogance as exemplified in H. L. Mencken's caricatures of the South as a cultural wasteland in his essay, 'The Sahara of the Bozart' (1920), and in the news media's caricatures of Southern fundamentalists during the Scopes 'monkey' trial of 1926. The 'Twelve Southerners' also hit out at Northern industrialism and its presumed puppet-mastery of New South activism. For the Agrarians, it was primarily 'industry' that doomed the New South project and the future of America, just as – in their selective revisionism – 'industry' (and not abolition or Federalism) had been the South's prime antagonist in the Civil War. One Agrarian, Frank Owsley, parodied Lincoln's famous 'House Divided' speech in order to make this point:

> This struggle between an agrarian and an industrial civilization ... was the irrepressible conflict, the house divided against itself, which must become according to the doctrine of the industrial section all the

one or all the other. It was the doctrine of intolerance, crusading, standardizing alike in industry and in life. The South had to be crushed out; it was in the way; it impeded the progress of the machine ('Twelve Southerners', 1977: 91).

The Agrarian arguments against industrialism were habitually impressionistic and often unsupported. Davidson, for example, declared industrialism 'anti-art', and art 'anti-industrial', with no other basis than a metaphorical crystal ball: 'The making of an industrialised society will extinguish the meaning of the arts, as humanity has known them in the past, by changing the conditions of life that have given art a meaning' (Ibid.: 29–30). For Ransom, 'malignant' Northern industrialism was a 'contemporary form of pioneering' that employed 'the latest scientific paraphernalia [to] sacrifice comfort, leisure, and the enjoyment of life to win Pyrrhic victories from nature at points of no strategic importance' (Ibid.: 15). John Gould Fletcher saw the destruction of Southern leisure and culture by industrial education, as well as by 'the present plague of factories and rash of cheap automobiles' (Ibid.: 96). John Donald Wade and Andrew Nelson Lytle respectively conjured up a victimised son and daughter of the New South. Wade's tragic victim was his impoverished Georgia cousin, Lucius, duped into believing 'that an agricultural community could fare well in a dance where the fiddles were all buzz-saws and the horns all steam-whistles' (Ibid.: 284). Lytle – who had himself chosen to abandon agriculture for Vanderbilt University, a year abroad in France and two years at the Yale Drama School – pitied the Southern milkmaid in her leisure:

> Industrialism gives an electric refrigerator, bottled milk, and dairy butter. It takes a few minutes to remove it from the ice to the table, while the agrarian process has taken several hours and is spread out over two or three days. Industrialism saves time, but what is to be done with this time? The milkmaid can't go to the movies, read the signboards, and go play bridge all the time (Ibid.: 223).

Robert Penn Warren co-opted Booker T. Washington and, by extension, the entire community of former slaves as allies against rampant industrialism. Washington, he wrote,

> realised that the masses of negroes, both then and for a long time thereafter, had to live by the production of their hands ... The most urgent need was to make the ordinary negro into a competent

workman or artisan and a decent citizen. Give him whatever degree of education was possible within the resources at hand, but above all give him a vocation (Ibid.: 250).

Warren had no comment on the possibilities for black aspiration that might have extended beyond his and Washington's limited horizons, or indeed the relationship between slavery, the plantation system and the poor 'resources at hand' that had ensured the underdevelopment of the South's educational sector.

As John Stewart notes, the Agrarians' 'abstractions', born out of 'naive parochialism', were constructed into a collective 'symbol made up of the most hideous features of New York, Chicago, Pittsburgh, and Detroit and representing all of America north of the Mason-Dixon line' (Stewart, 1965: 150). Such abstractions were misleadingly selective: 'Conveniently, the writers ignored the farmers of Indiana, New Jersey, and upstate New York; they forgot the men who raised dairy cattle in Ohio, sheep in New Hampshire, and apples in Maine; they overlooked the small tradesmen and self-employed craftsmen in countless villages of the North' (Ibid.: 151). Moreover, their invocations of the Old South – particularly its commitment to leisure – carried the whiff of hypocrisy:

> The gentlemen of the Old South who built fine mansions, whose sons knew enough Horace to season a political address, and whose daughters could play Mozart, lived off the culture of Northern and European mercantile-industrial societies, from whence came their education, books, fine china, musical instruments, furniture, draperies, and fashions (Ibid.: 201–02).

Nonetheless, the Agrarian Fletcher argued that the poor whites and subsistence farmers who, before the Civil War, could not avail themselves of such comforts, should be denied a post-bellum education system if it meant turning them into moral monstrosities of the Northern type:

> We shall not ... reproach our own mountaineer, poor white folk, for their little schooling and simpler manners, and for lacking those arts and graces that make the public-school product of New York City or Chicago a behaviorist, an experimental scientist in sex and firearms, a militant athiest, a reader of detective fiction, and a good salesman ('Twelve Southerners', 1977: 95).

By so selectively regionalising their objections to industrial culture – as did their antebellum predecessors – the Agrarians not only redefined the motives for the Civil War, but they also perpetuated the cycle of stereotype that had prompted their manifesto in the first place.

The Agrarians' stubbornly localised focus also led them to misperceive national and transnational problems as purely sectional ones, such as in their attempt to regionalise a cultural malaise – alienation – that actually pervaded transatlantic modernism. The dislocated, enervated New Southern subjects of (for instance) Tate's poem, 'To the Lacedemonians' (1936), are cut off from their past – as represented by the inaccessible Confederate dead – and are imprisoned in a restored United States, 'the country of the damned', with 'streets hard with motion' and 'dull commotion' (Tate, 1936: 85–8). Yet the old Confederate veterans do not hold the monopoly on dislocation and enervation: they share it with Eliot's waste-landers in London, with Joyce's Dubliners, with Svevo's Zeno in Trieste, as well as with the farmers and orchard-keepers in Frost's rural New England. This is perhaps one of the most paradoxical aspects of the Agrarian project, on the one hand opening itself to currents that transcend the concerns of region, and on the other hand determined to regionalise the afflictions it identifies.

In at least one instance, their attempted regionalisation of global complexities brought the Agrarians to the brink of ridicule, as demonstrated in Allen Tate's original intention – fortunately overruled by his colleagues – to title the Agrarian manifesto *Tracts against Communism*. As Tate explained in the introduction to *I'll Take My Stand*:

> The true Sovietists or Communists – if the term may be used here in the European sense – are the Industrialists themselves. They would have the government set up an economic super-organization, which in turn would become the government. We therefore look upon the Communist menace as a menace indeed, but not as a Red one; because it is simply according to the blind drift of our industrial development to expect in America at last much the same economic system as that imposed by violence upon Russia in 1917 ('Twelve Southerners', 1977: xlii).

This wilful, impossible equation of American industrialism with Soviet communism, ignoring or crudely ironing out the political and other systemic differences between the two, at least partially indicates the desperation with which the Agrarians sought to valorise aspects of antebellum Southern history and yoke them to contemporary problems.

In so doing – and especially in their near-total sidestepping of race – they 'avoided hard questions about the South itself' (King, 1980: 56). Nonetheless, they – like Harris, Dixon, Griffith, Mitchell and Disney – helped to pave the way for a revival of Confederate nationalism (see Chapter 5) whose adherents continue to invoke their names, prejudices and philosophy to an ever-widening and increasingly receptive white audience.

CHAPTER 3

Martyrdom and Memory

On 14 January 1995, a nineteen-year-old husband and father from Kentucky, Michael Westerman, was shot while driving in a pickup truck sporting the Confederate battle flag. He was white, and the alleged assailants were four black males. The leading neo-Confederate organisation, the League of the South (see Chapter 5), elegised Westerman as a 'Southern Patriot and Martyr' (League of the South, 1998). The League's designation of Westerman as such suggests both the attraction of invoking the concept of Civil War martyrdom for contemporary partisan purposes and the tendency to apply the label where it might not belong. For, as Jan Willem Van Henten emphasises, there must be an important element of choice in acts of martyrdom: 'A martyr is a person who in an extremely hostile situation prefers a violent death to compliance' (Van Henten, 2002: 3). In spite of the tragic senselessness of Westerman's death, there is no evidence that he chose to die for the Confederate flag – a choice more likely to have been made by the dead comrades of Allen Tate's 'old soldier' (see Chapter 2), who murmurs: 'Because I am here the dead wear gray' (Tate, 1936: 85). In this reading of 'To the Lacedemonians', the old soldier's very presence is enabled by his dead Confederate comrades who chose to die for their cause. In alluding to or invoking martyrdom – either legitimately, as does Tate, or illegitimately, as does the League of the South – these parties perpetuate one of the earliest and most important cultural tasks emerging from the Civil War: the construction of its martyr figures.

This task, of course, was not restricted to the Confederacy: by nearly all accounts, martyrdom is the basis of the preserved Union and its 'new birth of freedom' as uttered by Lincoln in the Gettysburg Address (1863), which dedicates the battlefield 'as a final resting place for those who here gave their lives that that nation might live' (in Basler et al., 1953: VII, 23). In his exploration of what he calls 'Gettysburg and the Culture of Death', Garry Wills points to 'the function of the cemetery as a training of the sensibilities' (Wills, 1992: 70). That function is shared by the interred dead who presumably chose the route to their 'final resting place'.

However, as the Civil War was the first American war in which conscription manned the armies of both sides, thus removing the crucial element of choice from the equation for thousands of war dead, even Lincoln's construction of martyrdom at Gettysburg opens itself to question – as, indeed, does that of Allen Tate. Nonetheless, martyrdom is inseparable from cultural expressions of the Civil War, and it is useful to examine a pair of case studies whose textual longevity has ensured their presence across a range of cultural forms well into the present day. These two cases – the anti-slavery guerrilla, John Brown, and the Confederate general, Stonewall Jackson – raise important considerations about the cultural uses and, perhaps, abuses of martyrdom.

John Brown's Body

The first of the Civil War's martyr figures was John Brown, who even before the war was the subject of a great descriptive crisis. He was either a terrorist or a freedom fighter, a madman or a genius, a treasonous criminal or God's avenging angel. After his aborted Harper's Ferry raid, his hanging was either the appropriate outcome of a well-functioning civil machine (as Lincoln, among many others, believed) or a veritable crucifixion (as Frederick Douglass, again among many others, believed). In the six-week interval between Brown's capture and his execution, Henry David Thoreau – in his 'Plea for Captain John Brown' (1860) – was already predicting the part that culture would play in fixing his status: 'I foresee the time when the painter will paint that scene [of Brown's trial], no longer going to Rome for a subject; the poet will sing it; the historian record it; and, with the Landing of the Pilgrims and the Declaration of Independence, it will be the ornament of some future national gallery' (Thoreau, 1860a: n. p.). To be sure, the visual images alone – from the gallows-bound saint kissing a black baby in Thomas Hovenden's oil painting, 'The Last Moments of John Brown' (c. 1884), to the ten-foot-tall avenger in John Steuart Curry's mural adorning the Kansas State Capitol, 'Tragic Prelude' (1937–42), to Raymond Massey's wild-eyed fanatic in the films *Santa Fe Trail* (1940) and *Seven Angry Men* (1954) – reflect the extremes to which Brown's historical reputation has been polarised in culture. The conflicting representations make Stephen Vincent Benét's question a crucial one: 'You can weigh John Brown's

Figure 3 *John Brown Executing His Hangman* (Jefferson Davis in drag), lithograph, 1865 (Library of Congress, Rare Book and Special Collections Division, LC-USZ62-92053).

body well enough, / But how and in what balance weigh John Brown?'
(Benét, 1990: 47).

Given that, in the oral version of his 'Plea', Thoreau was speaking
while Brown still lived, he was most likely the earliest – besides Brown
himself – to seize upon the trope that has brought John Brown into more
explicit kinship with the martyred Christ than any other American
figure, including Lincoln: his body, hanged and – as many subsequently
refigured it – resurrected. Thoreau declared: 'When a man stands up
serenely against the condemnation and vengeance of mankind, rising
above them literally *by a whole body* ... the spectacle is a sublime one'
(Thoreau, 1860a: n. p.). In another address, 'After the Death of John
Brown' (1860), Thoreau dwelt on the martyr's raiment – 'the clothes, all
cut and torn by sabres and by bayonet thrusts, in which he had been
taken prisoner' (Thoreau, 1860: n. p.). Brown's own part in engineering
his transformation from terrorist to martyr is well known. He viewed his
own hanged body as more valuable than his living one (as he wrote to his
friends and family from his prison cell), and the imagery of Golgotha in
his self-defence was carefully chosen: 'If it is deemed necessary that I
should forfeit my life for the furtherance of the ends of justice, and
mingle my blood further with the blood of my children and with the
blood of millions in this slave country whose rights are disregarded by
wicked, cruel, and unjust enactments, – I submit; so let it be done!' (in
Du Bois, 2001: 216).

Consequently, Richard Marius cites 'John Brown's Body Lies A-
Mould'ring in the Grave' as the Civil War's first important 'ideological
poem', the origins of which are – like its subject – a matter of conflicting
legend (Marius, 1994: xix). One version has it written by members of a
Massachusetts infantry regiment 'which had a sergeant by the name of
John Brown' (Watson and Dudley-Smith, 2002: 366). Another has it
coming from a quartet in the Boston Light Infantry who 'first sang it
publicly when it ... marched past the scene where Crispus Attucks fell'
(Du Bois, 2001: 224–5). A third version traces it to the composer
Thomas Bingham Bishop, who, upon learning of Brown's execution,
hastily rewrote the words of his camp-meeting hymn, 'Gone to Be a
Soldier in the Army of the Lord' (Brogan, 1990: 319). Less arguable is
the apotheosis of John Brown through the lyrics of the song, which has
his soul marching on even as his body lies 'a-mould'ring', and which
inspired Julia Ward Howe to recast it as the North's war anthem, 'Battle
Hymn of the Republic'.

More explicitly, Herman Melville's 'The Portent' (1859) invokes the wounds of Christ to turn the gallows into a cross for 'Weird John Brown ... The meteor of the war':

> Hanging from the beam,
>   Slowly swaying (such the law),
> Gaunt the shadow on your green,
>   Shenandoah!
> The cut is on the crown
>   (Lo, John Brown),
> And the stabs shall heal no more.
>   (Melville, 2000: 11)

Indeed, memorialists – white and black, male and female – looked to John Brown's body, his corporeality, as a metaphor for a route to the country's redemption. Just as no one could get to God but through eating of the body and drinking of the blood of Christ, so would the chained body and spilled blood of John Brown (mingled, terribly, with that of both the innocent and the guilty) save the Union, as W. E. B. Du Bois implied in his hagiographic biography (1909):

> 'I, John Brown, am quite certain that the crimes of this guilty land will never be purged away but with blood. I had, as I now think vainly, flattered myself that without very much bloodshed it might be done'.
>   These were the last written words of John Brown, set down the day he died – the culminating of that wonderful message of his forty days in prison, which all in all made the mightiest Abolition document that America has known' (Du Bois, 2001: 219).

It was left, however, to Benét to offer the first real epic of John Brown. As Alfred Haworth Jones argues, 'No American writer had ever undertaken a more ambitious poetic treatment of a national theme than Benét in *John Brown's Body*' (Jones, 1974: 32). Published in 1928 and selling over 100,000 copies in its first year, Benét's Pulitzer Prize-winning recreation of the Civil War acquired – for poetry – a uniquely popular status. As Cullen notes, Benét anchored John Brown's body to all subsequent US history: 'From Brown's grave came a united nation and a powerful beacon of hope' (Cullen, 1995: 28).

One of the great paradoxes of *John Brown's Body* is its sceptical treatment of the martyr-making process even as it succumbs to it. It is true that 'Martyr Day ceremonies were held across the North and in

Canada on December 2 [1859], the day John Brown was executed'
(Humez, 2003: 39). But Benét explicitly rubbishes the foundations of the
popular martyr lore surrounding Brown on the day of his execution:

> The North that had already now begun
> To mold his body into crucified Christ's,
> Hung fables about those hours – saw him move
> Symbolically, kiss a negro child,
> Do this and that, say things he never said,
> To swell the sparse, hard outlines of the event
> With sentimental omen.
>   It was not so.
> He stood on the jail-porch in carpet-slippers,
> Clad in a loose ill-fitting suit of black,
> Tired farmer waiting for his team to come.
>   (Benét, 1990: 51)

For Benét, John Brown's power lies less in his symbolic movement
toward the gallows than in his symbolic repose after he is cut down:

> John Brown's body lies a-mouldering in the grave.
> Already the corpse is changed, under the stone,
> The strong flesh rotten, the bones dropping away.
> Cotton will grow next year, in spite of the skull.
> Slaves will be slaves next year, in spite of the bones.
> Nothing is changed, John Brown, nothing is changed.
>
> *'There is a song in my bones. There is a song*
> *In my white bones'*
>   (Ibid.: 52)

Ultimately, the 'song' that emanates from 'the skeleton pipes of music'
within John Brown's grave is the Emancipation Proclamation, prior to
which there is merely 'the sound of armies / And that is an old sound'
(Ibid.: 53, 183). Through John Brown's body the nation is washed clean
of its cardinal sin – slavery – and is reborn as a distinctly masculine,
godlike industrial colossus:

> Out of John Brown's strong sinews the tall skyscrapers grow,
> Out of his heart the chanting buildings rise,
> Rivet and girder, motor and dynamo,
> Pillar of smoke by day and fire by night,

The steel-faced cities reaching at the skies.

(Ibid.: 335)

With such a legacy, it is understandable why such Southern Agrarian writers as Robert Penn Warren and Frank Owsley regretted the perpetuation of John Brown's name into the 1920s and 1930s, given their disgust with the victorious industrialism that had turned their beloved Old South into a Yankee-dominated New one (see Chapter 2). While the popular and critical acclaim for Benét's epic was still fresh, Owsley lamented: 'As time rolled on, the chorus of "John Brown's Body" swelled ever louder and louder until the lusty voice of grandchildren and great-grandchildren of rebels joined in the singing' ('Twelve Southerners', 1977: 65). The year of Benét's Pulitzer Prize, Warren responded with *John Brown: The Making of a Martyr* (1929), deploring the process through which 'the gallows' had been made 'glorious like the cross' and thereby obscured a critique of Brown's fanaticism, monomania, egotism, and his dangerously arrogant appeal to 'higher law' (Warren, 1929: 391).

John Brown's cultural uses extended even further, into the early stages of the Second World War, when the partisans of active US intervention were pitted against those of cautious domesticism or isolationism. The year 1940 saw three noteworthy productions: two poems by Muriel Rukeyser and Norman Rosten, and Michael Curtiz's film, *Santa Fe Trail*. Rukeyser's starkly interventionist 'The Soul and Body of John Brown' evokes the crusader for justice as the United States stands idle in the face of Hitler's gathering power, while 'Slaves under factories deal out identical / gestures of reaching' (in Marius, 1994: 128). The explicitly noble fanaticism of Rukeyser's Brown must surmount 'Not mountains, but men and women sleeping' to awaken (in the words of the epigraph from the Book of Joel) 'Multitudes, multitudes in the valley of decision!' (Ibid.: 123, 125). In unison with Rukeyser, Rosten rhetorically asks – by way of his poem's title – '*Where was Lincoln when they hanged John Brown?*' (Rosten, 1940: 39, italics in original). The substance of Brown's true 'Americanism' (which, to Rosten, shamed the US government by contrast) lay in his determination to act: 'if something wasn't on the true level / a man always had his two arms and a gun / to set it right – if the law didn't help' (Ibid.: 39).

Yet, in spite of progressive voices like these, the combined talents of Michael Curtiz, Errol Flynn, Ronald Reagan and Raymond Massey – backed by the budget of Warner Brothers Studios – ensured that the dominant image of John Brown in 1940 would be that of 'a fiery psychopath brutally interfering in a system gently in the process of reforming itself' (Newman, 1990: 21). Chasing Brown (Massey) and his sons through Kansas and ultimately to Harper's Ferry, the West Point classmates and rivals in love, the Southern-born J. E. B. Stuart (Flynn) and the Northern-born George A. Custer (Reagan), make the case for non-intervention. 'Jeb, there's a purpose behind that madness,' says Custer of Brown, 'one that can't easily be dismissed.' Stuart chides him: 'It isn't our job to decide who's right and who's wrong about slavery, any more than it is John Brown's.' Suitably chastened, Custer replies: 'I guess you're right, Jeb. I'm sorry.' Brown perishes on the gallows, uttering on screen the words of Christ – which he did not utter in real life – 'God forgive them for they know not what they do', earning the final ironic judgement from Robert E. Lee (Moroni Olsen): 'So perish all such enemies of the Union, all such fools of the human race.' The implication is that John Brown's interference provoked a greater crime than slavery itself, as Stuart's fiancée, Kit Holliday (Olivia DeHavilland) implies as she looks up at the gallows: 'I see something else up there. Something much more terrible than just one man' (Curtiz, 1940).

In the same year, Massey gained critical acclaim for exchanging his role of Brown for that of Lincoln in John Cromwell's film version of Robert Sherwood's play, *Abe Lincoln in Illinois* (see Chapter 4). The role-reversal is instructive: Massey plays Lincoln as a decidedly reluctant interventionist dragged towards his destiny as the Great Emancipator, illustrating Benét's assertion that Lincoln completed Brown's unfinished work – an assertion more explicitly underlined in the film when, under arrest at Harper's Ferry, Brown (played by Cromwell himself) is told by his dying son, 'It's no use, Pa. You gotta give in. Somebody else has gotta finish this job' (Cromwell, 1940). However, Massey's Lincoln is the epitome of caution and compromise, driven ultimately to intervention, but not precipitously. Cromwell's Brown, by contrast, is as wild-eyed and fanatical as Massey's own in *Santa Fe Trail*.

As if to further discredit Brown's interventionism – this time in the context of the 1950s and the desegregation struggle – Massey returned to the role of John Brown in Charles Marquis Warren's *Seven Angry Men* (1954). This film challenges the political credibility of Brown's activism through emphasising the tragedy he wreaked upon his family through his abolitionist obsession – a challenge made in the very year of the Supreme Court's *Brown* v. *Board of Education of Topeka* decision striking down the 'separate but equal' doctrine, which the court subsequently shied away from enforcing in spite of its express order for the South to desegregate 'with all deliberate speed' (Lieberman, 1987: 306–07).

Amidst such signals that militant activism amounted to an intrusion or outrage upon an otherwise peaceful body politic, John Brown proceeded towards what must be his nadir in popular culture, Paul Bogart's comedy film, *Skin Game* (1971), in which Brown's progression from holy martyr to laughing stock is all but complete. In this farce, stripped of political didacticism, Brown (Royal Dano) blunders into a scam played by a white confidence man, Quincy (James Garner), and his black partner, Jason (Lou Gossett). The scam works by Quincy selling Jason to wealthy slave-owners and then rescuing him; they make a fortune repeating the confidence game all over Missouri. When they stray into Kansas, Jason is 'rescued' by the unwelcome avenger, John Brown, from whom he is obliged to escape if he wants to continue with the scam. Again, the implication is that all would be well if John Brown had not come a-meddling.

John Brown's subsequent appearances in cultural texts have been few, if more complex. The British author, George MacDonald Fraser, threw his roguish Victorian hero, Flashman, into the company of Brown at Harper's Ferry in *Flashman and the Angel of the Lord* (1994), in which 'old J. B.' modulates – as he did in popular commentary – between the extremes of 'murderous rustler' and 'Christ with six-guns' (Fraser, 1999: 89). Flashman, in spite of his trademark irreverence for anything except the saving of his own skin, is keenly aware of the political and cultural work to be done by Brown's martyrdom, including its deliberate function of obscuring the man's earthly history:

> Aye, if there's a company of saints up yonder, they'll be dressing by the right on J.B., for when the Recording Angel has racked up all his crimes and lies and thefts and follies and deceits and cold-blooded killings, he'll still be saved when better men are damned. Why? 'Cos if he wasn't, there'd be such an almighty roar of indignation from the Heavenly Host it would bust the firmament; God would never live it down. That's the beauty of a martyr's crown, you see; it outshines everything, and they don't come any brighter than old J.B.'s. I'm not saying he deserves it; I only know, perhaps better than anyone, how he came by it (Ibid.: 19).

'How he came by it' is also the concern of the novelist, Russell Banks, whose massive *Cloudsplitter* (1998), told from the point of view of John

Brown's aged son, Owen, attempts to demythologise and humanise the historical figure while critiquing the construction of his martyrdom. Brown's martyrdom, Owen admits, indeed had its practical uses: 'Father's progression from activist to martyr, his slow march to willed disaster, can be viewed, not as a descent into madness, but as a reasonable progression – especially if one consider the political strength of those who in those days meant to keep chattel slavery the law of the land' (Banks, 1998: 675). But Brown's martyrdom also has its price for others caught up in the making of the martyr. At one point, while addressing a research assistant helping to prepare Oswald Garrison Villard's great biography of Brown, Owen acknowledges that his father had been 'celebrated and sung by all the most famous poets, writers, and philosophers here and abroad'. Still, he asks:

> But who amongst your new, young historians and biographers, even amongst those who loathe him or think him mad, has considered the price paid for that sort of greatness by those of us who were his family? Those of us who neither examined him from a safe distance, as you do, nor stood demurely in his protective shadow, as we have so often been portrayed, but who lived every single day in the full glare of his light? (Ibid.: 103)

Ultimately, Owen must conclude that John Brown's martyrdom could not obliterate his crimes at Pottawatomie and elsewhere – 'the wasted deaths of all those others whose bodies lie now before me' (Ibid.: 532). The martyrdom of John Brown as explored by Banks and his predecessors thus carries obvious resonance in the twenty-first century, in which the combination of martyrdom and murder continues to complicate political activism around the globe.

Children in North America and Britain now sing a parody of 'John Brown's Body' – 'John Brown's baby had a cold upon his chest, / So they rubbed him with camphorated oil' – certainly without being aware of the origins of that song in American slavery, murder and deliberate, highly orchestrated martyrdom. This is a significant indication of Brown's potency as a cultural figure who has been worked into the consciousness of the oblivious as well as the knowing. Just as children continue to sing 'Ring-a-ring-a-rosy' knowing nothing of the Black Death that inspired it, their song of 'John Brown's Baby' is freighted with history and dripping with blood.

The subject of the following case study, Stonewall Jackson, cannot claim the same popular currency among juveniles (although he has been treated in children's literature), but among adults his name is synonymous with martyrdom in the service of the Confederate cause. Consequently, he has – with the aid of American culture – been lifted from the ranks of the merely human, to the great satisfaction of his defenders and to the disgust of his detractors who associate his cause with the perpetuation of white supremacy and slavery. In one case – as we shall see – Jackson, as an icon, demonstrates a potential for interracial habitation, although he has yet to approach John Brown in his capacity for cultural appropriation by blacks as well as whites. Nonetheless, he shares with Brown an aura of holy martyrdom, the preparations for which he, too, witnessed in his lifetime.

Stonewall Jackson's Way

In Ronald Maxwell's film, *Gods and Generals* (2003) – based on Jeff Shaara's novel of the same name (1996) – Thomas 'Stonewall' Jackson is brought to the screen for the first time since the silent film era. Played by the New York actor Stephen Lang, who dominates the film, Jackson alternates between ruthlessness and gentleness, but is always a determined, devout Christian soldier. Most importantly, he appears deliberately constructed to diminish the mythic haze obscuring the historical figure. As Maxwell explained in an interview, 'I am not interested in putting Jackson or (Robert E.) Lee or (Joshua Lawrence) Chamberlain or any of these people on a pedestal. I am not interested in deifying them. I am interested in presenting them in their full humanity' (quoted in Collier, 2003: D1). This suggests that the contemporary historical film, as a genre, may seek deliberately to reduce the inflated, iconic status of historical figures – to make them realistic and humanly believable again – thereby enhancing, if all goes well, the professional iconic status of the actors who portray them.

In Jackson's case, this marks a reversal in a hagiographic process that began in the very midst of the Civil War. Jackson was a celebrity before his death, and his larger-than-life image pervades the war's popular-culture output even today. A glance through the latest monthly or seasonal issues of glossy magazines such as *Blue and Gray* ('For Those Who Still Hear the Guns'), *America's Civil War* and *Civil War Times* will reveal a wealth of Jackson merchandise – prints, crockery, ceramic statues and beer mugs all bearing his image. Popular artists such as Mort Künstler, Don Troiani and Don Stivers have built lucrative careers around the readership of such magazines, with Jackson surpassed only by Robert E. Lee as a favourite subject (Gallagher, 1998: 103–04).

In terms of iconic status, however, Stonewall Jackson has the edge over Lee in one respect: his martyrdom. Shot by his own men at the battle of Chancellorsville in 1863, Jackson – whom Lee called his 'right arm' – became 'the first icon, the ultimate offering for the Southern cause' (Robertson, 1997: ix). With Jackson, so innumerable elegies repeated, went the Confederacy's hopes for independence. As a clergyman intoned in 1881 at the unveiling of a New Orleans monument: '*And Thou knowest O Lord, that when Thou didst decide that the Confederacy should not succeed, Thou hadst first to remove Thy servant, Stonewall Jackson*' (in Shaara, 2002: 491). Thus, even before his death, with his celebrity firmly established in the first two years of the war, Jackson was the South's own Christian martyr in the making – not, it must be said, in the self-conscious manner of John Brown, who placed a higher value on his own dead body then on his living one. Stonewall Jackson did not actively seek his own death, although, as an enlisted frontline general wholly committed to the Confederate cause, he was willing to accept it.

Members of the white Southern population actively, if unwittingly, played their part in ensuring that, in the event of Jackson's death, it would be that of a holy martyr. Southern women would 'come to him with children in their arms to ask for his blessing upon the infants' (Robertson, 1998: 71), while an Alabama soldier went so far as to elevate Jackson's holiness over that of his greatest rival in martyrdom: 'If Jesus Christ were to ride along the ranks on the foal of an ass … there would not be half the cheering and huzzaing that there is when General Jupiter Stonewall Jackson rides along our ranks' (in Robertson, 1997: 628).

It is important to recognise the complex process by which an individual, in becoming first a legend, and then a martyr, often draws his aura from the anonymous, conflicting sources around him. Jackson earned his captivating nickname from one of a number of possible utterances at the first battle of Manassas. The most commonly quoted is, 'Look at Jackson, men, standing like a stone wall'; but as Hugh Brogan cites it, it was 'Look at Jackson's men, standing like a stone wall', conferring the honour more upon his men than upon Jackson himself (Brogan, 1990: 330). Ken Burns's documentary, *The Civil War* (1990; see Chapter 7) quotes a more ambiguous utterance that lies somewhere between the first two: 'Look, there's Jackson with his Virginians, standing like a stone wall' (Burns, 1990: episode 1). It is not clear here who is standing like the proverbial wall – Jackson or his Virginians. Such questions are not meant to detract from Jackson's well-earned reputation as a battlefield commander and tactician (acknowledged even in his lifetime by observers across America and Europe), but rather to interrogate the processes by which an iconic aura is assumed and then built upon.

The Alabama soldier quoted above remarked of Jackson, 'The soldiers cheer him as if they think him to possess some supernatural power' (in Robertson, 1997: 628). As both Robertson and Robert Tanner suggest, Jackson's deliberate secrecy as a strategist enhanced his supernatural aura in the midst of the war. Robertson notes that Jackson 'veiled all of his great movements in mystery' (Robertson, 1998: 75); consequently, 'his army seemed to simply drop from sight' (Tanner, 1994: 779). Adding to Jackson's carefully maintained aura of mystery was a host of personal eccentricities that were circulated and popularised across the print media. Gary Gallagher writes: 'He was the "lemon sucker", a fanatic about health who sat bolt upright to keep his internal organs aligned, held one hand aloft so his blood would run down and establish equilibrium, refused to eat pepper because it weakened his constitution, and so on' (Gallagher, 1998: 116). Such exaggerations and half-truths 'gained wide circulation during the war and have remained firmly embedded in the literature ever since' (Ibid.: 116). As Michael Shaara's fictionalised James Longstreet says of Jackson in *The Killer Angels*, 'A little eccentricity is a help to a general. It helps with the newspapers' (Shaara, 1996: 139).

In the end, Robertson attempts to encapsulate Jackson's aura in one word: 'charisma' (Robertson, 1998: 72). However, Clifford Geertz has highlighted aspects of 'charisma' – drawn from Max Weber – that, at the very least, problematise any such easy explanation:

> At once 'a certain quality' that marks an individual as standing in a privileged relationship to the sources of being, and a hypnotic power 'certain personalities' have to engage passions and dominate minds, it is not clear whether charisma is the status, the excitement, or some ambiguous fusion of the two (Geertz, 1993: 121).

What is more clear is the importance of the particular aspects of a subject's history that have contributed to, but may also be obscured by, the charismatic aura surrounding him. In Jackson's case, three major aspects are his 'obsession with honor, concern for salvation, and genius for destroying his fellow men' (Stewart, 1965: 322).

Figure 4 Women Mourning at Stonewall Jackson's Grave, c. 1866 (unknown photographer: courtesy of Virginia Military Institute Archives).

The first two are commonly combined in Jackson iconography, as indicated by more than one reconstruction. In the 1930s, the Southern Agrarian Frank Owsley chose to depict Ulysses Grant as so moved by the spectre of Jackson that he could – at least for a moment – cease his depredations of the South and reflect upon Jackson's holiness. Hatless at the threshold of the house where Jackson died, Owsley's Grant mutters, 'General Jackson was a gallant soldier and a Christian gentleman' ('Twelve Southerners', 1977: 61–2). In the immediate aftermath of the war, in her memoir of four years in the Lincoln White House, Elizabeth Keckley (see Chapter 6) put similar sentiments about Jackson into the mouth of the US president: '"He is a brave, honest, Presbyterian soldier", were his words; "What a pity that we should have to fight such a gallant fellow!"' (Keckley, 1868: 137).

Relatively few of Jackson's memorialists have allied his gallantry and Christianity with his 'genius for destroying his fellow men', but those who have done so have – deliberately or otherwise – brought out the paradox inherent in the phrase 'Christian soldier'. The first popular poem in Jackson's honour, John Williamson Palmer's 'Stonewall Jackson's

Way' (1862) – quickly adopted as a Confederate marching song – has him

> Appealing from his native sod,
> *In forma pauperis* to God –
> 'Lay bare thine arm; stretch forth thy rod'

before darkly warning,

> The foe had better ne'er been born,
> That gets in Stonewall's way
>   (in Marius, 1994: 296–9).

In *John Brown's Body* (1928), Stephen Vincent Benét likewise fuses the martial with the holy in describing the 'Cromwell-eyed' Jackson and the 'Presbyterian sabre of his soul' (Benét, 1990: 51, 169), while Jeff Shaara's Jackson vows, 'General Lee, if it will please God, we will kill them *all*' (Shaara, 2002: 396).

The fact that Jackson distinguished himself by his ruthlessness in killing rather than capturing, and executing rather than pardoning, is unsurprisingly downplayed in the cultural iconography, Northern as well as Southern. John Greenleaf Whittier's 'Barbara Frietchie' (1863) has Jackson's troops marching through Maryland, confronted by a local woman, 'old Barbara Frietchie ... Bowed with her fourscore years and ten', who defiantly waves the US flag in their faces (in Marius, 1994: 307). Improbably shamed in his rebellion against that flag, Whittier's Jackson has a 'nobler nature within him stirred', but – still full of menace and incipient savagery – he warns his troops, 'Who touches a hair of yon gray head / Dies like a dog!' (in Ibid.: 308). Only in the Southern poet Sidney Lanier's 'The Dying Words of Stonewall Jackson' (1865) can the words themselves 'miniature his deeds', as though Jackson's battlefield ruthlessness could ultimately be spoken away (in Ibid.: 311).

The Union victory initially inspired contrasting sectional responses to Jackson before he was adopted by the victorious Northerners in the service of what Nina Silber has called 'the romance of reunion' (Silber, 1993: passim). In the poetry collection, *Battle Pieces* (1866), Herman Melville forbade 'the grandchildren of General Grant' to 'pursue with rancor, or slur by sour neglect, the memory of Stonewall Jackson' (Melville, 2000: 262). Melville's two poems for Jackson balance respect for the man's earnestness with contempt for his cause and scepticism about his martyr status. Thus, in 'Stonewall Jackson', 'We drop a tear on the bold Virginian's bier, / Because no wreath we owe' (Ibid.: 80), while in 'Stonewall Jackson: Ascribed to a Virginian', the South itself is depicted as weeping for the hero who 'fell in the South's vain war' (Ibid.: 83).

Walking a tightrope between Confederate patriotism and fealty to the restored Union, certain white Southerners strove to perpetuate Jackson's memory for the instructive benefit of all the nation's children, Southern and Northern. Thus, Sarah Randolph's juvenile biography, *The Life of General Thomas J. Jackson* (1876), promises its readers 'who are striving to make headway against a sea of troubles in their walk through life, what encouragement it offers, what lessons in patient perseverance!' (Randolph, 1876: 354). Similarly, Mary L. Williamson's *The Life of Thomas J. Jackson ('Stonewall'), In Easy Words for the Young* (1899) is

DEDICATED
TO ALL YOUTHS WHO
ADMIRE THE CHRISTIAN VIRTUES
AND MILITARY GENIUS OF
THOMAS J. JACKSON

– virtues 'upon which the young people of our day will do well to build' (Williamson, 1899: i). Works such as these do not wholly avoid references to the political causes and consequences of the war, but in general they choose to emphasise Jackson's martyrdom as a holy example of a reunified America's claim to greatness.

Yet, for all attempts at incorporating Jackson into the narrative of reunion, he cannot be wholly separated from the Confederate cause, which in turn cannot be separated from the defence of slavery and white supremacy. At the dedication to the first major post-bellum monument to Jackson, in Richmond, Virginia, in 1875, Governor James L. Kemper declared: 'It revives no animosities of the past ... to honor and revere the memory of Jackson ... His example belongs to mankind, and his deeds and virtues will be cherished by all the coming generations of the great American republic as among the proudest memories of a common glory' (in Randolph, 1876: 360). Yet, black participants were excluded from this unifying ceremony, save for 'a contingent of former slave workers who had been in the Stonewall Brigade during the war'; such 'racial ordering', in David Blight's words, shows 'much of what was at stake in Southern memorialization as it went public' at the end of Reconstruction (Blight, 2001: 83).

If indeed 'Jim Crow danced his steps at hundreds of Confederate monument unveilings' in the wake of the Richmond ceremony (Ibid.: 272), at least once black American has recently chosen to stake a claim upon Jackson in a fashion that would not be appreciated by his white supremacist champions. In 1995, David Jonathan Sawyer published a book entitled *My Great-Grandfather Was Stonewall Jackson: The Story of a Negro Boy Growing Up in the Segregated South*. Sawyer's claim is based on research that, he argues, validates a rumour long denied by Jackson's white champions, that as a young cadet Jackson fathered an illegitimate child by a black woman. Ironically or not, Sawyer seized on Jackson for the very reasons urged by those Reconstruction-era biographers writing for the white children of the South. As he explains:

> Though there's not a Confederate bone in my body, my hero for all of my boyhood and most of my adult life was Thomas Jonathan 'Stonewall' Jackson ... Since he had been my kin, I thought it my right to call on his spirit in times of trouble ... How better for a boy to grow up than with Stonewall Jackson at his side? (Sawyer, 1995: 292)

Read symbolically, Sawyer's appropriation of Jackson may be the most successful of all attempts to effect a 'union' or 'reunion' in his name, at least in racial if not in national terms.

Certainly, the same cannot be said for such failed attempts as that by the Virginia state legislature to establish 'Lee-Jackson-King Day' in the early 1990s – a brief, 'bizarre fusion of the Civil War and civil rights', argued on the grounds that 'all three men were "defenders of causes"' (Horwitz, 1998: 41). In his travel narrative, *Confederates in the Attic: Dispatches from the Unfinished Civil War* (1998), Tony Horwitz encounters a young black preacher from Virginia named Michael King:

> I asked King if there was any way for white Southerners to honor their forebears without insulting his. He pondered this for a moment. 'Remember your ancestors', he said, 'but remember what they fought for too, and recognise it was wrong. Then maybe you can invite me to your Lee and Jackson birthday party' (Ibid.: 44).

As a black Southerner without the benefit of Stonewall Jackson's blood running in his veins, Michael King offers less scope than does David Jonathan Sawyer for the universal embracing of this particular martyr figure, either in the South or the United States at large.

The assertion and the denial of martyrdom are part of the Civil War's cultural history. Building upon this discussion of John Brown and

Stonewall Jackson, the next chapter is devoted to the Civil War's (and America's) greatest martyr figure, its Ur-martyr, about whom, it is likely, more words have been written, more images graven and more feet of film exposed than about any other American historical figure. At the extreme of his deification, he is religiously inscribed into the American landscape itself – at Mount Rushmore, South Dakota, where Gutzon Borglum carved his image into the pantheon of the 'great white fathers' dominating the conquered holy lands of the Sioux (Taliaferro, 2002: 26–7). In Washington, DC, he has his own 'temple', in which 'the memory of Abraham Lincoln is enshrined forever', designed – as its architect, Henry Bacon, phrased it – to enable Americans to internalise 'the words of this inspired man who "though dead, yet speaketh"' (in Thomas, 2002: 70, 130). At his most degraded, Lincoln, through his body, has been dragged down to earth in vulgar contrast to his heavenly resurrection. Carnivalised in the doggerel still circulating throughout the South, the martyred civic god is mocked through the irreverent baring of 'the lower stratum of [his] body' (Bakhtin, 1984: 21):

> *Abraham Lincoln was a son of a bitch,*
> *His ass ran over with a seven-year itch,*
> *His fist beat his dick like a blacksmith's hammer,*
> *While his asshole whistled the Star-Spangled Banner*
> (in Horwitz, 1998: 147)

In between these two extremes of exaltation and debasement lies a wealth of cultural and political uses to which Abraham Lincoln has been put since the Civil War.

CHAPTER 4

Abe Lincoln's Mixed Reviews

When the US novelist Kurt Vonnegut lamented an increasing inability for writers to connect with modern readers through points of historical reference, he chose as an example 'the murder of the greatest President this country will ever have, Abraham Lincoln, by the twenty-six-year-old ham actor, John Wilkes Booth ... Who is there left under the age of sixty, and not in a History Department, to give a damn?' (Vonnegut, 1997: 193–4). In fact, American popular culture has long assumed a degree of cultural interest in, and literacy about, Lincoln, enough to sustain an entire parodic industry. This is most important, as parody always relies upon a 'historical awareness' of the subject being parodied (Hutcheon, 2000: 4).

Thus, in *The Simpsons* (to choose one of the most recent examples), when Homer is thwarted in his attempts to find 'Lincoln's gold' buried in the White House grounds, his characteristic outburst – 'That lying, rail-splitting, theatre-going freak!' – assumes a common knowledge about the particulars of Lincoln's iconography, if not his biography (Greaney, 2000). A second, very witty, *Simpsons* episode assumes a common knowledge about Lincoln's place in popular culture. When Lisa appeals to Lincoln's statue for advice in an episode entitled, 'Mr. Lisa Goes to Washington' (Meyer, 1991), it is a direct reference to Frank Capra's film, *Mr. Smith Goes to Washington* (1939), in which the idealistic junior senator, Jefferson Smith (James Stewart), gazes at the Lincoln Memorial, murmuring in awe, 'That Mister Lincoln, there he is. He's just lookin' right straight at you as you come up those steps. Just sitting there like he was waiting for somebody to come along' (Capra, 1939).

Thus, like John Brown, Lincoln is a figure who has endlessly inhabited American culture since his death. He functions, for instance, as a science-fiction character: the writers of *Star Trek* beamed him aboard the starship *Enterprise*, where he famously purred to Lieutenant Uhura, 'What a charming Negress', only a few months after the same show

Figure 5 Marilyn Monroe with Her Portrait of Lincoln, Los Angeles, 1954 (Milton H. Greene: courtesy of MHG Archives, www.archivesmhg.com).

premièred US television's first interracial kiss (Daugherty, 1969). In Philip K. Dick's novel, *We Can Build You* (1972), Lincoln, as a sentient automaton, uses his legal skill to protect his inventors amidst sinister corporate skulduggery – a rendering very likely to resonate in the minds of those familiar with one of Disneyland's most famous attractions, the Lincoln simulacrum 'capable of performing 275,000 possible combinations of facial expressions and body movements' (Morris, 1991: 6).

More intriguingly, American culture has succeeded in casting Lincoln as a sexual icon – suggesting that he is potent enough to be resurrected through sex as well as through the invocation of his words. Joshua Logan's *Bus Stop* (1956) has cowboy Don Murray attempting to seduce cabaret singer Marilyn Monroe by murmuring the Gettysburg Address into her ear. The seduction is foiled by Monroe's protective landlady calling through the door, 'If you go any further, *Mister Lincoln*, you're gonna miss the parade' (Logan, 1956). Arguably, some of the scene's sexual tension is informed by Monroe's own publicly acknowledged hero-worshipping of Lincoln. As Gloria Steinem relates: 'Until the end of her life, she displayed a portrait of Lincoln in each place she lived, and usually a copy of the Gettysburg Address as well' (Steinem, 1987: 169). Monroe maintained that she was first attracted to her husband, the playwright Arthur Miller, for his resemblance to the young Lincoln, while she believed – as she told the British journalist, W. J. Wetherby – that her alleged lover, John F. Kennedy, would 'be another Lincoln' (Wetherby, 1989: 206).

Arguments over Lincoln's sexuality still simmer in public discourse, largely fuelled by the playwright and gay rights activist, Larry Kramer, who has claimed that Lincoln had an extensive affair with his closest friend, Joshua Speed. As one of Lincoln's chief defenders, Gabor S. Boritt, argues, Kramer's purpose was to force 'the country, indeed the world, [to] contemplate the possibility that its greatest son was gay', leading to a ceremony in 2000 in which over a thousand gay people held 'a mock marriage' at the foot of the Lincoln Memorial (Boritt, 2001: xv).

Thus, what Vonnegut perhaps perceives is not a contemporary indifference to Lincoln, murdered 140 years ago, but rather the ruthless ability of popular culture to absorb, re-work, and play with Lincoln, murder and all. The comedian Lenny Bruce sensed as much in the early 1960s when he claimed:

> I definitely know that I could do a satire on the assassination of Abraham Lincoln and really get screams with it on television. Although Abraham Lincoln was a wonderful man ... Satire is tragedy plus time. You give it enough time, the public, the reviewers will allow you to satirise it (Bruce, 1975: 204).

Within living memory of Lincoln's assassination, such a satire would have been practically unthinkable – at least in the North. As Lloyd Lewis argued in 1929, Lincoln was still 'the dying god of America':

> After the fashion of older dying gods in older worlds, he had come stalking up from among the people, often mocked, unrecognised for what he was until death had claimed him. It was not until Abraham Lincoln had been killed and his body shown to the people that he was understood by the American masses to have been their long-awaited folk god (Lewis, 1941: 351–2).

However, it is clear that Lewis cannot have been speaking for the South. In spite of Vonnegut's complaint that there is no one left to 'give a damn' about Lincoln, that is precisely what many Southerners are still prepared to give, judging from Borrit's report of public reactions to the opening of the Lincoln Center for American Studies at Louisiana State University in 2001. As one citizen wrote in protest: 'An International Abraham Lincoln Center? To honor the mass murderer who slew 300,000 southern men, women, and children? That precursor of Lenin, Hitler, and Stalin? Are you out of your mind?' (in Boritt, 2001: xxvi). The polarised opinions here – from Vonnegut's 'greatest President' to this protester's 'mass murderer' – appear to give the lie to the chorus-like character, the Balladeer, in the Stephen Sondheim/John Weidman musical, *Assassins* (1991). Confronting the washed-up 'ham actor', John Wilkes Booth, the Balladeer chides him: 'Lincoln, who got mixed reviews, / Because of you, John, now gets only raves' (Sondheim and Weidman, 1991: 22). Clearly, Lincoln still gets 'mixed reviews' rather than all 'raves', but the Balladeer is right in dating the 'raves' to Lincoln's assassination, the first of any American president. The Virginia novelist James Branch Cabell sarcastically congratulated Booth for ensuring Lincoln's deification – 'He was killed, treacherously, upon Good Friday: and was duly buried' (in Wilson, 1966: 97–8) – after which the references to Calvary and Good Friday proliferated in over a century of poetry, fiction, oratory and film about Lincoln.

Lincoln's detractors have been up against a monumental cultural project in canonisation. Hence the responses to just one attempt, that of the US historian, Frank Klement, to present Lincoln 'as a historical figure rather than as a national hero' in his study of Lincoln's Northern critics: 'The headlines … screamed the news – "Abe Lincoln myth shred by historian", "Abe's halo is slipping", "Lincoln no saint, professor says"' (Klement, 1999: xxviii, 183). The fact that this hagiographic project has been largely limited to north of the Mason–Dixon line does not diminish its power. Still, as Michael Davis notes, 'the South, more than any other part of the nation, has remained immune to the apotheosis of Lincoln':

> The South remains the most fertile source of anti-Lincoln jokes and anecdotes ranging from the humorous to the vulgar. Those vestals who guard the temple of Southern tradition still deny that Lincoln may be mentioned in the company of Jefferson Davis and Stonewall Jackson; certainly, Lincoln cannot approach Robert E. Lee in the Southern pantheon … His statue is seldom found in the South, and

only a few communities in the states of the late Confederacy are named for Lincoln. Few schools below the Mason-Dixon line bear his name (Davis, 1971: 4).

As argued by two of the most strident neo-Confederate apologists, the brothers James and Walter Kennedy, founders of the League of the South (see Chapter 5): 'Little wonder … that the modern world should have been introduced to the cruel and inhuman concept of total war not by rampaging Nazis but by the heartless brigades of Abraham Lincoln's army of Northern aggression and occupation' (Kennedy, 2001: 240).

At the bar of public and critical opinion, the tug-of-war over Lincoln's reputation rages back and forth across a number of divides. In one illustrative case – the debate over the Minnesota Sioux uprising of 1862, upon which Lincoln sanctioned the death sentences of 39 Native Americans – one charge (from the Kennedys) reads: 'Lincoln is America's only president to order a mass execution!' (Ibid.: 31). In Lincoln's defence, Boritt claims that by reducing the number of executions from 303 to 39, he 'cheated the gallows of 264 Indians. He performed by far the largest act of executive clemency in American history' (Boritt, 2001: xxiv). Charge: Lincoln was a dictator; he restricted civil liberties, suspended the writ of habeas corpus, suppressed the press and free elections, and arrested 'virtually anyone who disagreed with his views', resulting in the gaoling of 'over thirteen thousand American civilians' (DiLorenzo, 2003: 132). Rebuttal: 'Lincoln was not a dictator: elections occurred on schedule throughout the war, and the Democratic press continued to flourish. Restrictions on civil liberties in no way matched the massive repression during World War One' (Foner, 2003: 14).

More emotionally charged and complex is the debate that pits Lincoln the Great Emancipator against Lincoln the white supremacist. It is frequently argued that Lincoln's Emancipation Proclamation (1863) was a mere gesture – rather late in the day, at that – or a political sleight-of-hand that freed no slaves where it could have done so (the loyal, slave-holding Border States) while euphemistically 'freeing' those only where it could not be enforced (Confederate territory). Defence: Lincoln had to prevent the Border States from pitching themselves into the Confederate camp or the war would be lost. He could hardly just abolish slavery by executive fiat, since it was protected by the Constitution he was sworn to uphold, and as Commander-in-Chief he couldn't issue a proclamation as a military measure without a Northern victory to back it up – and he didn't get anything *close* to that until Antietam in September 1862. At any rate, Lincoln engineered the Thirteenth Amendment, which outlawed American slavery forever. Rebuttal: Not so, for the Thirteenth Amendment

> was authored and pressured into existence not by Lincoln but by the great emancipators nobody knows, the abolitionists and congressional leaders who created the climate and generated the pressure that goaded, prodded, drove, *forced* Lincoln into glory by associating him with a policy that he adamantly opposed for at least fifty-four of the fifty-six years of his life (Bennett, 2000: 19).

Charge: Lincoln said, 'I am not, nor ever have been, in favor of bringing about in any way the social and political equality of the white and black races ... [W]hile they do remain together there must be the position of superior and inferior, and I as much as any other man am in favor of having the superior assigned to the white race' (in Basler, 1953: III, 145). Defence: 'Had he not [said] so, we would never have heard of Abraham Lincoln. America's most effective antislavery champion would have disappeared from history. For such was antebellum Illinois, such was the United States' (Boritt, 2001a: 5). Lincoln said – and he meant – 'If slavery is not wrong, then nothing is wrong' (in Basler, 1953: VII, 281). Rebuttal: Lincoln said – and he meant – 'If I could save the Union without freeing *any* slaves I would do it ... What I do about slavery, and the colored race, I do because I believe it helps to save the Union; and what I forbear, I forbear because I do *not* believe it would help to save the Union' (Ibid.: V, 388). Summation: 'Lincoln as president was actually a better safeguard for the continued existence of slavery in the South than secession' (Guelzo, 2001: 102).

The accusations and rebuttals can be taken much further than this. In their totality, the combined words and deeds of Abraham Lincoln are suspended in a hall of mirrors, so targeted were they at particular constituencies at particular times. Above all, as Lincoln was thoroughly a political animal (which is by no means to say an amoral or immoral one), and 'probably the most plastic figure in US history', his legacy includes not only the preserved Union and the revised Constitution but also 'the man/hero and fact/myth dialectics' (Cullen, 1995: 41). These dialectics have played a crucial part in both the cultural and political uses of Lincoln, and the twenty-first century has shown early signs that more use is yet to be made of him.

What would Lincoln do?

The Welsh travel writer, Jan Morris, writes of the man she pursued in *Lincoln: A Foreigner's Quest* (1991): 'I think of his legacy to the world as equivocal: and perhaps Puccini did, too, when in 1904 he made the cad Benjamin Franklin Pinkerton, USN, sail to the ruin of Madame Butterfly in a battleship named *Abraham Lincoln*' (Morris, 1999: 199). If there is an irresistible parallel between the 'ruin' brought to Japan in *Madame Butterfly* in the early twentieth century and that brought to Iraq in the early twenty-first, it is inscribed into the moment on 1 May 2003, when, from the deck of the USS *Abraham Lincoln*, President George W. Bush prematurely announced the end of major combat operations. Inevitably the question arose – as it does in the title of Patrick Gavin's *Counterpunch* article (2003) – 'What Would Lincoln Do?'

Gavin asserts, 'If Bush finds it appropriate to conclude his own war on the deck of a ship named after Mr. Lincoln, it's worth asking what Lincoln might think of our current President' (Gavin, 2003: n. p.). Gavin surmises that 'Lincoln would support Bush and Ashcroft's efforts with regards to the PATRIOT Act and civil rights restrictions during a time of war [and] … find little wrong with our detainment camp in Guantanamo Bay'. However, given Lincoln's care in ensuring that it was the Confederacy that fired the first shot of the Civil War, he 'may have taken exception to a few of Bush's actions, especially preemptive strikes' (Ibid.). At the other end of the political spectrum, in a *National Security Outlook* article for the right-wing think-tank, the American Enterprise Institute, Thomas Donnelly muses on 'Planning for War Against Iraq and for Its Aftermath: What Would Lincoln Do?' (2003). He concludes: 'Postwar Iraq must be thoroughly purged of Saddam's Ba'ath party, as Germany was of Nazis and the South was of the "slaveocracy"' (Donnelly, 2003: n. p.).

The Iraq war is only the latest in a series of American national crises to trigger an apparent political and cultural reflex, what David Donald called 'Getting Right with Lincoln' – that is, the tendency for (white) politicians and policy-makers to square their decisions according to their conceptions of what Lincoln would have done (Donald, 1961: 3–18). This at least partially explains the invocation of Lincoln on the first anniversary of the September 11th atrocities, when – controversially – New York Governor George Pataki chose the Gettysburg Address as the official memorial utterance, drawing questions about that particular text's relevance to a twenty-first-century terrorist attack. The decision, perhaps, had less to do with the choice of words than with the invocation of Lincoln himself, as in Capra's *Mr. Smith Goes to Washington*, or as in John Ford's last western, *Cheyenne Autumn* (1964), in which a US politician (Edward G. Robinson) mournfully appeals to Lincoln's portrait, rather than his words, for advice. This device – the appeal to Lincoln's portrait or to another graven image of him – is a startling feature of more than one Hollywood production, indicating a cultural desire to draw upon an inarticulate aura rather than upon Lincoln's conflicting words or upon his compromised, problematic political history.

Cultural and political appeals to Lincoln can be traced backwards like a thread running though the twentieth century. According to *Time* magazine, Bill Clinton's 'private bible about how to govern' is Donald T. Phillips's *Lincoln on Leadership* (1993), with its chapters advising all CEOs to 'Get Out of the Office and Circulate Among the Troops', 'Persuade Rather than Coerce' (except, presumably, when dealing with secessionists), 'Build Strong Alliances' and 'Keep Searching Until You Find Your "Grant"'. As Phillips explains: 'Lincoln was the man who really knew how to lead. Lincoln is the leader who genuinely has something new to offer contemporary business and political leaders' (Phillips, 1993: 9).

Oliver Stone's film, *Nixon* (1995), anchors the mentally disintegrating President (Anthony Hopkins) to the Lincoln Sitting Room in the White House, where he washes down pills with Scotch and, with the Vietnam War raging around him, mumbles – yet again – to Lincoln's mute portrait: 'How many [dead bodies] did you have? Hundreds of thousands. Where would we be without death, huh, Abe?' In Stone's recreation of Nixon's disastrous meeting with antiwar protesters at the Lincoln Memorial, the President gestures to the seated statue and says, 'That man up there lived in similar times. He had chaos and civil war and hatred between the races. Sometimes I go to the Lincoln Room at the White House and just pray.' The ironic, if improbable, parallel between Lincoln and Nixon is secured when Nixon's daughter, Julie, pleads with him as Watergate unfolds: 'You can't resign! You just can't. You're one of the best presidents this country's ever had! You've done what Lincoln did. You've brought this country back from civil war!' (Stone, 1995)

In November 1963, the political cartoonist, Bill Mauldin – who had himself portrayed a Union soldier in John Huston's *The Red Badge of Courage* (1951) – famously pictured the seated Lincoln Memorial figure sobbing into his hands to articulate the national grief at John F. Kennedy's assassination (Library of Congress, 2005: n. p.). Mauldin was building on a cartooning tradition that extended at least as far back as 1904, when *Puck* magazine presented an imperialist Theodore Roosevelt bullying his way through Latin America, the Caribbean and the Philippines, and wondering guiltily, 'What Would Lincoln Do?' (Zwick, 2005: n. p.)

As for the first President Roosevelt, so for the second. Merrill Peterson argues that 'the shadow of Lincoln the war President was never far from [Franklin] Roosevelt's mind', and repeats an exchange at a 1941 presidential press conference. '"Mr. President", a reporter piped, "if you were going to write a lead ...?" "I'd say", Roosevelt interrupted, "President Quotes Lincoln" – (Laughter) – "and Draws Parallel"' (Peterson, 1994: 323). Nor was Lincoln excluded from Roosevelt's great pre-war crisis, the Depression. Alfred Haworth Jones describes Lincoln's biographer, Carl Sandburg, campaigning for FDR in 1936 in the midst of national economic misery: 'In a speech entitled "What Lincoln Would Have Done", [Sandburg] insisted simply that the Great Emancipator would have done exactly what Roosevelt was doing' (Jones, 1974: 77). As Eric Foner writes, 'Every generation reinvents Lincoln in its own image' (Foner, 2003: 12), but the crisis-ridden generation of Franklin Roosevelt demands special attention for the intensity of its cultural and political uses of Lincoln.

Lincoln's New Deal

In the immediate aftermath of Lincoln's assassination, as David Donald notes, 'the Great Martyr was Republican property'. By the First World War, however, Woodrow Wilson could tell his fellow Democrats, 'I sometimes think it a singular circumstance that the present Republican party should have sprung from Lincoln, but that is one of the mysteries of Providence' (Donald, 1961: 8, 12). More belligerently, Franklin Roosevelt declared in 1929, 'I think it is time for us Democrats to claim Lincoln as one of our own' – which he proceeded to do with a vengeance, explicitly yoking Lincoln to the New Deal project by avowing: 'I believe with Abraham Lincoln, that "The legitimate object of government is to do for a community of people whatever they need to have done but cannot do at all or cannot do so well for themselves in their separate and individual capacities"' (in Jones, 1974: 65–6).

In seizing Lincoln for the Democrats and the New Deal, Roosevelt found his first cultural ally in Sandburg, whose two-volume biography, *Abraham Lincoln: The Prairie Years* (1926), had already achieved popular acclaim before the Wall Street Crash of 1929 and Roosevelt's first election. Sandburg followed with the four-volume Pulitzer Prize winner, *Abraham Lincoln: The War Years* (1939) in the midst of Roosevelt's second term. The combined six-volume opus was a 'sprawling' literary milestone about which Edmund Wilson sneered: 'The cruellest thing that has happened to Lincoln since he was shot by Booth has been to fall into the hands of Carl Sandburg' (Wilson, 1966: 115). In contrast, Mark Neely observes: 'Sandburg himself did more to promote Lincoln's reputation than any other person since John Wilkes Booth' (Neely, 1995: 124). In doing so, Sandburg became the most influential of 'Roosevelt's image brokers', as Jones calls them in the title of his 1974 study.

Sandburg's 'cultural work' in the finished Lincoln biography was to soothe public anxieties about the New Deal 'by turning to history and pointing out another occasion of unease: Abraham Lincoln's vast expansion of federal power during the Civil War. Sandburg demonstrated how it had been used for morally compelling purposes, just as, he believed, Roosevelt would do as well' (Cullen, 1995: 4, 46). An American folk icon in his own right, Sandburg was well known as a poet as well as a balladeer, guitarist and folksong collector, which places him in a popular and populist American bardic tradition inherited from Whitman (who figures largely in *The War Years*) and extending to such figures as Woody Guthrie, Bob Dylan and Bruce Springsteen. Self-consciously the songster of the common man and woman – his major work of poetry was *The People, Yes* (1936) – Sandburg stylised his Lincoln as an organic product of the American grain in spite of his ambition and lust for power:

> There could have been times when children and dreamers looked at Abraham Lincoln and lazily drew their eyelids half shut and let their hearts roam about him – they half-believed him to be a tall horse chestnut tree or a rangy horse or a big wagon or a log barn full of new-mown hay – something else more than a man, a lawyer, a Republican candidate with principles, a prominent citizen – something spreading, elusive, and mysterious – the Strange Friend and the Friendly Stranger (Sandburg, 1982: 147).

Crucially, Sandburg's Lincoln was no 'lackey of capitalism' – not the powerful railroad lawyer who had succeeded in absolving the Illinois Central Railroad from taxpaying, or whose services the Chicago and

Alton Railroad had rewarded by naming a town after him (Morris, 1999: 69–70). Instead, Sandburg picked up the baton from Vachel Lindsay's poem, 'Abraham Lincoln Walks at Midnight' (1914), which had earlier re-constituted Lincoln as the patron saint of 'the worker's earth' (in Marius, 1994: 356). As a lawyer, Sandburg's Lincoln accepts payment in 'groceries and farm produce' (Sandburg, 1982: 86) and damns the 'capitalists [who] generally act harmoniously, and in concert, to fleece the people' (Ibid.: 51). He rises in politics against a backdrop that could as easily be the 1930s as the 1850s: 'Processions of thousands of men marched in the Northern large cities with banners reading: "Hunger Is a Sharp Thorn" and "We Want Work"' (Ibid.: 137). As Cullen argues, Sandburg offers 'a classic example of Depression-era documentary' – not 'an avowedly objective work' but rather a highly emotive 'cultural form that begins with human records' and is 'of a piece with the photographs of Dorothea Lange, the ballets of Martha Graham, and the films of Pare Lorentz' (Cullen, 1995: 40).

Lincoln's work for Roosevelt, however, did not end with the Depression. Roosevelt became an overt war leader in 1941 with the bombing of Pearl Harbor, but by then he had already spent a number of years – with the help of his 'image brokers' – in steering Abraham Lincoln towards a confrontation with Adolf Hitler.

Lincoln's Second World War

After Carl Sandburg, the greatest of 'Roosevelt's image brokers' was the playwright Robert E. Sherwood, whose Pulitzer Prize-winning *Abe Lincoln in Illinois* (1938) drew upon Sandburg to depict 'Lincoln's transformation from indifference to commitment' in the years preceding the Civil War (Jones, 1974: 46). By 1938, the polarities of appeasement and war had become as stark as they had been in 1858, by which time (in Sherwood's words) Lincoln had 'turned from an appeaser into a fighter'. The play's leading actor, Raymond Massey – who went on to reprise his stage role in John Cromwell's 1940 film version (see Chapter 3) – declared: 'If you substitute the word dictatorship for the word slavery throughout Sherwood's script, it becomes electric with meaning for our time' (Sherwood and Massey quoted in Ibid.: 46).

Seizing on Sherwood's popularity and his facility with Lincoln's folksy allusions, Roosevelt drafted the playwright as a speechwriter in 1940 in a bid to stoke the fires of interventionist passion. Sherwood noted how 'Roosevelt was happiest when he could "reduce an enormous and even revolutionary issue to the familiar scope of a small town" by transforming a cloudy idea like Lend-Lease into the loan of a garden hose to a neighbor fighting a fire' (Stott, 1973: 96). Roosevelt was familiar with the Lincoln who begins Sherwood's play in affirming, 'I'm minding my own business – that's what I'm doing!', but who gradually gathers enough moral fibre to conclude: '"Let each State mind its own business". That's the safer course, for the time being. But – I advise you to watch out! ... [A]re you quite sure that the demon you have thus created will not turn and rend you? When you begin qualifying freedom, watch out for the consequences to *you!*' (Sherwood, 1966: 49, 63). It was no accident that Cromwell's film version premiered in Washington, DC, in 1940, with Eleanor Roosevelt at the head of a guest list that also included 'the secretaries of State, Treasury, Agriculture, and Navy, as well as the British and Italian ambassadors' (Jones, 1974: 47).

Ironically, Republican loyalists in Hollywood, led by producer Daryl F. Zanuck, had also seized upon Lincoln to challenge his appropriation by the Democratic machine, rushing John Ford's *Young Mr. Lincoln* into production in 1938 in anticipation of the filming of Sherwood's play. As the anonymous editors of the French Marxist film journal, *Cahiers du Cinéma*, argue in their landmark essay, 'John Ford's *Young Mr. Lincoln*' (1970): 'Twentieth-Century Fox ... because of its links with Big Business, also supports the Republican Party [and] participated in its own way in the Republican offensive by producing a film on the legendary character of Lincoln' (Editors, 1970: 499). In Henry Fonda's rendition, Lincoln is less a lawyer than a veritable people's conscience, proclaiming to a sneering prosecutor (Donald Meek) in a murder trial, 'I may not know so much of law, Mister Felder, but I know what's right and wrong.' He appeals to each juror's 'feelings' and 'heart' rather than to his grasp of the legal argument. However, careful not to take this appeal to the emotions too far, Lincoln is determined to check its spread from the individual to the collective. As he chides a lynch mob: 'We seem to lose our heads in times like this. We do things together that we'd be mighty ashamed to do by ourselves' (Ford, 1939). As Michael Tratner explains with reference to such scenes:

> The main Republican answer to Roosevelt's radical policies was the claim that the New Deal was socializing America, was giving in to collectivism and destroying capitalist individualism. Against such a political backdrop, the movie *Young Mr. Lincoln* gains most of its

political power from its portrayal of the dangers of out-of-control crowds pursuing mistaken solutions to local problems (Tratner, 2003: 62).

It is a mark of the Democrats' success in appropriating Lincoln that, as the 'local problems' of the Depression were overtaken by the gathering storm of a second world war, the final image of Fonda/Lincoln trudging alone uphill into a tempest brought *Young Mr. Lincoln* into a more comfortable ideological fellowship with *Abe Lincoln in Illinois* than its producers initially intended.

In the aftermath of Pearl Harbor, with the US for the most part united in the war effort, it remained for a third of Roosevelt's 'image brokers', the composer Aaron Copland, to yoke Lincoln more firmly to the military struggle against fascism through his tone-poem, *Lincoln Portrait, for Speaker and Orchestra* (1942). Against a folk-based, melodic score that indicated Copland's abandonment of avant-garde experimentation for a more popular form, the Speaker intones excerpts from the Lincoln oeuvre that give the Second World War 'a Lincolnian stamp' (Morris, 1999: 3). Copland claimed in his notes to the programme from the Cincinnati Symphony Orchestra's May 1942 première that his chosen excerpts 'seemed particularly apposite to our own situation today' (Copland, 1987). Thus, *Lincoln Portrait* aims to equate the nineteenth century's war against slavery with the twentieth century's war against fascism, and the struggle for American union with the struggle for global democracy, through such quotations as these from Lincoln's annual message to Congress (1862) –

> Fellow citizens, *we* cannot escape history. We of this Congress and this administration, will be remembered in spite of ourselves. No personal significance, or insignificance, can spare one or another of us. The fiery trial through which we pass, will light us down, in honor or dishonor, to the latest generation (in Basler, 1953: V, 537; Copland, 1987).

> The dogmas of the quiet past, are inadequate to the stormy present. The occasion is piled high with difficulty, and we must rise with the occasion. As our case is new, so we must think anew, and act anew. We must disenthrall our selves, and then we shall save our country (Ibid).

– and from the last of the Lincoln–Douglas debates at Alton, Illinois (1858):

It is the eternal struggle between two principles – right and wrong –
throughout the world ... It is the same spirit that says: 'You work and
toil and earn bread – and I'll eat it'. No matter in what shape it comes,
whether from the mouth of a king who seeks to bestride the people of
his own nation and live by the fruit of their labor, or from one race of
men as an apology for enslaving another race, it is the same tyrannical
principle (in Basler, 1953: III, 315; Copland, 1987).

Copland's *Lincoln Portrait* clearly helped to lay the groundwork for
what Morris witnessed as 'the zenith of Lincoln's myth' in 'the years after
the Second World War when he was regarded as a very metaphor of the
benign and victorious Republic ... flushed with success, gleaming and
glittering above the world's debris' (Morris, 1999: 2–3). Yet, in Lerone
Bennett's estimation, by seizing upon Lincoln, Copland failed to offer a
metaphor suitable to the Republic's black constituency, whose ancestors
Lincoln had once hoped to deport to Africa or the Caribbean, leaving an
ethnically cleansed America. Thus, what Bennett calls the 'fallacy of the
isolated quote' ensured that Copland's audience would be oblivious to
that part of Lincoln's Alton speech which the composer did not use – the
part acquiescing to the Fugitive Slave Law, in which 'Lincoln endorsed
"the same tyrannical principle", saying that it was necessary to maintain
the divine right of slaveholders in the South and to join with them in
"running and catching niggers" [Lincoln's own words] who escaped
from people who believed in the divine right of kings and slaveholders'
(Bennett, 2000: 126–7).

Bennett's is the most sustained and least forgiving African-American
critique of the 'vacillating president by the name of Abraham Lincoln', as
Martin Luther King called him in his 'I've Been to the Mountaintop'
speech the night before his murder (King, 1990: 279). It shows, along
with other black American responses, that Lincoln's champions have not
been entirely successful in establishing him as a totemic figure around
which the entire nation can always rally.

The White Man's President

In 1876, Frederick Douglass recalled in an otherwise complimentary
elegy:

> Abraham Lincoln was not, in the fullest sense of the word, either our
> man or our model. In his interests, in his associations, in his habits of
> thought and in his prejudices, he was a white man.

He was preëminently the white man's President, entirely devoted to the welfare of white men. He was ready and willing at any time during the first years of his administration to deny, postpone and sacrifice the rights of humanity in the colored people in order to promote the welfare of the white people of this country (Douglass: 1892: 588).

Addressing the country's white population, Douglass added: 'First, midst, and last, you and yours were the objects of his deepest affection and his most earnest solicitude. You are the children of Abraham Lincoln. We are at best only his step-children; children by adoption, children by forces of circumstances and necessity' (Ibid.: 589).

Ironically, however, in the midst of his presidency and in the realm of culture, Lincoln's detractors accused him of more than mere step-fatherhood: 'Lincoln was caricatured for his perceived support of abolition in various ways, including symbolic "blackening". Opponents suggested that he had "African" origins, while a related strand of satire caricatured the president as Othello, "Blacked ... all over to play the part"' (Young, 1999: 49–50). The German-born dentist and Confederate sympathiser, Adalbert Johann Volck, drew a series of widely circulated caricatures in 1862, including one of Lincoln as a 'Negro chief' with African features and Moorish costume, performing an elaborate orientalist dance (Lorant, 1969: 169). In 1863, William Russell Smith's 'anti-Lincoln play', *The Royal Ape*, accused Lincoln of a 'hidden blackness' that, far from being skin-deep, determined his entire political agenda (Young, 1999: 50). Yet, in spite of such pro-slavery charges against 'Lincoln the Black Republican' (as he was frequently called), African-American responses have tended to focus on his prioritising of Union over abolition and of legalities over justice, his acceptance of slaves as property (hence his plans for compensatory emancipation) and his devotion to the separation of races through deportation and colonisation.

Three relatively recent cultural treatments of Lincoln indicate the extent to which Frederick Douglass's nineteenth-century reservations have been shared in the late twentieth and early twenty-first centuries. Ishmael Reed's *Flight to Canada* (1976) parodies 'Lincoln the Player' (as a chapter is titled) using the enslaved black race as pawns or bargaining chips, only belatedly aware of slavery as the central moral and political issue of the Civil War. 'We change the issues, don't you see?' Lincoln plots. 'Instead of making this some kind of oratorical minuet about

States' Rights versus the Union, what we do is make it so that you can't be for the South without being for slavery ... That's it. The Emancipation Proclamation. Call in the press' (Reed, 1998: 49). Yet Reed's Lincoln is haunted by the blackness under his skin, less in the biological than in the metaphorical sense. 'I never even gave spooks much thought', he muses, 'but now that they've become a subplot in this war, I can't get those shines off my mind' (Ibid.: 47). In Reed's treatment, it is Lincoln and his schemes that are the real subplot to the Civil War; the larger story is represented by the escaped slave and poet, Raven Quickskill, who signifies resistance, self-preservation and the centrality of black Americans to the cultural and political destiny of the nation. As for Lincoln, he is so degraded as to complain at one point: 'I feel like a minstrel' (Ibid.: 45).

Such parodic themes have been extended more recently in Kevin Willmott's film, *CSA: The Confederate States of America* (2003), a faux documentary that premièred to great acclaim at the 2004 Sundance Film Festival (see Chapter 5 and Cnclusion). In this film, premised upon an ultimate Confederate victory in the Civil War, the ousted Lincoln attempts to flee to Canada disguised in a minstrel's blackface, under the guiding hand of Harriet Tubman. Captured en route (and with Tubman executed), Lincoln is imprisoned, eventually paroled and exiled to Canada. Remembered only as 'the man who lost the War of Northern Aggression', he sinks into obscurity, ending a long, sad life with the confession: 'I only wish that I had truly cared for the Negro – truly cared for his freedom, for his equality. I used him, and now I am used. Now I, too, am a Negro without a country' (Willmott, 2003).

The symbolism of amalgamating Lincoln's personal identity with that of African-Americans is most fully worked in two plays by the Pulitzer Prize winner, Suzan-Lori Parks. In her formally dense and abstract *The America Play* (1990–93), the main character, known variously as 'The Lesser Known' and 'The Foundling Father as Abraham Lincoln', reverses the Lincoln-in-blackface motif: he is a black gravedigger who moonlights in whiteface as a Lincoln impersonator at an amusement arcade, allowing himself to be shot on a daily basis by paying customers pretending to be John Wilkes Booth. The visual images of the Great Man (the historical Lincoln) and The Lesser Known blend into each other in a highly intimate mélange, although a bitter distinction remains, with the gravedigger being told from birth practically that he and the Great Man were dead ringers, more or less, and knowing that he, if he had been in the slightest vicinity back then, would have had at least a chance at the great honor of digging the Great Mans grave (Parks, 1995: 161).

Parks continued playing with Lincoln's relation to blackness in *Topdog/Underdog* (2001), creating – as she explained – 'another black Lincoln impersonator, unrelated to the first guy ... a new character for a new play'. In this more realistic play, the blending of identities is even stronger, if more ironic: 'This new Lincoln impersonator's real name would be Lincoln. He would be a former 3-card monte hustler. He would live with his brother, a man named Booth' (Parks, 2002: i). The associations between Lincoln and hustling, playing and confidence tricks are brought to the fore here, as in *Flight to Canada*, along with the ironic relation to minstrelsy. Booth tells Lincoln, who has surprised him in whiteface, '[T]ake off that damn coat, man, you make me nervous standing there looking like a spook, and that damn face paint, take it off. You should take all of it off at work and leave it there' (Ibid.: 11). Booth admits to great respect for Lincoln's moves – 'Scheming and dreaming. No one throws the cards like you, Link' (Ibid.: 20) – but he also forces Lincoln into a feeble defence of his own trickery:

> *Lincoln*
> I cant be hustling no more, bro.
> *Booth*
> What you do all day aint no hustle?
> *Lincoln*
> Its honest work.
> *Booth*
> Dressing up like some crackerass white man, some dead president and letting people shoot at you sounds like a hustle to me.
> *Lincoln*
> People know the real deal. When people know the real deal it aint a hustle.
>
> (Ibid.: 22)

In the aggregate, however, Bennett, Reed, Willmott and Parks – among other black critics – suggest that uncovering 'the real deal' about the contested myth of the Great Emancipator precisely means uncovering 'a hustle'. Many others, surely, will find it a harsh critique of the president who saved the Union, preserved the democratic process in the midst of civil war, sealed the fate of American slavery and gave his life in the process. However, it comes from the perspective of an American constituency openly and avowedly de-prioritised by Lincoln himself. Ironically or otherwise, in their scepticism over Lincoln's cultural canonisation, black American critics have found themselves sailing very close to an alliance with the neo-Confederates – the subjects of the following chapter – for whom Lincoln is nothing less than the devil incarnate.

CHAPTER 5

Rebels, Inc.

In 1930, the Nashville Agrarians (see Chapter 2) urged the South to resist surrendering 'its moral, social, and economic autonomy to the victorious principle of Union', but they stopped short of advocating another try at secession: 'Nobody now proposes for the South, or for any other community in this country, an independent political destiny. That idea is thought to have been finished in 1865' ('Twelve Southerners', 1977: xxxviii). Not so in 2001 for the twin brothers James Ronald and Walter Donald Kennedy, stalwart officers of the Sons of Confederate Veterans and founding members of the League of the South (see Chapter 4):

> We who grew up under the threat of a worldwide communist tyranny have lived to see the Berlin Wall come crashing down. We have seen the once mighty and *perpetual* union of the Soviet empire disappear from the world map ... For us die-hard Confederates, we feel as if God's vindication is just around the corner (Kennedy, 2001: 8).

'God's vindication', they invoke – *Deo Vindice*, the motto on the Great Seal of the Confederacy. In the Kennedys' neo-Confederate jeremiad, *The South Was Right!* (2001), Eastern European, Balkan, and Quebecois freedom-fighters equate with Jefferson Davis and Robert E. Lee, while Saddam Hussein equates with Abraham Lincoln for his invasion of Kuwait and his attempt to incorporate it forcibly into a greater Iraq. The end of the Civil War, they argue, turned the South 'into a colonial province of the Yankee empire', which it remains to this day, as 'big government' lords it over the people, imposing 'a huge deficit', 'tax-and-spend' policies, political correctness, 'a school system controlled by the liberal Supreme Court and the NAACP' and 'such insults as busing, racial quotas, minority set-asides, affirmative action plans, reverse discrimination, and a discriminatory South-only Voting Rights Act' (Ibid.: 11, 151, 234, 249).

For the League of the South, the exercise is more than speculative: 'If we cannot convince our Northern neighbors to reform this current, overgrown, and unresponsive government of their making, then we shall work for the re-establishment of a Constitutional Republic known as the Confederate States of America!' (Ibid.: 10–11). In 2004, the league published *The Grey Book*, its 'blueprint for Southern Independence' (League of the South, 2004). The league's website links over a million 'Southern Supporters' to a host of affiliates including the radio station WDXB (Dixie Broadcasting, 'The Powerful New Voice of Today's Southern Movement') and the League of the South Institute for the Study of Southern Culture and History – the latter 'made up of the South's finest unreconstructed scholars' and 'the South's best hope for properly educating Southern youth and for countering the political correctness that has infected our educational institutions all across Dixie' (League of the South, 2004a). Disturbingly or otherwise, the Kennedy brothers are not alone, nor are they part of an unbroken tradition.

Deo Vindice

It has not been left merely to strong, isolated Southern voices such as Thomas Dixon or Margaret Mitchell (see Chapter 2), or small collectives

Figure 6 Confederate Bikini, West Columbia, South Carolina, 2001 (Jeanne-Marie Kenny: courtesy of the photographer).

like the Agrarians, to wage war against the spectre of Northern dominance. As early as 1869, the Southern Historical Society was established
'to offset what was perceived as a pronounced Northern bias in accounts
of the Civil War, owing to the destruction or confiscation of Southern
records by conquering Yankees insistent on promoting their view of the
conflict' (Cullen, 1995: 110). This was the first of a number of organisations to promote what Gaines Foster, David Blight, Alan T. Nolan and
others have called 'the Lost Cause' project – in Foster's words, 'the
postwar writings and activities that perpetuated the memory of the
Confederacy' and 'helped shape southern perceptions of defeat' (Foster,
1987: 4–5). In 1889, the United Confederate Veterans and their
magazine, *The Confederate Veteran*, were founded, providing a voice 'for
both Confederate memory and reconciliation on Southern economic and
political terms' (Blight, 2001: 272). Soon renamed the Sons of Confederate Veterans (SCV), the organisation has continued to promote its
declared mission as uttered by its first 'Commander General', Stephen
Dill Lee, in 1906: 'the vindication of the cause for which we fought'
(SCV, 2004). In practical terms, this mission translates into the
sponsoring of 'memorial, historical, and educational activities' and the
recruitment of new members, backed up by a sophisticated Internet and
broadcast network promoting pro-Confederate activism, the boycott of
perceived non-Confederate-friendly institutions and the sales of Confederate texts and paraphernalia (Ibid.).

By far, however, the most powerful of the Confederate apologist
organisations has been the United Daughters of the Confederacy (UDC),
founded in 1894, and since then tirelessly dedicated to the project of
fundraising, monument-building, scholarship endowment and the rewriting of Southern school textbooks. As Blight notes, 'In all their efforts, the
UDC planted a white supremacist vision of the Lost Cause deeper into
the nation's historical imagination than perhaps any other association'
(Blight, 2001: 273). The UDC's juvenile branch, 'Children of the
Confederacy', boasts its own highly instructive creed, steeped in denial:

> To honor the memory of our beloved Veterans; to study and teach the
> truths of history (one of the most important of which is, that the War
> Between the States was not a rebellion, nor was its underlying cause
> to sustain slavery); and always to act in a manner that will reflect
> honor upon our noble and patriotic ancestors (CC, 2004).

It is no accident that the UDC chose to commission their gigantic monument to the Confederate leadership at, of all places, Stone Mountain, Georgia, where the Ku Klux Klan had rededicated itself in its second incarnation of 1915 (Taylor, 1989: 57). Across a vast granite bas-relief – '90 feet tall by 190 feet wide' – Robert E. Lee, Jefferson Davis and Stonewall Jackson charge on horseback in images carved by the sculptor of Mount Rushmore, Gutzon Borglum, and his successor, Walker Hancock (Jacobson, 1996: 112). Eulogised as 'the Southland's sacred mount' by the Georgia poet Lucian Lamar Knight in a twenty-four-part epic poem (1923), the UDC's monument and its Olympian heroes cast their shadow over the small town of Stone Mountain, with its African-American population of roughly fifty per cent (including its mayor) who are obliged to gaze upon them daily (Morse, 1999: 56; Knight, 1923).

Although the UDC and its fellow organisations are mostly associated with the period 1865–1913, when perceptions of the 'Lost Cause' argu-ably helped white Southerners to cope with the trauma of defeat, reunion and Reconstruction, they continue to provide a platform for today's Confederate revivalists. The Kennedys make clear in their manifesto: 'Every true Southerner should be an active member of an organization dedicated to the preservation and perpetuation of the truth about the Southern cause. The Sons of Confederate Veterans and the United Daughters of the Confederacy are two examples of such organizations' (Kennedy, 2001: 307). Recently, the Virginia state commander of the SCV, Henry Kidd, protested to the *New York Times*: 'Honoring my ancestors has nothing to do with racism' (Clines, 2001: A20).

Yet, as Nolan persuasively argues, white supremacy and a certain fond-ness for slavery cannot be dissociated from 'the Lost Cause Legend' per-petuated by neo-Confederate apologists. Elements of this legend include:

Southern denial that slavery was the central issue of the war; Southern blame on the abolitionists as 'troublemakers' and 'provocateurs'; Southern insistence that 'slavery would have been abandoned by the South on its own'; [and] the belief that slaves, by and large, were happy and protected in their bondage (Nolan, 1998: 29–30).

Hence the Kennedys' claim: 'Inner-city black-on-black crime is epidemic. In the United States of America more blacks die at the hands of fellow blacks in one year than ever died from lynching or beatings in *all* the years of Southern slavery!' (Kennedy, 2001: 116). The Kennedys are careful to maintain that 'if indeed the black people were better off in some respects under the system of slavery, that does not justify or warrant its return'. Their main objection, they claim, is that 'people who dare to speak about slavery in a light other than that demanded by the neo-Abolitionist left will find themselves an outcast from modern "P.C." society' (Ibid.: 114, 116).

Nolan identifies one further element of the 'Lost Cause Legend', a Southern essentialism based on 'purported binary oppositions between Northern and Southern culture (Anglo-Saxon-Norman vs Celtic; Puritan vs Cavalier, etc.)' (Nolan, 1998: 29–30). This has proved to be one of the most confusing and contested aspects of the legend, for while such Southern apologists as Wilbur J. Cash could write about 'the essential Southern mind and will', there is little agreement about what constitutes that 'essence' (Cash, 1991: 103). The Agrarian, John Crowe Ransom, claimed an undefined English culture as 'the model employed by the South' ('Twelve Southerners', 1977: 3), while the Kennedys crudely rework the essentialist thesis of Grady McWhiney's *Cracker Culture* (1988) to describe their *bête noire*, liberal guilt, as 'a typically Anglo-Saxon (English – and therefore Yankee) attitude as opposed to a Celtic (Welsh, Scottish, and Irish – and therefore Southern) attitude' (Kennedy, 2001: 249).

What is missing from this picture? As Helen Taylor explains, the League of the South 'was set up to defend the notion of the true South as Celtic, thus by definition white; other Souths (notably African American) thus become illegitimate and inferior' (Taylor, 2001: 16). W. J. Cash was at least flexible enough to acknowledge 'the pious Moravian brothers' and 'stolid Lutheran peasants from northern Germany' as elements of the Southern mix (Cash, 1991: 9), while Charles Joyner has more recently discussed 'the variety of European cultures – English, Scottish, Scotch-Irish, Welsh, French, German, Spanish' that have engaged with Caribbean, Native American, and most importantly, African cultures in forming whatever may be called the American South (Joyner, 1996: 14). It is here that an argument for Southern essentialism based on race must collapse under the weight of its own discrepancies. The Kennedys' manifesto, bizarrely, argues for the South's essentially Celtic identity while including photographs of Latinos, Jews and Africans who, they claim, were all good Southerners fighting for the Confederacy – as though, in spite of themselves, to admit the truth of what Richard King and Helen Taylor call the South's 'international eclecticism' (King and Taylor, 1996: 9).

Southern white supremacists have persistently appropriated Scotland in particular as a political and cultural touchstone, not merely because of Walter Scott's origins (see Chapter 1) but also because of the Scottish history of resistance to English domination. Helen Taylor recalls how, in its obsessive need to align Scottish nationalism with the neo-Confederate cause, the League of the South 'recommended that all "Southrons" (Walter Scott's pejorative term) should go to see *Braveheart*, a film also endorsed strongly by the Ku Klux Klan and John Birch Society' (Taylor, 2001: 17). Yet, as Alasdair Pettinger has argued, the South's white supremacists can make no exclusive claim to Scottish inheritance, regardless of such adopted symbols as the Klans and their burning crosses, or the Cross of St Andrew on the Confederate battle flag. In the 'important rhetorical struggle over "Scotland" and the South', Pettinger notes, Frederick Douglass staked his own claim:

> In changing his own name from Bailey to Douglass (after the hero in *The Lady of the Lake*), he 'signifies' on a characteristically Southern gesture ... His new name also allows him the pleasure of invoking 'the ancient "black Douglass"', another historical figure who also appears in Scott (Pettinger, 1999: 43, 49).

Alan Rice and Martin Crawford have observed how Douglass confounded any presumptions of a natural or automatic connection between Scotland and Southern white supremacists when, in Edinburgh in 1845, he inspired a popular protest against the Free Church of Scotland, which had enjoyed substantial contributions from slaveholders: '"Send Back the Money" became a popular rallying cry, chanted on street corners and scribbled on walls throughout the Scottish capital' (Rice and Crawford, 1999: 6).

Thus, to argue that the essential Southern heritage, culture, attitude or 'mind' can be so identifiably 'Scottish' or 'Celtic' is to imply that it is monolithically white (in spite of the multiracial origins of the Celtic societies themselves). This is the most striking 'black hole' (pun intended) in the neo-Confederate manifesto. The Kennedys argue, for instance, in starkly binary terms – 'Southern' versus 'black' – against the 'deification' of Martin Luther King: 'Southerners have generally taken the position that, if this is the type of man the black community desires to hold up as their hero, then let them do so – it is their business' (Kennedy, 2001: 295). Yet, as Leon Litwack most convincingly argues: 'In much that is written and filmed about the South, the perverse assumption persists that southerners are necessarily white ... If "southerners" is

defined to include blacks as well as whites, it becomes highly debatable
how many southerners actually supported the Confederacy' (Litwack,
1996: 133).

One can observe the selective convenience with which many white
Southerners *have* chosen to include blacks in their number, beyond
deeming them as three-fifths of a person for purposes of taxation and
representation in the original US Constitution. When Melanie in Mitchell's *Gone with the Wind* scoffs at the prospect of a slave insurrection,
she asks, 'Why should our people rise?' (Mitchell, 1993: 177). As Cullen
understates it, 'There is a striking duality in the commonly used
Southern phrase "our people", which here implies a familial sense of
closeness – and a sense of property ownership' (Cullen, 1995: 77).

It would, of course, be quite unfair to suggest that neo-Confederate
apologists speak for the entire white South. However, in their attempts
to subvert or challenge the power of neo-Confederate culture, progressive Southern groups and individuals are up against a movement
whose activities are truly corporate in scale and bear upon such diverse
cultural and commercial arenas as music, the heritage industry,
education and advertising, as well as upon the civic and public spaces of
the South. We turn first to music – particularly, but not exclusively, that
form most associated with Confederate iconography, Southern rock.

'The South's Gonna Do It Again'

In his study of 'Southern Rock and Nostalgic Continuities', Paul Wells
argues that the Confederate battle flag has become 'the symbol of
rebellion within the rock idiom' and, as such, is 'essentially depoliticised
in the historic sense and commodified in relation to southern music'
(Wells, 1996: 126). Thus, 'the flag represents "Lynyrd Skynyrd" or
southern rock, and not the emblem of the southern states' (Ibid.: 127).
To some extent, Wells is correct about the 'depoliticisation' of the
Confederate flag and its associated iconography in the musical arena, a
point also made by Cullen in his recollections of hearing the Charlie
Daniels band play their anthem, 'The South's Gonna Do It Again', in the
late 1970s: 'Just what is Daniels asserting that the South is going to do in
"The South's Gonna Do It Again"? Enslave blacks? That seems unlikely. Secede? No' (Cullen, 1995: 109). To be sure, the vagueness of
what constitutes 'being a rebel' in the Daniels song, which is essentially a
eulogy of fellow Southern rockers (the Marshall Tucker Band, Lynyrd

Skynyrd, Dickey Betts and others), makes a political stance hard to ascertain (Daniels, 1990). Even a more explicitly 'political' song such as Hank Williams, Jr's 'If the South Woulda Won (We'd Have Had It Made)' does not establish why the conservatism it espouses should be linked necessarily or particularly to a Confederate victory in the Civil War – Williams sings of taking Miami back from the drug pushers, relocating the Supreme Court to Texas and seeing that murderers get the noose instead of talk-show celebrity (Williams, 1990).

However, while Southern rock does not habitually make its political agendas or its relation to Confederate imagery crystal clear, scholars have charted its emergence in the 1970s against a host of conflicting political currents. To Bill Malone, it was the product of upbeat (white) Southern pride after the dark days of the civil rights battles of the 1960s, also reflected in the presidential election of Georgia's Jimmy Carter in 1976 along with a new batch of progressive Southern governors: 'With the disappearance or decline of the evils of southern society, along with the guilt that had accompanied them, young [white] southerners were freed to reaffirm or rediscover the good that lay in their culture' (Malone, 1979: 109). Wells and Cullen, however, do not share this positive inter-pretation. For them, Southern rock was not only a belligerent white male response to American impotence in the face of the military success of the Viet Cong, but it also emerged as a defensive backlash against progressive developments at home – feminism and affirmative action – and against perceived or actual criticisms of the South. Barbara Ching recounts the vicious battle sparked in 1970 by Neil Young's 'Southern Man', a scathing attack on 'the steamy, swampy South of antebellum white privilege', which brought in rebuttal four years later Lynyrd Skynyrd's 'Sweet Home Alabama' (Ching, 2004: 214; Young, 1990; King, et al., 1997). Cullen calls the Skynyrd song 'one of the most vivid examples of a lingering Confederate mythology in Southern culture', arguing that, while it 'makes no explicit reference to the Civil War or the persistent ideology of states' rights, both loom large over the song and any attempt to understand it' (Cullen, 1995: 125).

Given the racially charged background to the emergence of Southern rock, it is not surprising that the music should betray the telling political elision and formal paradox noted by Wells: 'The form of southern rock music borrows extensively from black music, while the content rarely addresses the racism that is an inherent part of championing "the southern way" as it was originally defined' (Wells, 1996: 121). In analysing the music of the Allman Brothers, Lynyrd Skynyrd, Charlie Daniels, Doc Holliday and .38 Special (among others), Wells identifies a number of 'chief thematic modes' informing Southern rock, including 'the contemporisation of a Civil War ethos as a mode of identity', 'the defence of a pre-Civil War ethos in the determination of gender roles' and 'the symbolic potency of "guitar" music in the definition of masculinity' (Ibid.: 117). As a genre, Wells concludes, 'southern rock has ... taken on the mantle of a resistance group, still metaphorically fighting the war by refusing closure and signifying an enduring alternative culture, perhaps most significantly embodied in the figure of "the Rebel"' (Ibid.: 118).

One of the great mysteries of the Southern rock genre is how its personalities have managed to locate themselves so firmly in the 'thematic modes' of the Confederacy and the Civil War when they send out such vague musical or regional signals. As Malone notes, 'Southern styles have become so enmeshed in American popular culture that it is now impossible to determine where their southernness ends and their Americanism begins' (Malone, 1979: 153). However, in analysing music with explicit Civil War themes – whether in Southern rock or related forms such as country and western – the desire to approach the material on an 'American' as opposed to a 'Southern' level can obscure provocative political stances that may be inscribed in a song. This problem can be explored through an examination of what are, arguably, the two best-known references to the Civil War in twentieth-century popular music, Robbie Robertson's 'The Night They Drove Old Dixie Down' (Robertson, 1969) and Elvis Presley's version of Mickey Newbury's 'An American Trilogy' (Newbury, 1971).

First recorded in 1969 by The Band before its circulation as a Southern rock, country and folk-rock anthem in numerous cover versions, 'The Night They Drove Old Dixie Down' is neatly summarised by Greil Marcus. The song's protagonist, Virgil Kane,

> is a poor white farmer from the Confederate side of Tennessee, probably not more than twenty years old, a survivor of the attacks made by General Stoneman's cavalry on the Danville train he defended. With the war over, a glimpse of Robert E. Lee is worth as much to him as the memory of his brother, who died fighting for the sense of place Virgil Kane's war was all about (Marcus, 1991: 55).

Marcus's personal response to the song is particularly instructive, as it appears to modulate from the perspective of a (presumably white) Northern listener to that of a (presumably white) American one. In effect, he argues, the song's greatest value is its capacity to facilitate a sense of kinship and reunion between North and South:

> It is hard for me to comprehend how any Northerner, raised on a very different war than Virgil Kane's, could listen to this song without finding himself changed. You can't get out from under the singer's truth – not the whole truth, simply *his* truth – and the little auto-biography closes the gap between us. The performance leaves behind a feeling that for all our oppositions, every American still shares this old event (Ibid.: 56).

As Cullen suggests, however, we can only achieve this reunion and the tragic catharsis the song invites 'by evading politics'; we are asked to 'suspend all our skepticism about the Confederate cause as irrelevant' in order to 'immerse ourselves in the human drama of Virgil Kane' (Cullen, 1995: 121).

In similar fashion, it has been argued that Presley's version of 'An American Trilogy' also attempts to 'evade politics' even as it explicitly acknowledges the separate Civil War constituencies in its conflation of 'Dixie', 'The Battle Hymn of the Republic' and the black spiritual, 'All My Trials'. According to this argument, the message – again – is the surmounting of tragedy and the blessing of reunion at the expense of political acknowledgement or reckoning. This is how Marcus interprets 'An American Trilogy', noticing here what he either fails to notice or does not admit to noticing in the song of Virgil Kane: 'Elvis transcends any real America by evading it. There is no John Brown in his "Battle Hymn", no romance in his "Dixie", no blood in his slave song ... The divisions America shares are simply smoothed away' (Marcus, 1991: 24). Linda Ray Pratt, however, sees the song as highly political – if 'domin-ated by "Dixie"' – in that it captures 'Southern history through the changes of the civil rights movement and the awareness of black suffering which had hitherto largely been excluded from popular white images of Southern history' (Pratt, 1979: 46). It must be said that if Presley's 'American Trilogy' is indeed 'dominated by "Dixie"' – if it is, in the final analysis, more of a Southern song than an American one, in spite of its title – at least it is a song that counts the South's African-Americans as 100–per cent Southerners. Acknowledging this goes beyond merely recognising the African-American foundations of Southern music or the

influence of black blues and gospel on Presley as an individual. It
assumes a different definition of 'Southerners' or 'our people' than that
offered by Margaret Mitchell, the Kennedy brothers and the League of
the South.

Barbara Ching claims, not necessarily with approval: 'To be Southern,
rock had to drape itself in a Confederate flag' (Ching, 2004: 214). We
turn now to that flag itself, for it remains a cultural flashpoint far beyond
its integration into Southern rock symbolism. The intense debate that
continues to surround the question of its public display goes to the heart
of any attempts to engage with the definitions of 'Southerner' or 'our
people'.

Figure 7 The Reverend E. Slave, Columbia, South Carolina, 2001
(Jeanne-Marie Kenny: courtesy of the photographer).

Rally Round the Flag

The Kennedys argue: 'Even though the Confederate flag never flew over a slave ship, and even though the United States flag did fly over slave ships, it is the Confederate flag that the left-of-center wordsmith refers to as the "flag of slavery". What kind of justice is this?' (Kennedy, 2001: 69–70) In order, they say, to 'instill (or re-instill) in *our people* a healthy dose of Southern pride' (Ibid.: 306; my italics), the Kennedys – along with all neo-Confederates – champion the display 'of the Confederate flag and other visible symbols of the Confederacy' (Ibid.: 296). Clearly, they resort to the same schizophrenic rhetoric that, in spite of its proclaimed inclusiveness, must exclude blacks from the fellowship of 'us' and 'ours': 'If you have never heard the response of a crowd of Southerners when our nation's emblem is proudly displayed, then you are in for a real treat' (Ibid.: 308).

If the Kennedys were right, however, there would be no motivation for at least one incontrovertible Southerner to have made his own peculiar display. On 17 April 2002, a 54-year-old black man named Emmet Rufus Eddy – calling himself the Reverend E. Slave – donned a black Santa Claus suit, climbed a ladder and set fire to a Confederate flag flying from the top of the South Carolina State House. In other acts of public protest he draped himself in chains and placed a noose around his own neck, bearing a placard proclaiming: 'I, too, am South Carolina' (Harris, 2002: A1). While Eddy's form of protest was unique, his protest was not. It followed by two years what the Columbia, South Carolina, *State* newspaper called 'the largest civil-rights gathering in [the] state's history', when '46,000 participants' marched against 'the Confederate flag waving across the State House dome' (Askins and Stroud, 2000: A1). As demonstrators raised placards saying, 'Your Heritage Is My Slavery', the bishop of the state's African Methodist Episcopal Church proclaimed: 'We are here to petition the South, and South Carolina to lead the South, to bring an end to the Civil War' (Ibid.: A9–A10).

The South Carolina flag controversy illustrates the complexities, if not the bizarreries, of the free speech debate in the Southern states. Six months after the NAACP rally – on 1 July 2000 – the South Carolina Legislature agreed to lower the Confederate flag from the Capitol and diminish its display, moving it to 'a less prominent flagpole on the Capitol grounds' (Firestone, 2001: B4). That day, the state's acknowledged 'barbecue kings', the brothers Maurice and Melvin Bessinger, commenced their own civil war. Outraged at the legislature's apparent capitulation, Maurice hoisted a Confederate flag above each of his nine restaurants in Columbia, sparking boycotts that ultimately scuttled a $20 million distribution deal for his bottled barbecue sauce. Melvin, in Charleston, jumped into the breach with his rival sauce, and issued a statement through his attorney: 'Melvin and his brother do not share political or social views. Despite their being brothers, they do not speak to each other. Melvin's views on the Confederate flag, slavery, and race relations are not those of his brother' (in Hitt, 2001: D1). As one observer said, 'Buying a barbecue sandwich is now a political act. You have to declare which side you're on' (Ibid.). In a further twist, Maurice found an unlikely ally in a local free-speech defender, Kevin Gray of the American Civil Liberties Union, who had exercised *his* freedom of speech the previous summer by burning the Confederate flag on the State House lawn (Guetersloh, 2000: 12).

While South Carolina's 2000 flag controversy may have earned the most column inches in the national press coverage, elsewhere in the South the debate was (and remains) pervasive and emotionally charged enough to prompt the Charleston *Post and Courier* to despatch its reporter, Brian Hicks, on a journey through five states 'in search of where the Confederate flag stands in the modern Deep South' (Hicks, 2000a: n. p.). In the wake of Spike Lee's popular film on Malcolm X, Hicks reported on an emerging fashion item that reflected a historically naive, if not ridiculous, alignment: 'For every black T-shirt or hat carrying a simple white "X" logo in honor of Malcolm X, there's another shirt or hat with the image of the flag reciting the closest thing there is to compromise here: "You wear your X, I'll wear mine"' (Hicks, 2000: n. p.).

At the official level, 'compromise' has in fact been the watchword in a number of states, most visibly Georgia, which in 1956 had 'added the Confederate battle cross to the flag, turning a state symbol into an officially sanctioned tool of protest that could be waved at the Democratic National Convention in defiance of federal desegregation orders' (Firestone, 2001: B4). In 2000, the black Georgia state representative, Tyrone Brooks, encapsulated his twenty-year campaign against the flag with the explanation: 'It is a symbol, and symbols are important. They are important to people's psyches, people's behavior. This isn't just something up there flapping in the wind. People put that up there to flaunt a bygone era. We just want it down' (in Hicks, 2000: n. p.). A year later, however, Brooks reversed his position, and in so doing, implied that black Southerners were in fact obliged *as* Southerners to accept the display of the flag: 'What I finally had to acknowledge was that Confederate history is a part of our history. We cannot erase it, and it needs to be preserved for history's sake. Just like I have no intention of removing the statues of Robert E. Lee or Stonewall Jackson, because as long as they're there, they will help us remember not to repeat our history' (in Firestone, 2001: B4).

What had happened in the intervening months was the re-design, by a bi-racial committee, of the flag that Brooks had previously called 'the Georgia swastika' and had successfully managed to have excluded from the 1996 Olympic Games in Atlanta. Crucial to the spirit of Georgia's compromise was the acknowledgement – so apparently alien to the UDC, the SVC and the League of the South – that many Southerners were African-Americans with 'a different view of Southern heritage' (Ibid.). This acknowledgement has indeed gained currency elsewhere across the South, as implied by Robert C. Khyat, chancellor of the University of Mississippi: '[There are some] symbols that are Confederate, not Southern. Somehow we need to ferret out things that are Southern from those that are Confederate' (in Lederman, 2001: 113). In Mississippi, such a 'ferreting' would require a re-design along the lines of Georgia's flag, as the Mississippi state flag still incorporates the Confederate battle flag as its canton. There is as yet no indication that such a re-design is in the offing.

Nonetheless, even if all the Confederate battle flags were assigned to the custody of the South's museums, and if all the state flags were re-designed in the spirit of racial awareness and compromise, there would still be an entire commercial sector left to fly its own flags of defiance and unreconstruction. The manufacturing and marketing of Confederate and associated images remains an industry in its own right, again with great implications for the public representation of region and race.

Fergit, Hell!

'Southerners', writes Linda Ray Pratt – and she can only mean white Southerners –

> do not love the old Confederacy because it was a noble ideal, but because the suffering of the past occasioned by it has formed our hearts and souls, both good and evil. But we celebrate the past with cheap flags, cliché slogans, decorative license plates, decaled ash trays, and a

glorious myth of a Southern 'way of life' no one today ever lived (Pratt, 1979: 51).

Amongst the merchandise to be purchased in Southern gift shops and market stalls are items – shot glasses, miniature and full-size flags, bumper stickers, T-shirts – bearing such messages as:

'If at First You Don't Secede, Try Try Again' (Horwitz, 1998: 51);

'Fergit, Hell!', 'We don't give a damn how they do it up North', and – in the case of a Rebel flag pin playing the tune, 'Dixie' – 'Warning: May Offend Idiots' (Hicks, 2000: n. p.);

'Happiness is a Northbound Yankee', 'I had rather be dead than a Yankee', 'Keep the history, heritage and spirit of the South flying' [with picture of the Confederate battle flag], 'Send more Yankees/ They are delicious' [with picture of a mosquito], 'Lest we forget the Civil War; America's Holocaust', 'American by birth/Southern by the grace of God', 'Welcome to the South/Now go home', and 'When I'm old/I'll move up North/& Drive like I'm dead!' (Cushman, 1999: 24).

Stephen Cushman suggests that the humour inscribed into such neo-Confederate paraphernalia provides a safety-valve for what is in fact 'a barely concealed continuation of hostilities' (Ibid.: 27). A less concerned Gaines Foster sees the 'paunchy, whiskered old Confederate veteran' on a bumper sticker, snarling 'Hell no, I ain't forgettin'!', offering nothing but an empty gesture:

The old veteran hardly appeared ready to fight, much less able to win … [He] offered no marching orders, reminded no one of a powerful ideology. That remained true even when his card or tag carried a slightly more assertive caption, 'The South shall rise again!' No one knew how or when or why it would (Foster, 1987: 3).

Nonetheless, Cushman is right in sensing that his more aggressive examples of Confederate imagery reflect a ratcheting up of the heat, a post-civil-rights-struggle phase of merchandising beginning in the early 1960s and considerably out of keeping with the more reconciliatory phases of advertising that preceded it.

As David Blight notes, 'in the 1880s many companies in North and South appealed to customers with elaborate advertisements that used themes of Civil War reconciliation'. He cites as an example 'the Duke Tobacco Company of Durham, North Carolina', which in 1889 began marketing their cigarettes with 'an elaborate multicolored souvenir album' juxtaposing Union and Confederate war heroes whose 'images were salable memories in the name of good will and good business' (Blight, 2001: 201). The object in such a campaign was to dissolve 'the war's causes and consequences' in the name of 'national reunion' (Ibid.).

The side-stepping of race and slavery in such commercial invocations of the Civil War is not surprising, as much of the merchandise was filtered through a Lost Cause prism that diminished or wholly excluded African-Americans from the recollection. Noting that liquor advertising marked 'the most persistent employment of Old South/Confederate themes', Jack Temple Kirby cites the marketing in the early 1930s of such brands as Richmond's 'Dixie Belle' gin, Four Roses whiskey – 'limned "soft as Southern moonlight" ... with a color picture of rebel colonels with juleps' – and Paul Jones whiskey, sporting 'two aged veterans, one Confederate, the other Union, sitting beneath a tree with their glasses, reminiscing: "It was back in '65"' (Kirby, 1978: 75). Deep Spring Tennessee Whiskey, marketed between 1903 and 1915 by the J. W. Kelly Company of Chattanooga, was advertised as 'The Whiskey Without an Unkind Thought' on labels and tin signs that have become popular items on eBay and other Internet auction sites. The richly coloured Deep Spring label presents the Lost Cause in all its romance and political evasiveness, with an immaculate Robert E. Lee on horseback, saluting his ragged, cheering white troops, while in the foreground a merciful angel of Southern white womanhood supports a wounded rebel soldier as she holds to his lips a medicinal draught of whiskey.

An equally significant example – because it has survived to this day – is Rebel Yell Kentucky Bourbon, created in 1936 at the behest of Charles P. Farnsley, the Democratic politician who not only served successively as mayor of Louisville, state representative from Kentucky and US congressman, but who was also a member of the SCV and publisher/ president of the Lost Cause Press (Anon., 2004: n. p.). The brand's current merchandising information states that the whiskey – with its label boasting 'a line drawing of a Rebel soldier, sword in hand, galloping off to fight' – was first devised to 'personify the South', and that Farnsley sought 'to create a bourbon specifically for the people of the Deep South' (Sherman, 2004: n. p.). This is, if anything, a telling mark of identification for a politician from a Border State in the 1930s. In fact, Rebel Yell was at first distributed only in the South, and 'discontinued for a while' before its reintroduction – in the spirit of romantic reunion – to mark the Civil War Centennial in 1961. Eventually, Rebel Yell became 'so popular that the company finally allowed it to be sold to Yankees in 1984' – namely, the David Sherman Corporation of St Louis (Ibid.).

Advertisements that chose not to evade the question of race and slavery are invariably highly shocking and offensive. Kirby cites another Four Roses ad from 1935, 'showing an eager black servant rushing with his tray of juleps' above the caption 'Yes, suh, Colonel, I'se comin'!', and another Paul Jones ad depicting 'a Dixie patriarch giving orders to his black servant: "Toby, fetch me the key to the springhouse"' (Kirby, 1978: 75). Such references and images did not stop with whiskey, nor were they restricted to Southern-based firms. Again, Kirby cites a 1931 campaign by the Virginia Commission of Conservation and Development to promote 'Hams from Ole Virginia' – 'as good as though you went to the plantation and had Mammy cook it' – as well an Illinois Central Railroad campaign that in 1934 promoted package tours to the 'Sunny South', the 'Land O' Lee where the "white man's burden" can be laid down' (Ibid.: 74–5). In a particularly incisive critique of the manner in which Northern and Southern white reunion was (and, in some cases, remains) effected at black expense in the commercial arena, Kevin Willmott's faux television documentary, *CSA: The Confederate States of America* (2003; see Chapter 4 and Conclusion), is punctuated with commercials advertising products that – as the film explains in a postscript – 'actually existed in the United States of America'. Willmott's captions include:

> 'The Gold Dust Twins', 1880s–1930s. Both black children and whites in blackface were cast as Goldie and Dusty in Gold Dust Washing Powder Advertisements. The popularity of the twins led to a radio show in 1925.

> 'Coon Chicken Inn', 1920s–1950s. The Inn was a successful restaurant chain in Salt Lake City, Seattle and Portland. The entryway was the mouth of a grotesque grinning black man in a porter's cap.

> 'Niggerhair Tobacco', 1870s–1950s. The B. Leidersdory Co. of Milwaukee, Wisconsin, produced Niggerhair Tobacco 'to smoke or chew'. Several decades later the name was changed to 'Biggerhair'.

> 'Sambo Axle Grease', 1870s–1980s. Nourse Oil Co., Kansas City, MO.
> (all in Willmott, 2003)

While the longevity of such products as 'Sambo Axle Grease' may be surprising and depressing in equal measure, Helen Taylor has explored more recent examples from the late 1990s, all of which indicate that

> the cultural industries, including tourism, have worked hard to market a South rich in heritage and cultural diversity, treading carefully to avoid the inevitable historical memories of uglier times and the ever present reality of minority group unemployment, poverty, and racial oppression in a region still caricaturable through God, guns, and the Confederate flag (Taylor, 2001: 12).

Taylor mentions in particular Memphis, New Orleans and Atlanta, 'all with large black populations and black mayors and city councils', obliged, as they promote themselves, to walk 'a careful line between the nostalgia market for the Old South of plantation homes and Civil War battle sites ("the Confederate Trail") and the New South market for younger visitors, with live music, multimedia museums and exhibits, and multicultural events' (Ibid.).

In the commercial arena, however, there is still some distance to travel, as Willmott observes at the end of his film: 'Today the use of slave imagery in the promotion of products often goes unnoticed. Just ask Aunt Jemima and Uncle Ben' (Willmott, 2003). The decision of the Quaker Oats Company executives in the 1980s to replace the slavery-time, handkerchief-headed Aunt Jemima with a modern, pearl-bedecked bourgeois model only goes part of the way. The insulting designation 'Aunt' still remains, inviting a frosty response akin to that of the black education activist, Mary McLeod Bethune, when addressed as such by a white man: 'And which one of my sister's boys are you?' (quoted in Bennett, 2000: 110).

The grim catalogue of racial defamation and exclusion that characterises so much of Civil War culture suggests that unreconstruction remains an influential, if virulent, response to the war and its legacies. However, it would be a mistake to conclude that Civil War culture has been wholly resistant to progressive inspiration. As the next chapter indicates, recent feminist writing and scholarship has opened up Civil War history and culture to fresh interpretations, amounting to a veritable regendering in which the war and its cultural legacies are reclaimed as women's space.

CHAPTER 6

The Regendered Civil War

In 2001, California's Huntington Library and Art Gallery published for the first time the diary of Eliza Ann Wetherby Otis, the co-founder and publisher of the *Los Angeles Times*. Decades before she became an American publishing magnate, the poet Eliza Otis poured into her diary all the frustrations of an active, creative intellectual held in check by the constraints of Victorian American propriety. In 1860, as she viewed the approach of civil war, she could only sit in her parlour and upbraid herself for a situation clearly not of her own making:

FRIDAY, JANUARY 6.
Every day should be a record of usefulness, and every night should find us higher in our progressive life. But my advance I fear is somewhat snail-like, and not always certain at that. My life, I fear, is one of *thought* more than action.

But it is earnest, active life that we need. Our *inner* life makes the world no better, be it ever so high and holy, unless we embody it in deeds (Otis, 2001: 25).

WEDNESDAY, JANUARY 18.
I'm a sort of good-for-nothing piece of humanity … I write letters and wash stockings and pocket handkerchiefs, and eat breakfast, dinner and supper, and walk out once a day, and this is about the sum total of my exertions both physical and mental.

Ain't I a glorious demonstration of the truthfulness of the quoted saying of Longfellow's – 'Life is real, life is earnest'. Would anybody doubt it after a glance even at my life? (Ibid.: 43–4)

TUESDAY, JANUARY 24.
I've spent the day in dreaming – dreaming of what I could be and do. Ah, why don't I act – *act* – that would be better (Ibid.: 47).

Within weeks, her husband, Harrison Otis, disappeared into the ranks of the 12th Regiment, Ohio Volunteers, assumed the 'action' that she so craved, and left her to continue observing and commenting in private.

Eliza Otis's diary is, at least in part, a testament to the crippling effects of American patriarchy, if that highly contested term can be accepted as meaning 'the economic, political and ideological domination of women by men' (Murray, 1994: 8). A potent agent of that domination was what feminist scholars, after historian Barbara Welter, continue to call 'the cult of true womanhood'. In her influential analysis of antebellum society, Welter described the middle-class American woman as 'the hostage in the home', with the appropriateness of her captivity reinforced through the 'women's magazines, gift annuals and religious literature' that also reinforced a 'true' woman's rightful qualities: 'piety, purity, sub-missiveness, and domesticity' (Welter, 1966: 152). The consequences of tampering 'with the complex of virtues that made up True Womanhood' would bring down damnation as 'the enemy of God, of civilization, and of the Republic' (Ibid). As the editor of Otis's diary, Ann Gorman Condon, makes clear, in spite of Otis's 'advanced education' and the fact that her husband was not 'an overbearing patriarch at home', the couple

Figure 8 'The Woman in Battle': Jill, 43rd North Carolina Infantry, 2004 (Will Kaufman).

'fit the typical Victorian image of the middle class: conspicuous politeness, religious piety, and a romantic ideal of the marriage bond' (in Otis, 2001: xxxvi–xxxvii). In this regard, Otis cannot have been immune from the potency of the 'cult of true womanhood'.

However, Otis's diary also reveals a countercurrent stirred up by the ironically liberating possibilities of civil war. Beneath her partisan condemnation of an alleged Confederate spy, for instance, is an acknowledgement of the brutal egalitarianism of martial law:

> Writing to Harry again this morning. Told him of Mrs. Cotton's arrest for treason. She was sent beyond our lines today. Glad that Government has begun to deal with these female traitors. If they will indulge in rampant treason, then sex should not shield them from punishment. Justice shouldn't deal with the grammatical distinctions of gender, and make treason either masculine or feminine, and I'm glad that they are not doing it (Ibid.: 146).

This stern call for equality under the law might not, on the face of it, reflect a particularly emancipatory impulse. But it came at a time when, in Abraham Lincoln's White House, a woman who dared to venture a political opinion could be dismissed with the presidential sneer, 'You're quite a female politician', as allegedly happened to Jessie Benton Fremónt in 1861 (Burlingame, 1994: 128). Still, there is a further paradox: in the very same White House, Lincoln reportedly 'blazed with anger' upon hearing that the Federal paymaster had refused to authorise wages for one Mary Ellen Wise, who had enlisted in an Indiana regiment in male disguise and had been seriously wounded at the Battle of Lookout Mountain (Ibid.: 182). This paradox – the simultaneous censure and validation of women who stepped out of the domestic sphere and into the public tempest of the Civil War – is only one indication of the war's destabilising impact upon patriarchal structures and assumptions. As Joan E. Cashin argues, 'the war unsettled, undermined, and sometimes destroyed traditional gender roles, in all regions, forcing people to reconsider their assumptions about appropriate behavior for men and women of both races' (Cashin, 2002: 3).

In order to explore how the Civil War challenged – and continues to challenge – the received definitions of 'true womanhood' as few American historical crises have done, we must distinguish between white and black as well as Northern and Southern 'womanhood', because the institution of slavery, as well as the visitation of total war upon the

South, had a profound impact upon constructions of womanhood and femininity. Yet even these markers – black, white, North, South – should be treated with caution, subject as they are to destabilisation, ambiguity and the presence of 'border states' both geographical and metaphorical (Young, 1999: 19). We can begin by addressing the most direct challenge to the 'cult of true womanhood' as it was uttered in the last decade before the Civil War by the ex-slave, abolitionist and women's rights activist, Sojourner Truth, and relate it to two African-American texts emerging from both sides of the Mason–Dixon line: from the North, Harriet Wilson's barely fictionalised autobiography, *Our Nig* (1859), and from the South, Harriet Jacobs's 'classic' slave narrative, *Incidents in the Life of a Slave Girl* (1861). In conversation with each other, all three texts open up debates as to the very definition of 'womanhood' while complicating many conceptions of race and region that commonly mark Civil War scholarship.

Ain't I a Woman?

Truth's famous two-pronged attack on the 'cult of true womanhood' is a useful counterpoint to Eliza Otis's diary in that it not only challenges the cult's presumption of female weakness and helplessness, but it also takes issue with the assumption that slave women should be excluded from any definition of 'true womanhood'. Truth's words, addressed to the 1851 Women's Rights Convention in Akron, Ohio, come primarily in two versions. The more widely circulated version – and the one most often anthologised today – was first reported in 1863 in the *New York Independent* by Truth's fellow abolitionist and women's rights activist, Frances Dana Gage, as follows:

> That man over there says that women need to be helped into carriages, and lifted over ditches, and to have the best place everywhere. Nobody ever helps me into carriages, or over mud-puddles, or gives me any best place! And ain't I a woman? Look at me! Look at my arm! I have ploughed and planted, and gathered into barns, and no man could head me! And ain't I a woman? I could work as much and eat as much as a man – when I could get it – and bear the lash as well! And ain't I a woman? I have borne thirteen children, and seen most all sold off to slavery, and when I cried out with my mother's grief, none but Jesus heard me! And ain't I a woman? (Gage, 1881: 116)

The second version comes from the Salem, Ohio, *Anti-Slavery Bugle* of

21 June 1851, which reported Truth's words a month after they were delivered to the convention:

> I am for woman's rights. I have as much muscle as any man, and can do as much work as any man. I have plowed and reaped and husked and chopped and mowed, and can any man do more than that? I have heard much about the sexes being equal; I can carry as much as any man, and can eat as much too, if I can get it. I am as strong as any man that is now.
>
> As for intellect, all I can say is, if woman have a pint and a man a quart – why can't she have her little pint full? You need not be afraid to give us our rights for fear we will take too much – for we won't take more than our pint will hold.
>
> The poor men seem to be all in confusion and don't know what to do. Why children, if you have woman's rights give it to her and you will feel better. You will have your own rights, and there won't be so much trouble (in Painter, 1997: 125–6).

While scholars have argued over which of these accounts is the most reliable, it is clear that each of them challenges, in its own way – whether through rhetorical refrain in the first or sly irony in the second – the assumption that 'true womanhood' relies on female weakness, or that Truth, as a former slave, should be excluded from the definition.

The case of Sojourner Truth also problematises the issue of the North–South divide as it relates to the 'cult of true womanhood'. Truth was born into slavery in the North – in New York – thirty years before its abolition in 1827. It is clear, however, that for Truth, emancipation did not translate into inclusive views of black womanhood in the North. This point is reinforced in Wilson's *Our Nig*, in which the brutalities visited upon the mixed-race indentured servant, Frado, take place in a New England setting where a quasi-free black woman is presumed to be beyond the bounds of 'true womanhood'. This results in the needless self-loathing that begins in the protagonist's childhood:

> 'Who made me so?'
>   'God', answered James.
>   'Did God make you?'
>   'Yes'.
>   'Who made Aunt Abby?'
>   'God'.

'Who made your mother?'

'God'.

'Did the same God that made her make me?'

'Yes'.

'Well, then, I don't like him'.

'Why not?'

'Because he made her white, and me black. Why didn't he make us *both* white?' (Wilson, 1859: 51)

The cruel psychic wound that begins in Frado's childhood is culturally reinforced throughout her adulthood, and is referenced through the entire novel, as Frado is 'watched by kidnappers, maltreated by professed abolitionists, who didn't want slaves at the South, nor niggers in their own houses, North. Faugh! to lodge one; to eat with one; to admit one through the front door; to sit next one; awful!' (Ibid.: 129) Wilson effectively dissolves the border between slave and free territory – actually mirroring the intent of the Fugitive Slave Law – in asserting that the 'shadow of slavery' (as she phrases it in her subtitle) falls even in New England. With that dissolution comes the denial of black women's protected domestic status and, thus, their exclusion from the realm of 'true womanhood' as it was then defined on both sides of the Mason–Dixon line.

Both Northern and Southern assumptions of 'true womanhood' are further exploded in Jacobs's *Incidents in the Life of a Slave Girl*, a complex narrative that challenges and at the same time succumbs to the power of the 'cult'. On the one hand, Jacobs rejects the slave woman's legal status as the 'property' of a sexually predatory master, and affirms the right of women to admit to sexual desire and make sexual decisions – a unique affirmation in relation to most nineteenth-century American women, black or white, slave or free. It seems a profoundly empowering gesture, but it is couched in language that indicates, yet again, a great blow to the protagonist's self-esteem. Hiding behind the pseudonym of 'Linda Brent', Jacobs begins her narration by throwing herself upon the mercy of public opinion, in particular that of 'the women of the North', amongst whom she has resided since her escape from slavery (Jacobs, 1861: 6). Her willing sexual liaison with a white bachelor, which she describes as a calculated effort to discourage her lustful master, is undeniably an act of desire through which she becomes (to adapt her fourth chapter title) 'the slave who dared to feel' like a woman (Ibid.: 28). However, an openly sexual woman obviously could not conform to the standards of 'true womanhood' – to repeat Welter, standards of 'piety, purity [and] submissiveness'. Thus, while with calm defiance Jacobs argues that 'the slave woman ought not to be judged by the same standard as others', her plaintiveness betrays her real fear of Northern women's social dis-approbation or even damnation: 'O, ye happy women, whose purity has been sheltered from childhood, who have been free to choose the objects of your affection, whose homes are protected by law, do not judge the poor desolate slave girl too severely!' (Ibid.: 83). Jacobs is arguing for, among other things, a black woman's access to a legally and socially protected private sphere and the attendant conferment of 'true womanhood' – access to which, at any event, black women were denied both in the North and in the South, as all these texts make clear.

Taken in the aggregate, these examples reflect black women's prob-lematic desire for, and wariness of, inclusion into the mid-nineteenth-century's sphere of passive, protected and pious womanhood. Yet other Civil War writings indicate the belligerence with which many women, black and white, fought with varying success to transcend that sphere, turning the home front into a virtual battle front and the act of writing into an act of war. Through such texts as Louisa May Alcott's *Little Women* (1868), Mary Chesnut's *A Diary from Dixie* (1905) and Elizabeth Keckley's *Behind the Scenes* (1868), we can further explore important uses of – and challenges to – constructions of American womanhood in the destabilising context of civil war.

'I Must Warn you, Mrs. Lincoln, I am Very Political'

During the mid-nineteenth century, American women writers were, if anything, highly visible. William Dean Howells, editor of the *Atlantic Monthly*, complained in 1871 that the literary market had long been dominated by 'lady writers' and their 'long train of bigamists, murder-esses, adulteresses, and dubiosities' (in Hiatt, 1993: 5). Given that Howells was virtually, if unconsciously, paraphrasing Nathaniel Hawthorne's legendary outburst of sixteen years earlier – about America's 'd****d mob of scribbling women' (in Pattee, 1940: 110) – it is clear that a male paranoia of considerable proportion spanned the US literary culture at mid-century, reflecting a fear of women's incursion into, and domina-tion of, the public space.

Louisa May Alcott, for one, was wholly prepared to take on the greatest public issue of her time – the Civil War – as a subject: 'I will write "great guns" Hail Columbia & Concord fight' (in Fahs, 2001: 21).

However, in her most popular Civil War text, *Little Women*, the battle is waged against the 'cult of true womanhood' rather than against slavery, secession or any battlefield adversary. In the novel, the March family's absent father figure, a chaplain in the Union army, makes clear his expectations in a letter to his wife: their daughters must 'do their duty faithfully, fight their bosom enemies bravely, and conquer themselves so beautifully that when I come back to them I may be fonder and prouder than ever of my little women' (Alcott, 1996: 9).

Consequently it is Jo March who most keenly feels the implied pressure to conform:

'I'll try and be what he loves to call me, "a little woman", and not be rough and wild, but do my duty here instead of wanting to be somewhere else', said Jo, thinking that keeping her temper at home was a much harder task than facing a rebel or two down South (Ibid.).

Jo is particularly aware that her enforced inaction is a highly gendered form of repression:

'I hate to think I've got to grow up, and be Miss March, and wear long gowns, and look as prim as a China aster! It's bad enough to be a girl, anyway, when I like boys' games and work and manners! I can't get over my disappointment in not being a boy; and it's worse than ever now, for I'm dying to go and fight with Papa, and I can only stay at home and knit, like a poky old woman!' (Ibid.: 4)

Thus, Jo channels her combative energies into her writing, which takes on openly martial connotations and at times transforms the home into a mirror image of the battlefield. 'I like good strong words that mean something', she says (Ibid.: 31), and when that channel is blocked – when Jo's sister Amy destroys the book that Jo has been writing in her garret – Jo's frustration pours forth in the novel's only moment of violence, which begins with Jo shaking Amy 'till her teeth chattered in her head' and ends with a *mêlée*: 'Meg flew to rescue Amy, and Beth to pacify Jo, but Jo was quite beside herself; and, with a parting box on her sister's ear, she rushed out of the room up to the old sofa in the garret, and finished her fight alone' (Ibid.: 63). In this fight, and with her novel burned, Jo's diary remains the only site where she can risk expressing her transgressive or belligerent thoughts without fear of censure.

As a site of belligerent expression, Jo's fictional diary has an important historical counterpart that demands our attention. The diary of the

South Carolinian, Mary Boykin Chesnut, has long been a prime source for scholars and students wishing to gain a first-hand account of the upper echelons of a Southern slaveholding society witnessing its own extinction. When Chesnut's diary was published in 1905, nineteen years after her death, it established her as the best-known diarist of the Southern home front. However, C. Vann Woodward and Elisabeth Muhlenfeld have proven Chesnut's famous diary to have been actually written retrospectively in the 1880s. The private journal that Chesnut kept throughout the Civil War was not intended for publication, and did not appear until 1984 (Woodward and Muhlenfeld, 1984; see also Woodward, 1981). This makes the 1905 diary all the more valuable as a cultural document, for it becomes a signal example of a post-Reconstruction version of Civil War history disguised as a contemporary response. Thus, as Stephen Cushman notes, it serves as a reminder that 'should keep us from being too gullible about the authenticity of what we're reading' (Cushman, 1999: 72).

Chesnut's 1905 'diary' also reveals one of the most troubling dimensions in the representation of the Southern home front: the selective and racially charged claims to women's status as victims of the war. Chesnut, for example, recreates with calculated pathos the desolation of white Southern womanhood in a passage that many will associate with the 'Atlanta is burning' scenes in *Gone with the Wind*:

> Camden, S.C. May 2, 1865
> — Since we left Chester nothing but solitude, nothing but tall blackened chimneys, to show that any man has ever trod this road before. This is Sherman's track. It is hard not to curse him. I wept incessantly at first. The roses of the gardens are already hiding the ruins. My husband said Nature is a wonderful renovator. He tried to say something else and then I shut my eyes and made a vow that if we were a crushed people, crushed by weight, I would never be a whimpering, pining slave (Chesnut, 1905: 384).

For all her skill in utilising the rhetoric of victimisation, one of the most astounding and frequently cited aspects of Chesnut's writing is her profound inability or unwillingness to acknowledge to any meaningful extent the victimisation of slave women, however willing she is to cast herself as a white Southerner stoically resisting enslavement by the Yankees. To Chesnut, the greatest crime of slavery lies in what it does to respectable, long-suffering white women whose husbands are lured into sexual infidelity by scheming, wily mulattoes. Thus, these slave women bear the brunt of her assault even as she purports to pity them:

> I have seen a negro woman sold on the block at auction. She over-topped the crowd. I was walking and felt faint, seasick. The creature looked so like my good little Nancy, a bright mulatto with a pleasant face. She was magnificently gotten up in silks and satins. She seemed delighted with it all, sometimes ogling the bidders, sometimes look-ing quiet, coy, and modest, but her mouth never relaxed from its expanded grin of excitement. I dare say the poor thing knew who would buy her. I sat down on a stool in a shop and disciplined my wild thoughts (Ibid.: 13).

Passages such as this (and there are many) are of a piece with the sinister renderings of mixed-race women in other post-Reconstruction texts such as Thomas Dixon's novels and D. W. Griffith's *The Birth of a Nation* (see Chapter 2). These texts imply a presumably tragic inversion of the antebellum order in which the former slaveholders become the true victims, and the former slaves the oppressors. In keeping with Dixon's accusation that the slaves were the 'Black curse' whose presence had destroyed the 'garden' of the South (in Lang, 1994: 9) and Griffith's charge that 'the bringing of the African to America planted the first seed of disunion' (Griffith, 1915), Chesnut casts the slaves as the true culprits in the South's tragedy, even prior to emancipation and Reconstruction. Chesnut implies that even from the depths of their enslavement, black women are the authors of white women's woes. In the end, Chesnut's 'diary' is indeed a war document, but what it really chronicles is not only a war against black women, but also a war against the post-bellum order in which it was written. Thus, Woodward makes a point of calling Chesnut's 1905 diary a 'memoir', given the fact of its covert retrospective authoring.

One further influential memoir – openly presented as such – opens a window onto another battlefield, a liminal place situated between the home front and the military front. Elizabeth Keckley's *Behind the Scenes; Or, Thirty Years a Slave and Four Years in the White House* was one of the earliest accounts of the interlocking of domestic and political life in the Lincoln White House, and has served as a major source for historians, novelists and film-makers. (The misspelling of her name in the first edition has ensured that she is rarely referred to as 'Keckly', her proper name.) As Elizabeth Young argues, nowhere is the equation of writing with combat more stunningly made than in this memoir by the ex-slave who became a fashion designer, dressmaker and estranged confidante of Mary Todd Lincoln. Young describes the memoir as an instrument of Keckley's 'political authority' and 'covert civil war' (Young, 1999: 23, 119).

Gore Vidal relied heavily upon Keckley for his fictional recreation, *Lincoln: A Novel* (1984), which firmly establishes Keckley's 'political authority' in the scene where Mary Lincoln first meets her and accepts her letters of reference:

> 'You worked for Mrs. Jefferson Davis. How strange! I was just speaking of Mr. Davis'.
> 'Yes, I worked for Mrs. Davis ... I was very fond of Mrs. Davis'.
> 'Then why didn't you go South with her?'
> 'Well ... Look at me'. Keckley gestured.
> 'I *am* looking at you'.
> 'I am colored'.
> 'But free'.
> 'Even so, I could never live in a slave state. I am an abolitionist. In fact, I must warn you, Mrs. Lincoln, I am very political'.
> 'Oh, so am I!' Mary was delighted (Vidal, 1984: 89–90).

Vidal here implies a gauntlet being thrown down by one willing combatant and joyously taken up by another. Yet, in turning to Keckley's own text, it is clear that part of her rhetorical strategy is to appear much less politically authoritative than she really is – an important dimension of her 'covert war'. In recounting one of her last meetings with Varina Davis on the eve of war, she affects ignorance and surprise at what the rest of the nation already knows:

> While dressing her one day, she said to me: 'Lizzie, you are so very handy that I should like to take you South with me'.
> 'When do you go South, Mrs. Davis?' I inquired.
> 'Oh, I cannot tell just now, but it will be soon. You know there is going to be war, Lizzie?'
> 'No!'
> 'But I tell you yes'.
> 'Who will go to war?' I asked.
> 'The North and South', was her ready reply. 'The Southern people will not submit to the humiliating demands of the Abolition party; they will fight first' (Keckley, 1868: 70).

In spite of her faux naïvety, however, Keckley reveals a political awareness and scepticism that makes this wide-eyed, breathless exchange with
Mrs. Davis all the less credible:

> I knew the North to be strong, and believed that the people would
> fight for the flag that they pretended to venerate so highly. The
> Republican party had just emerged from a heated campaign, flushed
> with victory, and I could not think that the hosts composing the party
> would quietly yield all they had gained in the Presidential canvass
> (Ibid.: 72).

Although it was as a politically naïve dressmaker that Keckley acted
in the service of both First Ladies, it was as an incisive author that she
ultimately vanquished them and, through them, the privileged, slaveholding, white society from which they came. For while Keckley admits
to nothing but veneration for the martyred poor white, Abraham
Lincoln, she shows little mercy to Mary Lincoln, the former belle of
Kentucky (in spite of the latter's heated opposition to slavery). Ironically
– if not, perhaps, hypocritically – Keckley explains that she went public
against Mary Lincoln precisely because Mrs Lincoln had breached the
boundaries of domesticity through her political intrigues and her well-
publicised extravagance, which resulted in a scandal that still raged even
as Keckley went to press:

> Mrs. Lincoln, by her own acts, forced herself into notoriety. She
> stepped beyond the formal lines which hedge about a private life, and
> invited public criticism … Had Mrs. Lincoln's acts never become
> public property, I should not have published to the world the secret
> chapters of her life (Ibid.: xiii, xv).

Similarly, through reference to a dress that she had made for Varina
Davis, Keckley modestly applies the *coup de grâce* to Jefferson Davis's
reputation – and, implicitly, to Southern manhood at large – by affirming the rumour that he had worn this dress while attempting to evade
capture in Georgia (see Figure 3, p. 40). Davis had in fact been captured
wearing a shawl or a cloak, but the rumour of Keckley's dress did its
political and cultural work for the victorious North, as Nina Silber
describes:

> P. T. Barnum, always eager to take advantage of a cultural
> phenomenon, exhibited the unfortunate Confederate at his New York

museum in a tableaux showing a hoopskirted Davis surrounded by his captor-soldiers. And countless cartoons and prints offered similar impressions of 'Jeff's Last Shift', 'The Chas-ed Old Lady of the CSA', and 'Jeffie Davis – the Belle of Richmond'. The prints frequently displayed soldiers in the very act of exposing the Confederate president, often depicting a single Union soldier using his sword to lift Davis's skirt, thereby revealing the hoopskirt and unseemly boots which had given him away (Silber, 1992: 297).

Keckley's confirmation of the rumour about Davis in drag fed into a more general anxiety about gender divisions and distinctions during the Civil War. Lincoln, too, faced his share of emasculating or feminising caricatures from opponents who knew how to exploit this anxiety. The fact that both Davis and Lincoln were commanders-in-chief of their respective armies brings additional significance beyond the acknowledgement that they were wartime presidents, for the regendering of the Civil War took place not only on the pages of American literature, but also on the military battlefield – with lasting implications for American culture in the next two centuries.

Fighting Like Demons

In Rita Mae Brown's novel, *High Hearts* (1986), one of Virginia's top horsewomen, Geneva Chatfield, resolves to follow her husband into the Confederate ranks. Brown's premise is based on historical fact, as studies by (among others) Mary Elizabeth Massey (1994), Richard Hall (1993), Lee Middleton (1993), Elizabeth D. Leonard (2001) and DeAnne Blanton and Lauren Cook (2002) demonstrate. These studies examine the hundreds of distaff soldiers – women disguised as men – who fought and not infrequently died in Civil War battles. Disguised women served as guards, scouts, medical orderlies, musicians and drummer boys, secret agents and battlefield soldiers. Some were discovered only when they gave birth in camp or as POWs, having fought in such notoriously savage battles as Antietam and Fredericksburg during their late terms of pregnancy. Others were never discovered at all during their military service, and maintained their male disguise as civilians in order to enjoy the civil rights denied to them as women.

One distaff soldier – Jennie Hodgers – was only discovered as a frail, 70-year-old disabled veteran in the Illinois Soldier's Home, after which she was removed to an insane asylum and forced after a lifetime in male attire to wear the cumbersome skirts that she had avoided for so long. Unused to this humiliating, strange apparel, Hodgers – known to herself and to her comrades as Albert D. Cashier – tripped on a hem, broke her hip, and spent her few remaining years bedridden. Still at war, she was obliged to fight for her soldier's pension – as though to affirm that the 'feminisation of poverty' was an official objective almost a century before the sociologist, Diana Pearce, coined the phrase (Pearce, 1978: 28). As the Hodgers/Cashier case indicated, a virtual conspiracy of silence ensured that the record of women's military participation remained secret; hence the US War Department's official denial to the journalist, Ida Tarbell, that any women had ever listed in the military ranks during the Civil War, although – as we have seen – Lincoln himself was aware of it (Hall, 1993: 202; Blanton and Cook, 2002: 191).

There may have been much more to the War Department's silence than mere patriarchal embarrassment or, indeed, a determination to further entrench the 'feminisation of poverty'. As Blanton and Cook imply, the latter was certainly a consideration, but there was more at stake than the economics of gender discrimination:

> Women who passed as men were, in large part, seeking economic privileges and social opportunities otherwise closed to them. Their transvestitism was a private rebellion against public conventions. By taking a male social identity, they secured for themselves male power and independence, as well as full status as citizens of their nation. In essence, the Civil War was an opportunity for hundreds of women to escape the confines of their sex (Blanton and Cook, 2002: 5).

In this context, the transvestitism of distaff soldiers was a highly destabilising and subversive social act, 'a movement of boundary itself', as Judith Butler describes it (Butler, 1993: ix). Consequently it is unsurprising that twentieth-century historians have largely perpetuated the silence over the participation of women soldiers during the Civil War (Blanton and Cook, 2002: 196, 198). Such wilful historical amnesia is all the more curious since during the Civil War itself the adventures of unmasked distaff soldiers were frequent items in newspapers and magazines, spawning the popular sub-genre of 'Female Warrior' fiction exemplified by such texts as Madeline Moore's *The Lady Lieutenant* (1862), *Pauline of the Potomac: or, General McClellan's Spy* (1862) by Wesley Bradshaw (pseudonym of Charles Wesley Alexander) and Edward Edgeville's *Castine* (1865).

While such works were readily accepted and enjoyed as pure fiction, the same cannot so easily be said of the two extant memoirs of distaff soldiers: Sarah Emma Edmonds's *Unsexed: or, The Female Soldier* (1864, retitled *Nurse and Spy in the Union Army*) and Loreta Velazquez's *The Woman in Battle* (1876). Read against each other, these two narratives – the first from the North, the second from the South – highlight both the risks and the rewards of daring to propose that '"being a man" and ... "being a woman" are internally unstable affairs' (Butler, 1993: 126–7).

As a Union veteran writing for a Northern audience, Edmonds – herself a Canadian – enjoyed a supportive readership, and the authenticity of her narrative has been generally accepted since its first publication. Her theme is precisely the 'movement of boundary' to which Butler refers. Rebelling against the restrictions of hospital nursing, Edmonds accepts her first dangerous espionage mission to Richmond, the Confederate capital, disguised in blackface and a wig as a 'contraband' slave boy – apparently, if the episode is to be believed, with more fidelity to African-American appearance than that habitually offered on the minstrel stage (see Chapter 1). Having destabilised both race and gender (as well as the boundaries between life and theatre), she proceeds further to dismantle assumptions of her nationality as she disguises herself as 'an Irish female peddler' and infiltrates Confederate headquarters (Edmonds, 1999: 83). Armed with information, she returns to the Union lines with her hair shorn and dressed as a young orderly, which initiates her into battlefield combat. In spite of such profound sexual and racial transgression, an evangelical Christian rhetoric pervades Edmonds's narrative, which undoubtedly added to its popular appeal and the credence with which it was received. Thus, Edmonds succeeded in ameliorating the disorienting, if not subversive, implications of her gender-, race- and nation-bending.

If Edmonds's loyalty to the Union, as well as her evangelical rhetoric, helped her to offer a tale of profound subversion with relatively little censure, her Confederate counterpart, Loreta Velazquez, was not so fortunate. Velazquez's narrative was damned as a scandalous fabrication from the moment of its appearance (particularly by ex-Confederate generals) and has been lamented as 'too good to be true' by later feminists such as Catherine Clinton (Clinton, 1996: 72). Its sexual border-crossings and destabilising effects are much more complex than those offered by Edmonds, and if anything, they prefigure the proto-lesbian potential of Jo March in her 'disappointment in not being a boy' (Alcott,

1996: 4). For while Edmonds makes no such admission, Velazquez openly admits:

> I was especially haunted with the idea of being a man; and the more I thought upon the subject, the more I was disposed to murmur at Providence for having created me a woman. While residing with my aunt, it was frequently my habit, after all in the house had retired to bed at night, to dress myself in my cousin's clothes, and to promenade by the hour before the mirror, practising the gait of a man, and admiring the figure I made in masculine raiment. I wished that I could only change places with my brother Josea (Velazquez, 2003: 42).

While the fictional Jo March holds her impulses in check, vows to remain her father's 'little woman' and channels her frustration and defiance into her private writings, Velazquez – if she is to be believed – acts upon them in a narrative that Young chooses to interpret as 'a picaresque novel' and 'a literary fantasy prompted by the real-life transformations of Southern white women during wartime' (Young, 1999: 161). Thus Velazquez sets the scene for an adventure in shape-shifting and gender-crossing firmly anchored to martial combat (in her stated identification with Joan of Arc) and the discovery of 'new worlds' (in her identification with Columbus and Captain Cook) (Velazquez, 2003: 41–2).

Whether interpreted as history, fantasy, picaresque novel or a mélange of all three, *The Woman in Battle* presents the Cuban-born Velazquez immigrating to the United States in the 1850s, establishing her as an outsider whose *raison d'être* is the repeated act of infiltration. She settles in the South and, at the outbreak of the Civil War, dons the grey uniform over her wire corset to become Harry T. Buford, veteran of Bull Run, Shiloh and other battles. Trading the garb of soldier for spy, she infiltrates the Union intelligence service disguised as a Northern woman, to be given the bizarre order to locate the 'woman who is traveling and figuring as a Confederate agent' – that is, herself (Velazquez, 2003: 516). Throughout her intrigues she also assumes the identity of a French Creole, an Englishwoman, a Spanish lady, a Canadian, a Spanish soldier and a would-be filibuster from Cuba set on colonising Venezuela for exiled Southerners and their slaves. In between, she invites and resists the sexual advances of both men and women. Ultimately, as Jesse Alemán points out, 'there is no genuine "self" for Velazquez to find' (Alemán, 2003: xxv), just as – so it would appear – there is no genuine Velazquez for a reader to find. However, the truth or fiction of Velazquez's narrative may well be beside the point – an observation missed by the majority of critics and historians who have taken such great pains since 1876 to establish its authenticity or falsehood. What matters about *The Woman in Battle* is the extent to which it illustrates and relies upon the disruption of conventionally recognised codes, not only of gender and nation but also of genre. Alemán sees Velazquez's narrative taking on the attributes of 'pulp fiction, diary, spy memoir, historical text, travel account, picaresque novel, and even a queer seduction narrative that reverses the usual heterosexual seduction plot' (Alemán, 2003: xxiii). Velazquez's cross-dressing, then, does not stop with clothing, whether in terms of masculine/feminine, soldier/civilian, Northern/Southern or American/foreigner, but extends to her literary performance across a series of genre boundaries.

Collectively, Velazquez, Edmonds, the anonymous distaff soldiers and the writers discussed earlier in this chapter challenge one of the most corrosive assumptions ever made: the inferiority and irrelevance of women as agents and actors in public history. Blanton and Cook make a point of situating their distaff subjects in the context of Elizabeth Cady Stanton's 'Declaration of Sentiments' from the Seneca Falls Convention of 1848, which argues that, among man's outrages against women, 'He has usurped the prerogative of Jehovah himself, claiming it as his right to assign for her a sphere of action' (Stanton, et al., 1881: I, 71). In spite of the irony that the 'Declaration of Sentiments' pre-dates the Civil War, the battle to reclaim that war as a women's 'sphere of action' has been ongoing.

As late as 1993, an anti-discrimination court case brought by Lauren Cook against the Antietam Battlefield Park indicated that women had yet to secure ownership of the Civil War as a part of their history. Under her married name of Burgess, Cook has been a dedicated Confederate re-enactor of Civil War battles (see Chapter 7). In 1989 she was discovered as a male impersonator at the Antietam battlefield in the midst of a re-enactment, and told either to dress in a woman's garb – nurse, laundress, camp follower – or leave the park altogether. Burgess refused and was subsequently banned from participating in future re-enactments. In 1993 she successfully sued the US National Park Service – the proprietors of the battlefield and the organisers of the event – both on the grounds of sex discrimination and historical accuracy: there *were* women in male attire fighting the battle of Antietam, and her research had proved it. As Stephen Cushman notes, a degree of hypocrisy informs male objections to women re-enactors:

To women who claim that these nineteenth-century precedents give them the right to perform as reenactors, many men respond that if a woman can pass as a man without detection, as women in the ranks did during the war, then she is truly authentic and can reenact. But if she cannot pass, then she is not authentic and should be excluded from an activity founded on the principle of authenticity. In response to this argument, a woman can always retort that neither army had many middle-aged TBGs, a reenactor abbreviation for 'Tubby Bearded Guys', in it either (Cushman, 1999: 60–1).

The value of Burgess's case goes far beyond establishing the authenticity of distaff soldiers on the re-enactment field. As Young argues:

As a translation of cross-dressing in terms of gender equity, Burgess's lawsuit employed the mechanisms of legal redress made possible by feminist activism of the last three decades. Her victory overturns the separate spheres of the Civil War reenactment, whose usual roles for women – nurse, seamstress, soldier's wife – implicitly ward off contemporary feminism with a return to the nineteenth century (Young, 1999: 288).

Thus, the Burgess victory, in the end, establishes the right, if not the obligation, to remember history and all its participants, and to link remembrance with the historical facts that many would prefer to suppress.

Representation of the Civil War in American culture is, as we have seen, often beset with the problem of historical amnesia, wilful or otherwise. The following chapters continue to explore this problem, as well as some of its solutions, over a widening field of cultural expression and across a number of boundaries – from the real to the virtual, and from the national to the transnational.

CHAPTER 7

The Virtual Civil War

The Civil War is a 'place of memory' as well as a historical topic or event. This concept is best explained by its originator, the French historian, Pierre Nora, in the introduction to the first volume of his monumental project on France's national and cultural history, *les Lieux de mémoire* (1984–93): 'Today France is its own memory or it is nothing. The country is not the end result or the uncertain outcome of the history of the state, but rather the summary and actualization of a series of representations that the French call *lieux de mémoire*' (Nora, 1999: xxxvii). Extrapolating from Nora's concept, if a nation's history, inasmuch as people can perceive it, is the summation of its *lieux de mémoire*, then each *lieu* – each 'place of memory' – is in itself 'the summary and actualization of a series of representations'.

The representations of the American Civil War come in a host of forms, from the textual to the performative – from the seen and heard (through reading, viewing and listening) to the smelt, tasted and touched (through re-enactment and 'living history') to the interactive and artificially intelligent (through computer games). For us, as for all those who did not live through it, the Civil War – if it is to be experienced at all – can only be experienced virtually, that is, through engaging with it as a representation.

The form of visual representation with which we are most familiar is most likely the still photograph. The Civil War was 'the first war to be extensively photographed from start to finish' (Zeller, 1997: 13). However, the war's representations in that form have been controlled by such problematic factors as deliberate manipulation of the *mise en scène* and the technical constraints characterising the mid-nineteenth century's modes of image production. Stephen Cushman and Tony Horwitz separately offer a series of observations that, when read against each other, impress upon us both the potency and the inescapability of the Civil War's photographed images. Cushman holds the war's photographers in equal importance to Lincoln, Davis and Lee, for they 'shaped our perception and imagination of [the] events. For many of us there would be no Civil War, let alone interest in the Civil War, without them' (Cushman, 1999: 13). Horwitz implies the same when he recalls what drew him as a young boy into his life-long preoccupation with the Civil War: 'For me, the fantastical creatures of Maurice Sendak held little magic compared to the man-boys of Mathew Brady who stared back across the century separating their lives from mine' (Horwitz, 1998: 4). To Cushman, 'the Civil War – the war of trains, corn fields and Minié balls – meant black-and-white photographs' just as 'Vietnam – the war of helicopters, rice paddies, and napalm – meant our black-and-white television' (Cushman, 1999: 117). This particular controlling factor – the tyranny of monochrome – seriously compromised Horwitz's recent attempt to recapture the reality of the terrain on which the Civil War was fought, perhaps confirming Jean Baudrillard's claim that the simulation ultimately overpowers the original in its autonomy: 'The territory no longer precedes the map [or, in this case, the photograph] ... Hence-forth, it is the map that precedes the territory ... it is the map that engenders the territory' (Baudrillard, 1983: 2). Thus, as Horwitz describes:

> To the west loomed the Blue Ridge, gentle and azure in the morning sun. There wasn't a single modern intrusion. Looking at the scene, I thought about Mathew Brady's black-and-white photographs, and the false impression they conveyed. The War's actual landscape was lush with color and beauty. The sky, always a featureless white in Brady's photographs, was a brilliant, cloud-tufted blue (Horwitz, 1998: 15).

Horwitz appears to have been sufficiently shocked by the impact of living colour to shake himself free of 'the false impression' created by Mathew Brady's representations; but for many others that impression has determined what, to them, the Civil War should 'look like'. When John Huston applauded the apparent credibility of his cinematographer's shots for *The Red Badge of Courage* (1951) – exclaiming as he peered through the viewfinder, 'Doesn't it look like a Brady, kid?' (in Ross, 1952: 46) – he referred to an apparent gold standard of authenticity conferred by posterity upon Brady's images. If you want to see the Civil War, Huston implied, go back to Brady.

It is indeed important that we go back to Brady, but with a critical eye, for there are many problems arising from Brady's dominance over the war's visual landscape. Not least is his reputation, which obscures, if not obliterates, that of other Civil War photographers. This is particularly true of the Southern photographers who in fact created the war's first photographed images. Battlefield and out-of-studio pioneers such as J. D. Edwards, George S. Cook, James Osborn and F. E. Durbec saw their enterprises choked by the Union blockade of the South, which cut them off from the chemicals they required. Consequently, 'Confederate field photography almost ceased to exist after 1861. Thus, the photographic record of the Confederacy is limited largely to formal studio portraits of its statesmen and military figures' (Ray, 1994: 413). Into the battlefield void stepped 'Brady of Broadway', determining – not without help or mischief – the visual perceptions of the war for the succeeding generations.

'A System of Intelligibility'

When the Civil War began, Brady was already established as America's premier portrait photographer. The stamp of 'Brady, N.Y.' on the back of a photograph signified the 'integrity' of both the portrait and its maker (Meredith, 1976: 3). However, the Civil War turned Brady into a 'stage manager of a new kind of theater', as Alan Trachtenberg calls him, and severely compromised his reputation for 'integrity' (Trachtenberg, 1989: 38). Given that many of the photographs bearing Brady's stamp were in fact taken by such eventually well known associates as George Barnard, Alexander Gardner and Timothy O'Sullivan – the latter two of whom ultimately broke with Brady over his refusal to give them credit – Trachtenberg considers the Brady name as 'part symbol, part trademark' (Ibid.: 38). More importantly, in terms of representation, each of the 'Brady' photographs amounts to its own 'system of intelligibility' (Ibid.: 82).

A series of complex factors plays into the interpretation of this 'system'. Among the most important is ideology, on the part of the viewer as well as the photographer. Our own reading must be informed by the fact that, as a New Yorker bearing the priceless handwritten note, 'Pass Brady. A Lincoln', to his battlefield sites, Brady was politically as well as 'physically on the Union side throughout the war' (Meredith, 1951: xii; Jackson, 1997: 11). Not only did Yankee photographers dominate the field, their presentation of the war was invariably filtered through their necessary identification with the Union cause during a time of martial law. Doranne Jacobson argues that Brady and his Northern colleagues thus hoped to ensure that the battlefield dead would be seen as

Figure 9 Brady studio, *Brady the Photographer, Returned from Bull Run*, 1861 (Library of Congress, Prints and Photographs Division, LC-BH8277-550).

'a noble and necessary feature of a just war to save the Union'. Consequently, 'the emphasis of the largely Northern cameramen was on the Confederate dead', while the Union dead, if photographed at all, were shown 'in more serene poses, as if they had recently departed to a just heavenly reward' (Jacobson, 1996: 90).

This focus on the battlefield dead is a second important factor in the 'system of intelligibility'. As Jacobson notes, 'what was truly new in Civil War photography was the depiction of death': Roger Fenton may well have been the world's first battlefield photographer – in the Crimea – 'but none of his 360 images included a corpse' (Ibid.: 90). To some extent there were technological reasons for this grim accomplishment by the Civil War photographers: due to the cumbersomeness of setting up the cameras and the long exposure times, they were more likely to depict the aftermath of a battle than the battle itself. However, in the large body of images depicting battlefield corpses, deceptive poses often complicate the reading. William Frassanito's studies of the Gettysburg and Antietam photographs reveal the extent to which bodies were moved and situated for dramatic or aesthetic effect, while soldiers and photographers' assistants sometimes posed as corpses for the camera (Frassanito, 1975; Frassanito, 1978; Frassanito, 1994). Trachtenberg pointedly describes this process as 'stagecraft' (Trachtenberg, 1989: 73).

Post-mortem deceptions such as these had their intended effect. Oliver Wendell Holmes, Sr, who had seen his share of corpses while tramping across the Antietam battlefield in search of his wounded son, praised Brady's exhibition, 'The Dead of Antietam' (actually photographed by Gardner and James Gibson): 'Let him who wishes to know what war is look at this series of illustrations' (Holmes, 1863: 11–12). Reviewing the same exhibition, an anonymous *New York Times* journalist was equally explicit in equating the virtual with the real, in apparent ignorance of the photographers' manipulations of the scene: 'Mr. Brady has done something to bring home to us the terrible reality and earnestness of war. If he has not brought bodies and laid them in our dooryard and along the streets he has done something very like it' (Anon., 1862: 5). In spite of their visual power and their unrivalled influence upon culture as source materials, Brady's photographs often demonstrate that manipulation, fabrication and 'stagecraft' are all part of the Civil War's history of representation, greatly problematising the function of both the war and its photographs as *lieux de mémoire*.

'Picturing' the Civil War with increasing verisimilitude has meant the construction of a cultural process taking the war along a path – in H. Bruce Franklin's words – 'from realism to virtual reality' (Franklin, 2001: 5). The still images by Brady and his colleagues are early milestones along that path. The technological developments that have followed – along with a growing sophistication of illusion – have been geared towards satisfying the desire of people to go beyond viewing the war from a distance, and entering into it vicariously.

'The Illusion of Depth'

Most Americans and Europeans had to wait until the 1880s to see any of the Civil War's photographed images, when developments in photoengraving and half-tone printing first enabled the mass publication of photographs in books and periodicals. Before then, the mass public had relied on the work of 'special artists' such as Winslow Homer, Thomas Nast, Edwin Forbes, Frank Vizetelly and Alfred and William Waud, who from the battlefields and encampments provided illustrations for a range of popular magazines – *Harper's Weekly*, *Frank Leslie's Illustrated Newspaper*, the *New York Illustrated News* and the *Illustrated London News* (Jacobson, 1996: 16, 74). However, Fort Sumter sparked a boom-time for photographers and the development of a market through which 'the economic potential of supplying war scenes to the public became self-evident' (Ray, 1994: 410). The Civil War thus 'created for the first time a mass audience bent to simulacra' (Trachtenberg, 1989: 89). Very quickly, the market demanded that these 'simulacra' appear more and more real.

Thus, for those who could afford it, one of the most popular formats of Civil War photography was the stereographic image, a visual deception in which two near-identical photos were viewed through a stereoscope or stereopticon to create 'the illusion of depth' (Zeller, 1997: 16). As Trachtenberg notes, 'stereographs brought the war home to Americans more effectively than other photographic modes, precisely because their illusion of closeness held the war at bay, at the distance of a spectacle performed as if for parlor viewing' (Trachtenberg, 1989: 89). Stereographic photography was thus the precursor to television, newsreels and motion pictures: such was its far-reaching, if embryonic, influence. However, the technology of the stereoscope often determined the very composition of a picture. Consequently, historical views that have come down to us, including such momentous images as 'The Dead of Antietam', were in some instances geared toward satisfying the demands of that technology:

The Confederate dead lay still where they fell ... Gardner opted to use his stereo camera exclusively for the historic first series of soldiers lying dead on a Civil War battlefield ... Gardner's first task was to compose the photograph. As he did this, he was thinking in three dimensions. He looked for scenes with a distinct element in the foreground, and a good deep background (Zeller, 1997: 37).

Regardless of its role as an agent of visual illusion, the stereoscope offers a useful parallel to our contemporary situation in viewing the Civil War. It is possible for us now to appreciate the extent to which particular visual representations of the war have not been shared either among or across the generations. During the war, most people saw no photographs at all. We, by contrast, have seen enough Civil War photographs to make what were the more familiar images to the wartime observers – the lithographs and woodcut illustrations – appear unfamiliar antiques to us. At the same time, to reiterate Horwitz, the actual landscape of the war can seem to us more strange, and less authentic in terms of what the war's terrain 'looked like', than the monochrome images that signify 'Civil War-ness'. Still, for all our familiarity with the photographic archive, it has been for the most part a two-dimensional experience not often sought by the original audience or photographers. Bob Zeller's collection of Civil War stereo images was not published until 1997; consequently, as he reminds us, 'our ancestors knew something that has been largely lost to us' (Zeller, 1997: 13). For us to view through a stereoscope even the familiar images of Brady and his colleagues, which we have generally known in 2-D, is to perceive a startling visual transformation that appears to breathe life into flat, dead images. The desire to enable such an apparent revivification did not end with the stereoscopic photographers of the nineteenth century, however. It resulted in one of the twentieth century's most influential and problematic projects of Civil War representation.

'The Beauty of the Film Silences the Critical Voice': Ken Burns's *The Civil War*

Perhaps not surprisingly, in the immediate aftermath of Appomattox, the war-weary American public lost its appetite for the visual record. Mathew Brady spent ten years trying 'to persuade Congress [that his pictures] were important enough to purchase, and for almost a generation they passed from public view' (Trachtenberg, 1989: 77). The

1880s witnessed a brief resurgence of interest, not only through such massive illustrated projects as *Century* magazine's *Battles and Leaders of the Civil War* (1888), which gave Stephen Crane his source material for *The Red Badge of Courage* (1895), but also through the great popularity of stereopticon slides and cycloramas – 'large panoramic paintings of Civil War events displayed in special cylindrical buildings' – for which large crowds paid between twenty-five and fifty cents' admission (Jacobson, 1996: 102, 110). The war's photographs and other visual representations then gradually settled into their more modest role as the staple of historians, film-makers and lay aficionados, which they remained for most of the twentieth century.

In September of 1990, however, America *en masse* re-awoke to the still images of Brady, Gardner and others through an extraordinary broadcasting event. Ken Burns's *The Civil War*, an eleven-hour documentary series for the US Public Broadcasting Service (PBS), 'achieved public television's highest ratings ever ... when 38.9 million people tuned in to at least one episode of the five-night telecast ... averaging 12 million viewers at any given moment' (Edgerton, 2001: 169–70). Robert Brent Toplin notes that 'millions more saw subsequent broadcasts on TV, purchased videos, or viewed the series in connection with school, college, or adult education classes. Additional millions enthusiastically watched *The Civil War* when it appeared on television in Great Britain, Germany, Japan, and other nations' (Toplin, 1996: xv). For media historian Gary Edgerton, *The Civil War* was public broadcasting's 'prototype of "event TV". The program was mentioned on episodes of *Twin Peaks, Thirtysomething*, and *Saturday Night Live* ... Ken Burns appeared on *The Tonight Show*, and he was selected by the editors of *People* magazine as one of their "25 most intriguing people of 1990"' (Edgerton, 2001: 170). Jim Cullen surmises that *The Civil War* 'probably reached more people than [the work] of any contemporary academic' (Cullen, 1995: 2). As Toplin observes, Burns's documentary strategy was, at the time, unique for 'event TV':

> Burns did not incorporate re-enactments by modern-day figures dressed as soldiers or feature actors in period costumes or draw upon dramatic excerpts from Hollywood movies. Instead, he focused on authentic sources from the war – photographs, lithographs, paintings, newspapers, letters, signs, handbills, and other items ... Burns's camera also took the viewer to the modern-day locales of the

battlefield, using present-day cinematography to show the sites where tragedy had occurred in the 1860s (Toplin, 1996: xx).

It is likely that no other historical documentary besides Leni Riefenstahl's homage to Nazism, *Triumph of the Will* (1935), has excited so much historical controversy. The unprecedented popularity of *The Civil War* has caused tremendous scholarly debate – not only over the subjects that Burns chose either to include or exclude, or about whether he demonstrated a pro-Northern or a pro-Southern bias, but also about his narrative approach to history. As Cullen explains, *The Civil War* reflected 'an effort to provide a coherent vision of the past that integrates a variety of elements in the culture into a single master narrative. Burns undertook this enterprise at a time when many professional historians had abandoned it' (Cullen, 1995: 12). Thus, commentators – usually academics – appear to have been most concerned, in Daniel Walkowitz's words, with 'the canonization of the narrative strategies embedded in the production' of *The Civil War* in particular and television histories in general (in Gallagher, 1998: 246).

Gabor S. Boritt is notably sensitive in weighing up the competing elements of Burns's narrative approach: 'I am disgruntled as a scholar but wonder about the possible artistic rationale that I may not understand. How to balance the historical loss against an artistic gain?' (Boritt, 1996: 87–8). On the one hand, Boritt identifies the frequent mismatching of narrative text and visual image:

> Voice: Chancellorsville; photo: Wilderness. Voice: Mrs. Chesnut; photo: unknown person ... How much mismatching is demanded or justified by art? We would rebel if Lincoln's words were attributed to Grant, or Sullivan Ballou's to another soldier. Yet photographs are as much historical documents as speeches or letters (Ibid.: 87).

Boritt's conclusion reveals both his aesthetic appreciation and his awareness of the damage that an emphasis on aesthetic representation, in all its seductiveness, can bring to a historical documentary: 'It contains errors of fact, perhaps errors of interpretation. But the beauty of the film silences the critical voice' (Ibid.: 99).

Judging from Burns's own statements, it appears that 'the beauty of the film' was indeed a controlling factor, if not the primary one. He referred to his series as 'a poem – selective, impressionistic, to be sure, but a legitimate form of historic expression' (in Woodward, 1996: 7). He called himself 'a historian of emotions' – emotion being 'the great glue of history' (in Toplin, 1996: xxii). Burns enjoys the support of the British historian, Simon Schama (himself a notable television personality), who argues that the historian's 'pressing task' is to recast history in 'the forms by which it can catch the public imagination. That form, as Ken Burns's stunning PBS series on the Civil War demonstrated, ought to be narrative; not to discard argument and analysis, but to lend it proper dramatic and poetic power' (in Lang, 1994: 14).

For Robert Lang, however, the danger is that 'when you attempt a "picturisation of history", you get melodrama' (Ibid.) – and many have singled out as the most melodramatic moment in the series the reading of the Sullivan Ballou letter that concludes the first episode, when Ballou's heartbreaking utterances to his wife on the eve of his death at Bull Run are read against a series of romantically charged domestic photographs and mournful violin music (Burns, 1990: Episode 1). Burns recalled receiving letters informing him that, following the episode's broadcast, the Sullivan Ballou letter was being read at funeral services across America (Burns, 1996: 178). Clearly, the emotional intensity of the broadcast ensured that this particular Civil War *lieu de mémoire*, the Ballou letter, took on a cultural life of its own – as no academic exegesis appears to have done – illustrating precisely the power of Burns's claim: 'We have begun to use new media and new forms of expression to tell our histories, breaking the stranglehold the Academy has had on historical exchange for the last hundred years' (Ibid.: 161).

To appreciate the plotting of the Sullivan Ballou segment is to appreciate the power of Burns's narrative strategies – however manipulative they may be – as well as the concerns of 'the Academy' over the proprietorship of history. As Edgerton implies, productions like *The Civil War* mark a sea-change in the public representation of history:

> Some historians ... have admonished Burns for emphasizing the empathetic and experiential aspects of history in *The Civil War* more than detailed analysis. What such criticisms overlook, however, is that the visual media's codes of historical representation are far different from, though often complementary to, those of print. The present image-based histories of Burns and other producer-directors feature the simulated experience of engulfing viewers in a sense of immediacy or 'being there', in contrast to the printed word's propensity toward logic, detachment, and reasoned discourse (Edgerton, 2001: 171).

Thus, if *The Civil War* indeed 'challenges our understanding of what history is' (Boritt, 1996: 100), then this challenge refers both to history-as-event (the Civil War) and history-as-practice (*The Civil War*), with the latter openly striving towards 'the simulated experience' that Edgerton mentions.

This giant step towards an ever-closer virtual reality is part of a 'paradigm shift' in both representation and interpretation: 'The historic transformations from orality to writing to printing to filming and televising are generally understood today as producing concurrent shifts in the way in which societies privilege certain forms of expression and knowledge over others' (Edgerton, 2001: 171). Thus, if Brady's images of the Antietam dead are a once-startling precursor to the contemporary images of massacres that have become depressingly familiar representations of conflict, then documentary historians like Ken Burns – in spite of their pioneering work of only a decade or so ago – must already be feeling the pressure of 'new forms of expression and knowledge' that mark the next shift in historical representation. One of the most sophisticated of these new forms – in spite of its putative function as a site of play – is the computer game, which offers a virtual immersion into the Civil War that goes beyond the merely visual and the aural, to the interactive.

Grognards

In declaring himself the first person to devise and publish a comprehensive set of rules for war games – which he called *Little Wars* (1913) – H. G. Wells describes the pleasure of total immersion that he feels as a grown man playing on his hands and knees with miniature soldiers:

> The combat grows hot round some vital point. Move follows move in swift succession. One realises with a sickening sense of error that one is outnumbered and hard pressed here and uselessly cut off there, that one's guns are ill-placed, that one's wings are spread too widely, and that help can come only over some deadly zone of fire (Wells, 2004: n. p.).

Wells was perhaps the first and most famous 'grognard', that is, a near-obsessive devotee of war games. The Civil War has inspired a host of game forms by which grognards have vicariously participated in history.

Of the manufactured (as opposed to homemade) versions, the Avalon Hill board game is the oldest and most popular. One of Avalon Hill's current games, *Battle Cry*, offers the opportunity – through the vagaries of dice, command cards, tiles and tokens – to 'step back in time and lead your armies in 15 classic Civil War battles' (Avalon Hill, 2004: n. p.). However, the 32–page rule book for *Battle Cry* indicates one of the great barriers to the experience of 'being there' in manual games: the faithful re-creation of battle requires such attention to detail that the game gets bogged down in complex references, records and small print.

Enter the PC and videogame, the X-Box and PlayStation 2, supported by an industry of grognard-designers who have turned the Civil War battlefield into an 'audiovisual diegetic space' – that is, an on-screen virtual world (Wolf, 2001: 103). Household names for Civil War computer gamers include Talonsoft and By Design, but by all accounts the emergent leader in Civil War games is HP Simulations (founded 1990), with their already legendary programmer, John Tiller, and equally celebrated scenario designers such as Drew Wagenhoffer, Doug Strickler and Richard Walker. In a series of interviews with Brett Schulte, a leading games tester, these designers reveal in great detail the processes by which they have endeavoured to extend the vicarious opportunities offered by the early board games that inspired them as youngsters. The most striking subject in their conversations is their assumed obligation to balance a game's 'playability' – the processes and outcomes allowed by the computer programme – with its historical accuracy. They design their scenarios based on research from a list of sources invariably topped by the 128–volume *Official Records of the War of the Rebellion* (1880–1901) for details on regimental strengths and orders of battle, as well as scholarly monographs and period maps. Wagenhoffer implies the level of historical detail that Civil War grognards – a highly demanding constituency – have come to expect: 'Slip-shod work is easy to spot since many wargamers are passionate about – and have intimate prior knowledge of – their subject matter' (in Schulte, 2002: n. p.). Thus, the more accurate the designer's historical research, the more highly praised is a game for its authenticity and integrity.

In their quest for verisimilitude, Civil War games designers update the visual deceptions of the stereopticon, dramatically enhancing a 2-D experience on a flat screen with a simulated 3-D one. In Tiller's Campaign Games, the flat period maps of the Gettysburg and Corinth battlefields are transformed into three-dimensional landscapes composed of interlocked hexagonal segments (hexes), each representing 125 yards, sporting the same roads, creeks, trees, houses and fences that the armies would have encountered. Weapons are modelled with accurate detail, vomiting out cannonballs, minié balls and fire, while the 'fog of war' emerges as both a literal event (battlefield smoke) and the situational event described by Clausewitz, in which confusion and partial blindness are programmed into the game turns. Mathematical programming ensures that units succumb to increasing fatigue and rout, while a sophisticated digital soundtrack enables weapons to crack, cannon to boom, and soldiers to yip and yell with ferocity. Behind all – as in Burns's documentary – 'period music plays ... and adds to the sense of immersion' (Andress, 2004: n. p.). It would appear that, through the magic of ingenious multiple command systems, the touch of a finger can transform a viewer into a participant in Civil War history as it happened.

Crucially, however – and in spite of the passing of the war as a historical event – there would be little attraction to a game in which the outcome of a battle is pre-determined by historical fact. Hence the appeal of, say, attempting to reverse the hopelessness of Pickett's Charge at Gettysburg through the application of variables that were available but not applied on the original battlefield. This constitutes what game designers call the 'What if?' scenario (see Conclusion), which opens up a host of narrative possibilities based on the circumscriptions of historical fact and the iron laws of binary coding. Henry Jenkins and Kurt Squire note that 'game designers draw a distinction between games with "hard rails", which tightly structure the player's movements to unfold a pre-determined experience, and those with "soft rails", which are multi-directional and multilinear' (Jenkins and Squire, 2002: 69).

The most advanced Civil War games clearly run on soft rails. Wagenhoffer's *Campaign Corinth* contains 197 different scenarios, while Strickler's *Campaign Gettysburg* offers 314, narrowed down from over 6,000 possibilities that the designer originally considered (Cobb, 2004: n. p.). Thus, as Schulte says of the latter: 'You could literally play this game for years and not run across the same set of scenarios in a campaign twice' – even though all the scenarios are based upon the limiting historical factors of landscape and orders of battle (Schulte, 2004a: n. p.). Judging from the online game 'design centers' posted by Schulte (Schulte, 2004), Rich Hamilton (Hamilton, 2004) and Rolf Hall (Hall, 2004), to name just a few, a growing cadre of Civil War scenario designers is at work ensuring that both the historical and the 'What if?' possibilities proliferate – illustrating how 'the line between gamers and designers begins to dissolve' (Jenkins and Squire, 2002: 75). Such websites offer links to literally thousands of free, downloadable 'add-ons' with which players can expand upon the original designs of the games.

Civil War gamers can play against their computer in Artificial Intelligence mode or against a partner with a two-player 'hot-seat'. They can play by e-mail (PBeM, in which players take turns exchanging files that download into defensive, offensive or other actions) or engage in multiplayer Network Play in which the gamers are organised into teams. Hyperlinks connect games sites to other Civil War sites exponentially, while gamers can join the online American Civil War Game Club, a portal to a 'virtual community' devoted to Civil War computer play (ACWGC, 2004: n. p.). The possibilities for 'total immersion', then, apply not just to a particular game or a particular *lieu de mémoire*, but apparently to an entire online subculture.

The question remains as to whether such 'total immersion' obfuscates what Celia Pearce calls the 'meta-story' of the game, that is, the 'specific narrative "overlay" or narrative metaphor that contextualises the game rules ... In chess, for example, the meta-story is a battle between two kingdoms; in *Monopoly* it is a contest between capitalist land barons' (Pearce, 2002: 118). The meta-story for Civil War games – computer or otherwise – is, at its most basic level, the military contest between two sections of the United States over a set of highly emotive political and moral issues. Games reviewer Michael Andress observes that, habitually, 'gamers are not hampered by real-life military and political considerations', although it is possible to play a game 'as if one is commanding a real force with real military and political restrictions' – what he calls 'reality-based restrictions' (Andress, 2004: n. p.). More often, however, gamers (like obedient soldiers on a battlefield) are 'goal-oriented ... score oriented, conflict oriented [and] task oriented' rather than politically oriented (Wolf, 2001: 105). Thus, if a Civil War board game offers, via a chance card, an opportunity to issue an Emancipation Proclamation, it is understood to be more of a tactical than an ethical measure (just as, arguably, it was in historical fact). When Schulte asks Strickler what side he prefers to play on – Confederate or Yankee – his answer is apolitical and wholly strategic: 'The south. They are usually outnumbered, and ... in all but a few of the games, are committed to offensive action. I just think it is more challenging' (Schulte, 2004a: n. p.).

It appears, then, that – tactically battle-focused as they are – Civil War games rarely allow for the player to express identification with a cause, whether Union, States' Rights, slavery or abolition; one sets out to emulate a strategist or combat soldier in the heat of battle, and empathises with him or her in that tense situation. The game, in its immediacy, obliges the player to evade or avoid the politics of the meta-story, just as the ultimate object of the game as a source of vicarious pleasure is to evade or avoid the real even as it faithfully simulates it. H. G. Wells admits as much with reference to his 'little war' on the eve of the Great War: 'How much better is this amiable miniature than the Real Thing!' (Wells, 2004: n. p.). This is one of the great paradoxes of virtual reality: the combination of total immersion and avoidance. In the virtual arena of the Civil War, this paradox can be further explored through one other popular practice, the battlefield re-enactment in which all the senses are brought together, but which aims to keep the war's meta-story at bay.

Hardcores, Authentics and Farbs

There is a major drawback to the vicarious pleasure of computer games. As Mark Pesce argues: 'Many a visitor to these virtual worlds emerges wishing for a more complete unity with the imaginary. For the moment, however, our bodies require that we stand outside our virtual worlds, apart from them' (Pesce, 2002: 133). Thus, the diegetic experience, for all its impressive speed and graphics, is incomplete and, to Pesce, ultimately unsatisfying:

> Realism is arrived at through more than the eyes, or the ears; it's touch, smell and a dozen other sensations and instincts that subtly tell us what is real. Here virtual reality fails us: computers might create a hallucination of the world, but it's other people outside the experience who convince us that the hallucination is real. This is the real draw-back of all the VR [virtual reality] techniques cooked up thus far by scientists and technologists: they allow for only one person (or at most, a handful) to experience the synthetic simultaneously (Ibid.: 133).

Hence the appeal of historical re-enactment, or 'living history'. The object of its practitioners is to 'perform "impressions" for themselves and others that are meant to recreate vanished experiences or ways of life' (Cullen, 1995: 177) – impressions that include the taste of the hardtack and salt beef, the smell of the wood smoke, the cold of the ground and the heat of the battle.

The representation of the Civil War in the form of 'living history' began with the war's Union veterans, who in the 1870s inaugurated the practice of re-staging battles in their old uniforms, notably under the umbrella of the veterans' organisation, the Grand Army of the Republic

(GAR). The GAR re-enactments expressed 'a highly sentimentalised view of the war' that increasingly enabled Confederate veterans to participate in the spirit of reconciliation and reunion (Ibid.: 182). Cushman argues that 'the very idea of reenactment presupposes reconciliation', and requires the evasion or burying of the political differences and stances that led to the war and continue to charge its aftermath (Cushman, 1999: 58). In his analysis of the most romanticised veterans' re-enactment, the Gettysburg reunion of 1913 (which both opens and concludes the Ken Burns series), David Blight surmises that the event was in reality 'about forging unifying myths and making remembering safe' (Blight, 2001: 9). With this, he could have been referring to all subsequent re-enactments (as well as turns on the PlayStation): 'Neither space nor time was allowed at Gettysburg for considering the causes, transformations, and results of the war; no place was reserved for the legacies of emancipation or the conflicted and unresolved history of Reconstruction' (Ibid.: 9).

This is not to say, however, that re-enacting is necessarily innocent or denuded of politics. On the contrary, as the neo-Confederate League of the South (see Chapters 4 and 5) makes clear through its founding spokesmen, James and Walter Kennedy:

> As an activist, you should make yourself available to the local schools to do living-history discussions and demonstrations for their history classes. We have found that … our involvement in War for Southern Independence re-enacting makes for a great opportunity to convey to local Southern school children, black as well as white, the truth about their ancestors and the real reason they fought the War for Southern Independence (Kennedy, 2001: 307–08).

Even at the other extreme – in the absence of an explicit political manifesto – a re-enactor donning a Confederate uniform 'cannot escape the associations of her costume with a history of determined efforts against black freedom', as Elizabeth Young argues with reference to Lauren Cook Burgess (see Chapter 6) (Young, 1999: 301). However, considering the divisiveness of what Horwitz calls in his subtitle 'the unfinished Civil War', it is not surprising that there appears to be an unwritten code in operation on the re-enactment field, one that links the experience of 'living history' with that of playing computer games: avoid, where possible (to repeat Blight), the political 'causes, transformations, and results of the war'. Civil War re-enacting could not take place

Figure 10 The Dead of Ackworth, battlefield re-enactment, Yorkshire, 2004 (Will Kaufman).

on such a grand scale – with hundreds of stagings annually across the United States and abroad, some supporting thousands of soldiers and spectators – without the deliberate evasion or avoidance of the contentious political dimension.

In lieu of professed politics, re-enactors (or 'living historians', as they prefer to be called) have built a subculture of their own based on the degree of authenticity they achieve. In preparation for what are generally weekend-long activities, they immerse themselves in the details of a particular battle, claiming membership of a particular unit whose history they attempt to absorb in full through the study of primary and secondary sources. They adopt a shared vocabulary and a recognised caste-system. At the top of the re-enactors' evolutionary scale is the 'hardcore', the living historian who strives for ultra-authenticity: 'These people are the most precise practitioners of the hobby; they eat hardtack and salt pork, remain in character for entire weekends, and frown upon anything that compromises accuracy' (Cullen, 1995: 186). At the bottom of the scale is the 'farb': 'Violations serious enough to earn the slur [include] wearing a wrist-watch, smoking cigarettes, smearing oneself with sunblock or insect repellent – or, worst of all, fake blood'

(Horwitz, 1998: 10–11). In between are the 'authentics' who 'pay careful attention to details, though they do cut some corners' (Cullen, 1995: 186). Habitually a re-enactor will adopt the identity of a real Civil War participant – a named drummer, private, artillery gunner or field surgeon – encountered through letters, diaries, memoirs or histories. For some, the adopted identity can even be a corpse, as Horwitz makes clear in a memorable passage introducing Robert Lee Hodge, the recognised guru of Confederate hardcores. Hodge's re-enactment is clearly a matter of life following art, in that his aim appears to be the faithful reproduction of Brady's or Gardner's wartime dead:

> As he drew near, Troy Cool called out, 'Rob, do the bloat!' Hodge clutched his stomach and crumpled to the ground. His belly swelled grotesquely, his hands curled, his cheeks puffed out, his mouth contorted in a rictus of pain and astonishment. It was a flawless counterfeit of the bloated corpses photographed at Antietam and Gettysburg that I'd so often stared at as a child.
>
> Hodge leapt to his feet and smiled. 'It's an ice-breaker at parties', he said (Horwitz, 1998: 8).

If simulation has the potential of blurring the line between past and present as well as that between the real and virtual, then – on the re-enactment battlefield, at least – this breaching of boundaries appears to approach psychotic proportions. As Cushman notes: 'Among some reenactors, the mystical bent has even led to a belief that they are reincarnated Civil War soldiers' (Cushman, 1999: 63). In charting the progression of Civil War representation from observation to immersion, it is perhaps not so odd that we should move from viewing the dead (Brady) to playing the dead (Hodge) to *being* the dead (battlefield reincarnation). The latter, after all, appears to be the logical conclusion of taking representation – to repeat Franklin – 'from realism to virtual reality'. However, it is also questionable whether 'living history' can be equated with 'intelligible' history (referring back to Pierre Nora) if the sensation of 'being there' comes at the expense of the analytical reflection and the broader political overview that can only be achieved at a distance and through immersion of a different sort, that is, into the meta-story behind the battlefield events.

Our discussion has been increasingly concerned with the transcendence, movement or breaching of boundaries, whether between genders, races and regions, or between the real and the virtual. We turn now to explore a further aspect of transcendence, the manner in which the Civil War, as a cultural event, has impacted beyond the boundaries of American history, geography and culture to become, in many respects, transnational property.

CHAPTER 8

The Transnational Civil War

The transnational impact of the Civil War was felt from the moment of its commencement, both at home and abroad. In England, one public figure felt this impact – literally – with every fibre of his body. In the midst of the war, the prospect of a Union victory drove Lord Salisbury, future Tory Prime Minister and 'Victorian Titan', to the edge of a nervous breakdown, as his wife recalled:

> She awoke one night to see him standing at the wide open window of their second-floor bedroom, fast asleep, but in a state of extreme perturbation. He was, she thought, 'preparing to resist forcibly some dreamt-of invasion of enemies – presumably Federal soldiers or revolutionary mob leaders' (Roberts, 1999: 48).

A partial reason for Salisbury's distress can be found in a letter that he wrote to his son in 1902, as the American financier J. P. Morgan prepared to seize control of the transatlantic shipping industry:

> It is very sad, but I am afraid America is bound to forge ahead and nothing can restore the equality between us. If we had interfered in the Confederate War it was then possible for us to reduce the power of the United States to manageable proportions. But *two* such chances are not given to a nation in the course of its career (in Ibid.: 50).

Lord Salisbury offers just one example of perceiving the Civil War as an event that transcends purely American history. The mobility of the Civil War does not stop there, however, for as a cultural event it has transcended time just as it has transcended national boundaries. Thus, the various European, Canadian and Australian chapters of the Civil War Round Table Association continue to hold regular meetings in which historical papers are presented and discussed. Their members regularly travel to the US, where they join fellow lay historians combing the battle-fields of Gettysburg, Antietam and elsewhere (Cullen, 1995: 180–1).

In the UK, the American Civil War Society (ACWS), the country's largest Civil War re-enactment society, is composed of a host of Federal, Confederate and bi-partisan units recreating companies from Virginia to Texas, from Wisconsin to Pennsylvania. Some of their members appear as extras in the battle scenes of films such as Edward Zwick's *Glory* (1989) and Ronald Maxwell's *Gettysburg* (1993) and *Gods and Generals* (2003). For their authentic reproduction forage caps, kepis, bayonets, haversacks, Enfields, flintlocks, Union and Confederate brogans, and full uniforms of every historical variety, these British re-enactors need go no further than Birmingham, Bournemouth or Dover, all of which support sutlers' businesses devoted to the expanding Civil War re-enactment industry in Britain and across the Channel in Europe (ACWS, 2004).

Off the re-enactment battlefield, the Civil War infiltrates other transnational sites. Business executives and tourists staying at Liverpool's posh Thistle hotel can walk under an archway boasting portraits of Jefferson Davis and Admiral Semmes of the CSS *Alabama*. The hotel occupies the site of the Confederacy's major European embassy, near the shipyard where some of the South's most deadly commerce raiders were built to wreak havoc upon Northern shipping. A short stroll down the waterfront brings the hotel's guests to the National Maritime Museum, where exhibits on the Atlantic slave trade testify to the foundations of Liverpool's fortunes: American slavery and the importation of American slave cotton. Meanwhile, the Lancashire Cotton Famine still resonates in Manchester's Lincoln Square, in which presides George Gray Barnard's statue of a craggy, beardless Lincoln (derided in the London *Times* in 1917 as 'the Tramp with the Colic') standing upon a pedestal bearing the President's words of thanks for 'the support the working people of Manchester gave in the fight for the abolition of slavery during the American Civil War' (in Blackett, 2001: 2). Barnard's statue was originally intended for London's Parliament Square, but the gift was blocked in a gesture of transatlantic muscle-flexing by Lincoln's son, Robert, who hated the statue. Thus, it was replaced by the 'deeply contemplative' figure by Augustus Saint-Gaudens, which still watches over the doors to Parliament (Cawardine, 2004: n. p.; see also Peterson, 1994: 209–14). In one instance, out of those same doors walked Prime Minister Margaret Thatcher to record the narration of Aaron Copland's *Lincoln Portrait* (see Chapter 4) – a performance described by at least one reviewer as 'the height of perversity' (Williams, 1994: n. p.).

Other examples of the Civil War's transnational infiltration can be

Figure 11 Maltese Labour, German Capital, American Civil War, Playmobil, 2005 (Derek Drummond: courtesy of the photographer).

found in a variety of forms, and in some initially unlikely places. Somewhere outside of the US this week, a child will be bought one or two of the latest additions to the 'Playmobil' range of toy plastic figures made in Malta and Spain by the German company, Brandstätter: a Union and a Confederate soldier, each with the smiling, juvenile, cherubic face that is Playmobil's signature. Why should Maltese and Spanish workers be turning out these Civil War figures now, at such a late stage in Playmobil's thirty-year history?

Possibly Brandstätter's research-and-development strategists have tapped into the revival of interest sparked by the recent international success of the English director Anthony Minghella's Civil War film, *Cold Mountain* (2003), starring the English actors Jude Law and Ray Winstone and the Australian actress Nicole Kidman in their roles as North Carolinians. *Cold Mountain*, some critics note, revives images from a preceding internationally-acclaimed Civil War film, *Ride with the Devil* (1999), directed by the Taiwanese martial arts film-maker, Ang Lee. Those two films will almost certainly have been screened in striking distance of the small town of Emmaboda, Sweden, where members of an informal drinking club gather annually to toast the Civil War ironclads, the *Monitor* and the *Merrimac*, raising their glasses to images of the sea battle projected on a wall. 'Many people in Emmaboda', says the club's founder, 'know much more about the *Monitor* and *Merrimac* battle at Hampton Roads than the average Swede' (Blomqvist, 2004: n. p.). At the same time, that claim can be made by the residents of Filipstad, to the north of Emmaboda, where the *Monitor*'s designer, entombed in his grand mausoleum, is honoured with an annual 'John Ericsson Day' that includes *Monitor* vs *Merrimac* battle re-enactments (Templeton, 1984: 9). Before the Swedes get too possessive, however, it should be remembered that one of the most popular attractions in the 108–year history of England's major seaside resort, Blackpool Pleasure Beach, was a series of *Monitor* vs *Merrimac* re-enactments that began in 1910 and were watched by daytrippers enjoying their refreshments in 'Uncle Tom's Cabin' overlooking the beach (Walton, 2004: 119).

   And today – as the members of the Tokyo Lincoln Center and the Taiwanese chapter of the Abraham Lincoln Association go about their monthly or bi-monthly business of discussion and remembrance – we can rest assured that neo-Nazis across the globe will continue to find solidarity by tapping into the more extreme neo-Confederate websites and message boards that swell the Internet. However, rather than continuing this dizzying whistle-stop tour across oceans, nations, decades and cultural practices, this chapter aims to anchor the Civil War more firmly in its transnational context through engaging extensively with three particular case studies: the journalism of Karl Marx, the cultural representations of the Irish in relation to the war and the projection of American Civil War imagery onto the Spanish Civil War of 1936–39. Together, these case studies enable an assessment of the role of cultural texts in reflecting the Civil War's importance as an event impacting upon the destinies of North America, Latin America, Europe, Africa and Asia. It is appropriate to begin with Marx, as he was among the first and most comprehensive to view the Civil War for its truly global significance.

Internationale

Although Lord Salisbury was unaware of it as he pointed his imaginary rifle at his imaginary Union soldiers, the greatest enemies, perhaps, to most of what he stood for had already intruded into the Queen's realm. In 1849, a year after Karl Marx and Friedrich Engels published *The Communist Manifesto*, the Manchester-based Engels welcomed his exiled colleague to England, where they began to write on European affairs and viewpoints for Horace Greeley's *New York Tribune*. Often re-working their *Tribune* material for the Viennese daily, *Die Presse*, the two founders of international communism continued with their Civil War journalism – sometimes in collaboration and sometimes separately – through 1862. Even before the war's end, Marx and Engels had come to view it as 'the first grand war of contemporaneous history' (Marx and Engels, 1984: 29–30).

While Engels for the most part restricted his Civil War writing to military affairs, Marx ranged across the social and political landscape in his analysis of the war's transnational ramifications. His complex reading of events such as the Lancashire Cotton Famine enabled him to look beyond the British domestic or even the transatlantic economy, towards an impending global crisis in which the Civil War was an interlocking factor. Marx analysed Britain's trade figures not only with the United States but also with Canada, the East Indies, Australia and elsewhere in Europe and Asia. Taking into account disparate events such as the over-importation of Chinese cotton, the 'ravages of cholera' in India's north-western provinces and flooding in Bengal, Marx concluded that it was not a 'cotton famine' but rather a glutted market that had led to economic catastrophe, not only for the Lancashire mill operatives but also for the cotton workers in suddenly not-so-far-away Asia (Ibid.: 19). The Civil War thus enabled Marx to imply that what many viewed as an Atlantic economy was in fact a global economy.

In similar fashion, Marx examined the *Trent* crisis in which the Federal seizure of a neutral British steamship brought Britain and the US to the brink of war in 1861. To Marx, this was a multinational rather than merely a British–American crisis, yoking together the concerns of Europe and all the Americas. With the French emperor, Napoleon III (Louis Bonaparte) engaged in an imperial war to overthrow Mexico's revolutionary Juárez government, Marx warned, Anglophobic war hawks in the US who were simmering over the *Trent* seizure 'ought to remember that they do the work of the Secessionists in embroiling the United States in a war with England, [and] that such a war would be a godsend to Louis Bonaparte' (Ibid.: 99). Thus, Marx saw the fate of American workers – black and white – dovetailing with that of Mexico's progressives, doggedly resisting the French takeover that finally came in 1864 with Bonaparte's bloody installation of the Austrian Archduke Maximilian I as the bogus 'Emperor of Mexico'.

Marx did not stop with Mexico, however. Fearing that the French and their monarchical Spanish allies might well persuade imperial Britain and Russia to join with them in a new 'Holy Alliance' that would use Mexico as a base for a military intervention to save the Southern 'slaveocracy', Marx concluded that such an allied European intervention would inevitably end with the conquering of more territory south of the Mexican border (Ibid.: 69–70, 265). Thus, with both the Union and the Monroe Doctrine in tatters, the groundwork would be prepared for a slave empire stretching to the South American tropics. Marx's extrapolation is less important for its historical probability or improbability than for its capacity to situate the Civil War in a global chain of cause and effect.

Marx was characteristically utopian in his assessment of why the European working class should view the American Civil War as a transnational, rather than a domestic, affair. When, in September 1864, Marx, Engels and others founded the Working Men's International Association (or the First International, effectively the birth of the Communist Party), one of their first measures was to publish in *The Bee-Hive* newspaper Marx's open address to Abraham Lincoln, whom he later referred to as 'the single-minded son of the working class' (Marx and Engels, 1985: 20). Marx was perhaps heavy-handed in his appropriation of Lincoln the working man over Lincoln the bourgeois railroad lawyer, but his opening statement accurately and immediately proclaimed the war's transnational significance:

> When an oligarchy of 300,000 slave-holders dared to inscribe, for the first time in the annals of the world, 'slavery' on the banner of Armed Revolt ... then the working classes of Europe understood at once ... that the slave-holders' rebellion was to sound the tocsin for a general holy crusade of property against labour, and that for the men of labour, with their hopes for the future, even their past conquests were at stake in that tremendous conflict on the other side of the Atlantic (Marx and Engels, 1985: 19–20).

Thus, as the first volume of *Das Kapital* (1867–94) argues, the surrender at Appomattox planted a seed almost unnoticed amidst the fanfare of the restored Union: 'Out of the death of slavery a new young life at once arose. The first fruit of the Civil War was the *eight hours agitation*' (Ibid.: 223, italics in original). It was a fruit, Marx hoped, that would be shared across the entire world: 'We propose eight hours work as the legal limit of the working day' (Ibid.). In the context of nineteenth-century wage-slavery (let alone the global sweatshops of the twenty-first century), this was no modest proposal.

Marx was also adept in identifying the Civil War's transnational associations even when commenting upon domestic American events. One of his more intriguing treatments of the war lay in an ironic comparison he related concerning the mass 'migration' of slaveholders from the Border States fleeing into the Deep South 'in order to bring their property' – black human beings – 'to a place of safety'. It was, he wrote, 'wholly reminiscent of the exodus from Ireland in 1847 and 1848' (Marx and Engles, 1984: 257–8). The comparison is ironic because, if it is the fleeing slaveholders who are being compared with the Irish, then it is they who become the victims, like 'the small tenant farmers in green Erin … flung half naked on the street and driven from house and home quite as if the Tartars had descended upon them' (Ibid.: 210). This is hardly a stance that Marx would have seriously taken. However, if it is the slaves with whom the Irish are compared, the irony lies in the progressively antagonistic relations between the Irish and African-Americans before and during the Civil War. These relations – and their impact on American culture – are in themselves central to the war's transnational dimension.

Paddy's Lamentation

As Noel Ignatiev describes in his study, *How the Irish Became White* (1995), black–Irish relations in the United States could be, initially, very close:

> On their arrival in America, the Irish were thrown together with black people on jobs and in neighborhoods, with predictable results. The Census of 1850 was the first to include a class it called 'mulattoes'; it enumerated 406,000 nationwide … In New York, the majority of cases of 'mixed' matings involved Irish women (Ignatiev, 1995: 40).

In terms of the rhetoric of American racism, there was also a figurative closeness, 'since it was by no means obvious who was "white". In the early years Irish were frequently referred to as "niggers turned inside out"; the Negroes, for their part, were sometimes called "smoked Irish"' (Ibid.: 41). With US cities being the most frequent ports of refuge during the mid-century Irish diaspora, when over a million fled from the great famine of 1846–51 (leaving behind another million dead), the urban mix was especially competitive, as Kirby Miller summarises it:

Often without capital or skills, unaccustomed to work practices in their adopted country, the Famine Irish usually entered the American work force at the very bottom, competing only with free Negroes or – in the South – with slave labor for dirty, backbreaking, poorly paid jobs that white native Americans and emigrants from elsewhere disdained to perform … Those who rose later to more remunerative or respectable employment remembered bitterly that as 'Labouring men' they were 'thought nothing of more than *dogs*' (Miller, 1985: 318).

The result of what Ignatiev terms the collision between 'the Irish effort to gain the rights of white men' and 'the black struggle to maintain the right to work' was 'perpetual warfare' in cities throughout the North and South (Ignatiev, 1995: 120). No other city, however, experienced the collision like New York. As Herbert Asbury noted in *The Gangs of New York* (1927), the early study upon which Martin Scorsese based his blockbuster film of the same name, the city hosted a foreign-born population of over fifty per cent, with the 'overwhelming' majority Irish who 'had settled principally in the Five Points and Mulberry Bend districts, which contained 310 persons to the acre' (Asbury, 2002: 110).

One of the most depressing dimensions to the Civil War era's black–Irish conflict was the extent to which the abolitionist forces had hoped to rely on support from Ireland – but here, as elsewhere, transnational issues helped to determine the course of events:

In 1841 sixty thousand Irish issued an Address to their compatriots in America calling upon them to join with the abolitionists in the struggle against slavery. Heading the list of signers was the name of Daniel O'Connell, known throughout Ireland as the Liberator. The Address was the first time Irish-Americans, as a group, were asked to choose between supporting and opposing the color line … Ireland had an old antislavery tradition, going back to the Council of Armagh in 1177, which had prohibited Irish trade in English slaves (Ignatiev, 1995: 6–7).

But Abolition in America came up against Repeal in Ireland (the movement to repeal the union between England and Ireland and set Ireland on the road to independence) when, as William Lloyd Garrison wrote, the South's 'slave plunderers' seized on 'the cause of Irish Repeal': 'The game is this: "You tickle me, and I will tickle you!" … the South shall go for Repeal, and the Irish, as a body, shall go for Southern slavery' (in Ibid.: 16). Perhaps no greater mark of the tragedy by which American

racism had turned these potential allies against one another was its impact upon – of all people – Frederick Douglass, who uncharacteristically
adopted a 'rhetoric of nativism' when speaking of the Irish, as Richard
Hardack relates:

> Douglass repeatedly remarks, recycling the stock images he accumu-
> lates for his speeches, that he 'saw Pat, fresh from the Emerald Isle,
> requiring two sober men to keep him on his legs, enter and deposit his
> vote for the Democratic candidate' ... With terms like 'element',
> Douglass responds with a kind of racial rhetoric to categorise Irish
> Americans as a competing, but emphatically more foreign, minority
> group (Hardack, 1999: 130).

Ignatiev makes it clear that Douglass was in fact responding to a perceived transformation of the Irish in America, as though they had been
somehow altered after a middle passage of their own. Douglass wrote in
1853, 'The Irish, who, at home, readily sympathise with the oppressed
everywhere, are instantly taught when they step upon our soil to hate
and despise the Negro' – a position echoed a year later by Garrison in
The Liberator: 'Passage to the United States seems to produce the same
effect upon the exile of Erin as the eating of the forbidden fruit did upon
Adam and Eve. In the morning, they were pure, loving, and innocent; in
the evening guilty' (both in Ignatiev, 1995: v).

The gruesome details of the Civil War's great black–Irish confla-
gration, the New York City 'Draft Riots' of July 1863, are well known.
Just as 150,000 Irish-Americans were serving in the Union forces, an
equal number of their civilian counterparts took to the streets in a week
of carnage that left, in Asbury's estimation, 'two thousand killed and
eight thousand wounded', among whom were those of the only racially
targeted group: 'Eighteen Negroes were hanged [and mutilated] by the
rioters, and about seventy others were reported missing. Five were
known to have been drowned when mobs pursued them into the East and
Hudson rivers' (Asbury, 2002: 154).

Given the historical significance of the New York riots, Jim Cullen is
surprised that they find no place in Edward Zwick's *Glory* (1989), arguably the most important film since *The Birth of a Nation* to put race at the
heart of the Civil War through its focus on the all-black regiment, the
Massachusetts Fifty-fourth, and their white colonel, Robert Gould Shaw:
'No mention of disorder in New York – or elsewhere – is made in the
movie ... The riots could have been worked in somehow had the

filmmakers considered this important; the movie's time frame had been manipulated in more arbitrary ways' (Cullen, 1995: 163). To be fair, *Glory* does engage with the black–Irish conflict through the character of Sergeant Mulcahy (John Finn), who racially abuses the recruits and of whom it is wryly observed, 'The Irish are not noted for their fondness for the coloureds' (Zwick, 1989). Nonetheless, the absence of the New York riots, even as a subject of discussion, is startling.

Consequently, it took another American film-maker to reflect their significance. However, while Martin Scorsese's *Gangs of New York* (2002) does not avoid attention to the black–Irish collisions – how could it? – it diminishes them behind what appears to interest Scorsese more: the tragic, ironic and complex love–hate relationship between the nativist bruiser, Bill 'the Butcher' Poole (Daniel Day-Lewis) and the avenging son of the Irish priest he has killed, Amsterdam Vallon (Leonardo DiCaprio). There is no shortage of visual and oral references to the realities of Irish-American racism, such as the unapologetic racial slurs throughout, and unflinching footage of the lynching and torching of black bodies during the riots. We also see the broader Civil War context in such scenes as that of the newly arrived, newly uniformed Irish soldiers filing aboard a ship, destined for cannon fodder, as behind them rows upon rows of pine coffins are unloaded and stacked on the wharves, and a plaintive voice on the soundtrack sings the strains of the ballad, 'Paddy's Lamentation':

> Myself and a hundred more to America sailed o'er,
> Our fortunes to be made, we were thinkin'.
> When we got to Yankee Land they shoved a gun into our hand,
> Saying, 'Paddy, you must go and fight for Lincoln.'

Nor is the intimacy and great potential of black–Irish relations in a multicultural America neglected, to a soundtrack including the music of the fusion group, the Afro-Celt Sound System. In a telling scene, the knee-jerk disgust of Bill the Butcher vies with his fascination and desire to be included in this America of the future, as he sits in a Chinese opium den, watching a black New Yorker skilfully and joyously dancing to Irish music. 'Look at that,' he sneers, already a dinosaur. 'What in Christ's name is that? The rhythms of the Dark Continent thrown into the kettle with an Irish shindig, stirred around a few times and poured out as a fine American mess' (Scorsese, 2002). But for all such acknowledgements, the film's most powerfully plotted vector is the one leading inexorably to the Oedipal gladiatorial combat between Bill the Butcher and Vallon. In reality, Bill Poole never saw the New York riots or the Civil War: he died in 1855, fourteen days after being shot in a New York barroom, gasping his last words – as in the film – 'I die a true American' (Asbury, 2002: 90).

These words, however, have been given almost identical voicing in a significant attempt to depict an alternative history of the Irish in Civil War America – an attempt to wrest that history from Bill the Butcher, the rioters of New York and Margaret Mitchell's Irish slaveholder, Gerald O'Hara, and present an Irishman uncorrupted by the passage to America. The attempt is all the more significant because it comes from the pen and the voice of a Southerner. On his album, *The Mountain* (1999), the politically progressive country and bluegrass musician, Steve Earle, includes a song called 'Dixieland'. Earle bases the song's protagonist on the character of the Irish veteran of Gettysburg, Buster Kilrain, from Michael Shaara's *The Killer Angels* (1974). In the novel, Kilrain doggedly confronts his own racism and ultimately fights it down, affirming his solidarity with the racially oppressed: 'What matters is justice. 'Tis why I'm here. I'll be treated as I deserve … I'm Kilrain, and I God damn all gentlemen' (Shaara, 1996: 188). Building on this potential for transformation, Earle gives Kilrain a striking political history not written into the novel: fleeing County Clare under a British death sentence for Fenianism, he arrives in America to join Joshua Chamberlain's Twentieth Maine regiment. After Gettysburg, Kilrain prepares to march on 'Dixieland' with the vengeance of John Brown: he, too, damns 'all gentlemen / Whose only worth is a father's name and the sweat of a working man'. The 'working man' of whom Kilrain sings is unambiguously an enslaved black American. As for himself, he wrests the claim of 'American' from Bill the Butcher and all other nativists: 'We come from the farms and the city streets of a hundred foreign lands. / We spilled our blood in the battle's heat, now we're all Americans' (Earle, 1999) – the last a direct quote from Ely Parker, the Seneca Indian on U. S. Grant's staff who so responded to Robert E. Lee's quip at Appomattox, 'I am glad to see one real American here' (in McPherson, 1988: 849).

By dovetailing Kilrain's words with those of Ely Parker, Earle ensures that a powerful, non-racist Irish voice has a place in the great multicultural expression of the Civil War. Moreover, given that Earle has written songs eulogising, among others, Woody Guthrie, Martin Luther King, Malcolm X and Emma Goldman, it is clear that he places Buster Kilrain in a progressive fellowship for whom 'the battle's heat' does not end with Appomattox but rather is taken into the broader international struggle for democracy and racial justice. Into a later site of that struggle, the Spanish Civil War, the ghosts of Gettysburg also intrude.

¡No pasaran!

In John Dos Passos's *Adventures of a Young Man* (1938), an American anti-fascist, Glenn Spotswood, slips into Spain against the wishes of his own neutral government and eventually finds his clandestine contact. 'Glenn found himself looking into a pair of eyes as green as olives set in an oval brown face that had a little light down around the chin and on the cheeks. The boy smiled and came forward showing very white teeth. "Abraham Leencoln", he said very low' (Dos Passos, 1967: 311). The origin of this cryptic utterance is neatly encapsulated by Steve Earle's songwriting compatriot, John McCutcheon, whose first line echoes almost verbatim Earle's Buster Kilrain:

> From the farms, from the cities, from every land
> Came the Abe Lincoln Brigade;
> With a dream in their hearts and a gun in their hands,
> The Abraham Lincoln Brigade.
> *No pasaran! No pasaran!*
> So sang the Abe Lincoln Brigade;
> 'Cross the years and the oceans, we still sing the song
> Of the Abraham Lincoln Brigade.
>
> (McCutcheon, 2003)

No pasaran – 'They shall not pass' – was the war-cry of the international fighters attempting to block the seizure of Madrid, and thus all of Spain, by the fascist forces under General Francisco Franco, who had launched a *coup d'état* against the Second Spanish Republic on 17 July 1936. As the Irish fighter, Frank Ryan, described it before his capture at Aragón, one of Franco's major objectives was to restore 'the estates of the grandees' so that '20,000 landowners would again dominate 20,000,000 people' (in Tisa, 1985: xiii). This, then, is the second reverberation – after the invocation of Lincoln's name – of the American Civil War: an oligarchy of landowners is challenged by an army championing the rights of labour over property. However, on 31 March 1939, Franco 'announced the end of the Republic and the annihilation of its military forces. Hostilities had lasted nine hundred and eighty-seven days and had resulted in an estimated 410,000 violent deaths' (Eby, 1969: xix). Spain's fascist dictatorship

continued until 1975, ending only with Franco's death. On the losing side
– and subsequently creating their own Lost Cause mythology – were the
50,000–odd international fighters who had come to the defence of the
Republic. Of these, approximately 3,200 were Americans. Nearly all of
them fought – and half of them died – under the banner of the Abraham
Lincoln Battalion (often misnamed the 'Lincoln Brigade').

American conservatives – Ann Coulter (2003) is only the most recent
– have derided the Lincoln Battalion as a communist organ and an insult
to the name of Abraham Lincoln. They are correct in pointing out that
the Comintern – the Communist International – had indeed organised
the International Brigades, which included the Lincoln Battalion, and
that the Lincolns were themselves organised by the US Communist
Party. They have good reason to be suspicious of the cynical appropriation of Lincoln and other American icons by the Stalinists of the
1930s and their Popular Front operatives who issued such slogans as
'Communism is Twentieth Century Americanism' (Eby, 1969: 102).
They would most likely deride the comparison made by George Witter
Sherman in his poem, 'Moon Over Spain' (1938), which has the moon
'sorrowing at Lincoln's tomb in Springfield and / At Lenin's tomb in
Red Square' (in Guttman, 1962: 154). However, as Maxwell Anderson
makes clear in his play, *Key Largo* (1939), the Lincoln Battalion was no
communist organ. In the play, Nimmo, a Lincoln volunteer, explains:

> They're Anarchists, Communists, Leftists, Rightists, Leftist-rightists,
> Rightist-leftists, Socialists, Leftist-Socialists, Rightist-Socialists, Anti-
> clericals, Clerical-Communists, Loyalist soldiers, police, crazy people,
> and once in a while just a plain farmer, all fighting Franco! (Anderson,
> 1939: 9)

Ernest Hemingway echoed these sentiments in what many would
consider the major work of American literature to emerge from the
Spanish Civil War, the novel *For Whom the Bell Tolls* (1941). Hemingway's protagonist, Robert Jordan – based on the Lincoln Battalion's
charismatic leader, Robert Hale Merriman – admits to himself: 'You're
not a Marxist and you know it. You believe in Liberty, Equality and
Fraternity. You believe in Life, Liberty and the Pursuit of Happiness.
Don't ever kid yourself with too much dialectics. They are for some, but
not for you' (Hemingway, 1978: 288).

The political complexities of the Spanish Civil War were precisely
what enabled both American interventionists and non-interventionists to

draw on Abraham Lincoln and the American Civil War for their symbolic ammunition. Thus, Franco's most ardent American champion, Theo Rogers, wrote in *Spain: A Tragic Journey* (1937) that only the fascist general could protect 'the Washingtons, Franklins, and Lincolns of Republican Spain' from the menace of 'Soviet dictatorship' (in Guttman, 1962: 44). On the other side, no American commentator was as determined as Hemingway to yoke Lincoln and his war to the struggle against Franco. This project included Hemingway's war journalism, through which, in 1937, he confessed his guilt at having escaped harm in Madrid while visiting a less fortunate Lincoln volunteer blinded in battle: 'And it still isn't you that gets hit but it is your countryman now. Your countryman from Pennsylvania, where once we fought at Gettysburg' (Hemingway, 1967: 266). The following year, and in contrast to the appeasers of fascism, Hemingway described the Lincoln Battalion's commander, Milton Wolff, as

> tall as Lincoln, gaunt as Lincoln, and as brave and as good a soldier as any that commanded battalions at Gettysburg ... He is a retired major now at twenty-three and still alive and pretty soon he will come home as other men his age and rank came home after the peace at Appomattox Courthouse long ago. Except the peace was made at Munich now and no good men will be home for long (in Wolff, 2001: xli–xlii).

Hemingway reinforced the Lincoln imagery in his play, *The Fifth Column* (1939), in which the Hemingway-like figure, Philip Rawlings, intercedes on the part of a Lincoln Battalion volunteer about to face the firing squad:

> Listen, Mi Coronel ... This boy is all right ... He just went to sleep, and I'm not justice, you know. I'm just working for you, and the cause, and the Republic and one thing and another. And we used to have a President named Lincoln in America, you know, who commuted sentences of sentries to be shot for sleeping, you know. So I think if it's all right with you we'll just sort of commute his sentence. He comes from the Lincoln Battalion you see – and it's an awfully good battalion. It's such a good battalion and it's done such things that it would break your damn heart if I tried to tell you about it (Hemingway, 1968: 49).

Most explicitly and extensively, however, the American Civil War finds its place in *For Whom the Bell Tolls*, in which the exhausted Jordan tells himself, 'Your grandfather fought four years in our Civil War and you are just finishing your first year in this war. You have a long time to go yet and you are very well fitted for the work' (Hemingway, 1978: 316). Jordan repeatedly bolsters himself with recollections of such Civil War icons as Stonewall Jackson, William T. Sherman, Phil Sheridan, Jeb Stuart and – as an inveterate hard-drinker in the Hemingway mould – Ulysses Grant:

> Do you suppose Grant really was a drunk? His grandfather always claimed he was. That he was always a little drunk by four o'clock in the afternoon and that before Vicksburg sometimes during the siege he was very drunk for a couple of days. But grandfather claimed that he functioned perfectly normally no matter how much he drank except that sometimes it was very hard to wake him. But if you *could* wake him he was normal (Hemingway, 1978: 223).

While it is true that one Lincoln Battalion volunteer – from Arkansas – is reported to have snarled, 'Why not a Jeff Davis Battalion?' (in Eby, 1969: 88), a large mass of American writing associates the Spanish Civil War with black emancipation and civil rights in the United States. To some degree this is due to the history of the Lincoln Battalion as the first racially integrated American fighting force – a point made by its black captain, Oliver Law, who before his death on a Spanish battlefield 'reminded a visiting Southern colonel that [his] status would have been impossible in the then segregated United States Army' (Guttman, 1962: 100). However, the nature of the Lincoln Battalion's adversary practically ensured that the echoes of the American Civil War and Reconstruction would sound across Spain.

As Langston Hughes wrote from Spain in 1937, in *The Afro-American* newspaper: 'Give Franco a hood and he would be a member of the Ku Klux Klan, a kleagle. Fascism is what the Ku Klux Klan will be when it combines with the [right-wing, nativist] Liberty League and starts using machine guns and airplanes instead of a few yards of rope' (Hughes, 1977: 129). Of all black American participants and commentators, it was Hughes who most vied with Hemingway in determining how the Spanish Civil War would be remembered in print – and, as did Hemingway, Hughes ensured that it would be intimately linked with its American predecessor, in particular as a war for black emancipation. Two of Hughes's poems – 'Letter from Spain, Addressed to Alabama' (1937) and 'Postcard from Spain, Addressed to Alabama' (1938) – are purportedly written by a black Lincoln Battalion volunteer named Johnny. As he writes to the 'Dear Folks at home' in the latter poem, 'Folks over here don't treat me / Like white folks used to do'; rather, they would 'fight for me now / Like I'm fightin' now for Spain' (Hughes, 1996: 203).

The earlier poem best demonstrates the perspective that Hughes – virtually alone among commentators – brought to the major racial dimension of the Spanish Civil War, the plight of the Moorish conscripts drafted in from Spanish Morocco to fight Franco's battles for him. Habitually demonised even in anti-fascist posters as sinister, terrifying, coal-black figures through images that inverted the buffoonish caricatures of American minstrelsy (see Chapter 1), the Moors were, in Hughes's words, Franco's 'pawns' and 'cannon fodder' – in an analogous position to the blacks drafted in to fight for the Confederacy as the tide turned stronger against it (Hughes, 1977: 106). 'They are illiterate African colonials forced to obey the commands of the Fascist generals in power', Hughes wrote back to *The Afro-American*: 'To keep up their morale, they are spurred on by promises of loot, rape, and the doubtful pleasure of killing some of those Spaniards who in the past have taken so many shots at them' (Ibid.: 127).

Thus, in 'Letter from Spain', Johnny writes to 'Dear Brother at home' from the Lincoln Battalion positions on 'November Something, 1937', describing his challenge to a wounded Moorish captive: 'Boy, what you been doin' here / Fightin' against the free?' (Hughes, 1996: 201). Johnny emphatically structures *his* war as a war for black liberation, regardless of any other objectives for which the white anti-fascists might be fighting – again, re-playing the conflicting motives for involvement in the American Civil War, where the fight for union was not always the fight for abolition. Looking across the sea towards Africa, Johnny sees 'foundations shakin'', for Franco's defeat means the liberation of Morocco, where 'something wonderful'll happen / To them Moors as dark as me' (Ibid.: 201–02).

Hughes's hopeful vision was thoroughly crushed in 1939 when Franco declared the end of Spanish democracy. With the defeat of the Lincoln Battalion in their celebrated last stand in the Jarama Valley came the final, ironic inversion by which the associations with the American Civil War drew closer to those of the vanquished South and its Lost Cause than to Lincoln and emancipation. Milton Wolff recalls the romantic names of the conflict – 'The Good Fight, The Pure War, The Wound in the Heart' (in Tisa, 1985: ix) – while Dos Passos has his protagonist write pathetically on the wall of his prison cell: '*I, Glenn*

Spotswood, being of sound mind and imprisoned body, do bequeath to the international working-class my hope of a better world' (Dos Passos, 1967: 337). To John Tisa, the last of the Lincoln Battalion volunteers to escape from Spain, the sights on the retreat to France as 'the peasants and their families watched from fields in apparent disbelief ... made vivid the pictorial scenes of our own war-torn country during the fratricidal War Between the States' (Tisa, 1985: 213–14). The journalist Martha Gellhorn could have been referring to the people of Richmond, Atlanta, Savannah and Vicksburg when she wrote: 'What was new and prophetic about the war in Spain was the life of the civilians, who stayed at home and had war brought to them' – in which case she was misguided in writing: 'The people of the Republic of Spain were the first to suffer the relentless totality of modern war' (Gellhorn, 1959: 13). The same is habitually said of Sherman's civilian victims, while the cause for which they suffered – at least from the viewpoint of Lost Cause partisans – might be recalled in Gellhorn's elegy: 'All of us who believed in the *Causa* of the Republic will mourn the Republic's defeat and the death of its defenders, forever, and will continue to love the land of Spain and the beautiful people, who are among the noblest and unluckiest on earth' Gellhorn, 1959: 13).

Yet, to Langston Hughes's Johnny, writing his third letter 'From Spain to Alabama' in 1949, the outcome for the oppressed people of Spain is more akin to a Confederate victory than a defeat, if not just another day in the Jim Crow South. The Spanish are left to 'sing / Their *flamencos*', while the blacks of the South are left to 'sing / Their blues' (Hughes, 1996: 252–3). Hughes implies that Franco's own brand of Reconstruction was already serving as an ironic contrast to the brief American experiment that – for all its hardship to the South's former slaveowners – had marked the beginning of African-American citizenship and empowerment.

As a source of symbolic invocation and a cultural point of reference, the American Civil War contributed to the articulation of the Spanish struggle through its appropriated images of contest, victory and defeat. The nature of the American struggle as a transnational source of inspiration is yet another example of its capacity to be taken beyond the boundaries of its original situation, whether in terms of geography, history or culture. The next and final chapter considers an apparent cultural desire to further uncouple the Civil War from its position in history and to project it into another dimension where time is no barrier, where alternative histories are played out, and where a final armistice may at last be signed.

'History Is my Starting Point'

The last Civil War veteran, Walter Washington Williams, died in 1959. When that happened, writes Stephen Cushman, 'we lost access to the first group of witnesses' (Cushman, 1999: 8). Strictly speaking, Cushman is not correct, for included in that 'first group', surely, should have been Charlie Smith, the last American slave, who died in 1979 at 137 years old (AARC, 2004: n. p.). Still, in itself, Cushman's argument gathers considerable force:

> When the last civilian who could have had even childhood memories of the war also died, a death that may have occurred as late as the 1980s and probably went unrecognised for what it was, we lost a second link. Soon, with the passing of those who knew members of either of these groups we will lose a third (Cushman, 1999: 8).

On 20 January 2003, one of the third group, the last surviving widow of a Union veteran, died. Ninety-three-year-old Gertrude Janeway had married her husband, John, when he was 81 and she was 18: the Civil War had been over for 62 years (BBC, 2003: n. p.). When she died, many eyes turned southward to Alabama, where the oldest surviving Confederate widow, Alberta Martin, had long been enjoying celebrity-goddess status, particularly fetishised by neo-Confederates (she had married 81–year-old veteran William Martin when she was 21). The Sons of Confederate Veterans had already adopted Mrs Martin as their 'matriarch' and, as one SCV member said, 'She became a symbol like the Confederate battle flag' (CNN, 2004: n. p.). By the time she died on 31 May 2004, thousands of dollars had been collected for what would virtually be a Confederate state funeral: 'Mrs Martin will lie in state in the parlor at the First White House of the Confederacy in Montgomery, Alabama' (LCW, 2004: n. p.). Alberta Martin's death was the final function in Cushman's mathematical equation of loss: 'With each group lost, the remoteness of the Civil War increases not arithmetically but geometrically … We depend more heavily on records, representations, reproductions, re-creations and reenactments of one kind or another' (Cushman, 1999: 8).

Cushman is quite right in his conclusion but, as we have seen throughout this study, 'records, representations, reproductions, re-creations and reenactments' have always been the raw materials of the Civil War as a *lieu de mémoire* – a place of memory (see Chapter 7) – just as they contributed to the cultural divisions that led to the war itself (see Chapter 1). In many ways, those who lived through the Civil War were no less reliant upon, and no more immune to, such representations than we are. Nonetheless, Cushman identifies – particularly in relation to his 'third group' of witnesses – a cultural phenomenon that cannot be ignored, what we might call the 'aura of association', both a source and an object of great desire, and an agent of profound historical deception.

The Aura of Association

If one touches the hand of someone who has touched the hand of someone who lived through the Civil War, then – so it would appear from the celebrity of Alberta Martin – one has managed to secure a palpable connection with the historical event. This assumption is of course wrong, but it is no less culturally powerful or pervasive for that. One of the more celebrated Civil War novels of the past two decades, Allan Gurganus's *Oldest Living Confederate Widow Tells All* (1989), is a precise comment on the aura of Civil War association and the cultural commodification that it engenders. Loosely based on the celebrity surrounding Alberta Martin, Gurganus's novel has as its narrator Lucy Marsden, who proclaims to her interviewer: 'I'm the last living veteran of the last living veteran of that war' (Gurganus, 1990: 11).

Among the many burdens that Lucy confronts through the accidents of her birth, marriage and longevity is the weight of having become a conduit to something called 'history' – '"History", who's she? I been breathing a while, never met her once … What you call history is really just the luxury of afterwards' (Ibid.: 151). Adding to Lucy's burden is the fact that, even though she was born twenty years after Appomattox and had married old Captain Marsden at the age of fifteen, the historical event with which she is associated through marriage happens to be the national epic owned collectively and still jealously fought over: 'Around here, on the subject of the Civil War, every filling-station man's a expert' (Ibid.: 11).

Consequently, it dawns on Lucy that she and her husband have become commodities, although she is unable to determine precisely which epic has turned them into merchandise – the Civil War itself, or a cultural representation such as *Gone with the Wind*: 'Especially after that big Civil War moving picture come out in '39, folks couldn't get enough ... Got so I tacked up paper arrows in our hallway. Wrote out "Oldest surviving", etc., like pointing tourists to Mount Rushmore' (Ibid.: 4–5). Lucy's own epic story of survival is, among other things, about her refusal to remain a victim to the commodification of history by virtue of her association with a Civil War veteran. She learns to resist being part of the commercial phenomenon though which the 'wads of useless Confederate money' are sold at flea markets 'at higher than face value' (Ibid.: 41). In the end she will not be commodified, but – both physically and mentally – she has many scars to prove it (some of them at the hands of her ex-Confederate husband, for whom the continued re-fighting of the war is his *raison d'être*).

Scarring, of course, is a resounding Civil War trope, with the savaged back of the slave circulated in textual treatments from abolitionist literature and photography to such contemporary texts as Toni Morrison's *Beloved* (1987). Marcus Wood discusses the proprietary impulses generated by just one ubiquitous image, that of the scarred back of the escaped slave, Gordon, distributed by abolitionist agencies throughout the war:

> This whipped back, so carefully stretched out in an elaborate pose presenting the slave as scientific data, was printed in thousands and passed out to Northern troops as a testimony to the barbarity of the slave power. This figure is a victim of the South, but a patient of the North, cleaned up, sanitised, recorded and displayed ... His whipped back existed at the centre of a narrative of redemption (Wood, 2000: 268).

By the late twentieth century – that is, after the death of Charlie Smith – it was no longer possible to appropriate living slaves in the interest of any narrative whatsoever. However, the aura of association with former slaves has persisted, and it remains an equally powerful and problematic cultural phenomenon.

One example, Ken Burns's *The Civil War*, highlights the 100–plus-year-old Daisy Turner, daughter of a former slave and Union soldier, Alex Turner. Having located the blind and nearly deaf woman in a Vermont nursing home, Burns filmed her recitation by memory of 'The

Soldier's Story', an epic poem of Gettysburg in rhyming couplets. Afterwards, he likened Daisy Turner to 'a cinematic Greek chorus' able to 'connect the past with the present and so perpetuate that magnificent drama we call history' (Burns, 1996: 156). As we have seen (see Chapter 7), this is a characterisation of history that has earned the worry of academic historians who fear the loss of critical engagement at the expense of drama and aesthetic pleasure. Still, in 1997, yet another Daisy – Daisy Anderson – was honoured at a Gettysburg ceremony solely because she had been married to a former slave and Union soldier, Robert Ball Anderson (CNN, 2004: n. p.). The aura of association, once again, had turned an individual into a presumably precious living link with the Civil War and, as such, a valuable cultural commodity.

These references to Cushman's 'third group' of witnesses, black and white, indicate the high cultural value placed on any living connection with the Civil War past. However, with human memory and perception being the fallible functions that they are, even with living connections it is often the case – to adopt one of Robert S. McNamara's 'eleven lessons' – that 'belief and seeing are both wrong' (Morris, 2003). This raises an obvious question of historical reliability that attaches to the living witness just as it attaches to the textual representation. As if in warning, Gurganus launches his novel through reference to one of the roughly two thousand slave narratives collected in the mid-1930s for the Works Progress Administration, that of 91-year-old Fanny Burdock, who remembered seeing Abraham Lincoln walking through Georgia in the midst of the Civil War. To Gurganus, it is beside the point that Lincoln could never have been in Georgia during the Civil War. What matters, he says, is that 'such scenes were told by hundreds of slaves. Such visitations remain, for me, truer than fact' – and he concludes with his oft-quoted line, 'History is my starting point' (Gurganus, 1990: xiv).

It is difficult to ascertain what Gurganus means with his cryptic assertion that 'such visitations' are 'truer than fact', but it implies both seductive power and untrustworthiness. As such, it is a comment on the risks of interpretation involved in the sending and receiving of historical messages or representations, particularly as they are filtered through memory and a process of deliberate selection. In the case of the WPA slave narratives – as Bruce Fort makes clear in introducing his online anthology for the University of Virginia – interpreters must ever be on their guard. With reference to a particular narrator, Emma Crockett, Fort writes:

We might discern a number of reasons for her inability or unwillingness to name names, to be more specific about brutalities suffered
under slavery. She admitted that her memory was failing her, not
unreasonable for an eighty-year-old. She also told her interviewer
that under slavery she lived on the 'plantation right over yander', and
as it is likely that the children or grandchildren of her former masters,
or her former overseers, still lived nearby, the threat of retribution
could have made her hold her tongue (Fort, 1998: n. p.).

It is perhaps such silences as these that have permitted neo-Confederate
apologists to perpetuate the myth of benign slavery. Other interpretive
risks and challenges are explicitly addressed in a second epic that in many
ways prefigures and compliments Gurganus's own: Ernest J. Gaines's
fictional *Autobiography of Miss Jane Pittman* (1972), also a purported
narrative of a woman who carries Civil War memories into the twentieth
century. Born a Louisiana slave and having lived through emancipation
and Reconstruction – the latter of which Gaines calls black America's
'flicker of light' (Gaines, 1972: 67) – Jane is battered by the post-
Reconstruction resurgence of white supremacy. At 110 years old, she
becomes active in the civil rights struggles of the 1960s. One lesson she
has learned is that people will resist information and stories as much as
they will resist an opposing army. As she advises her young activist-
protégé, Jimmy:

> 'I have a scar on my back I got when I was a slave. I'll carry it to my
> grave. You got people out there with this scar on their brains, and
> they will carry that scar to their grave. The mark of fear, Jimmy, is
> not easily removed. Talk with them, Jimmy. Talk and talk and talk.
> But don't be mad if they don't listen. Some of them won't ever listen.
> Many won't even hear you' (Ibid.: 242).

However, it is people's reluctance or inability to tell – to represent –
that compounds the failure to hear, and both Gaines and Gurganus
engage with this problem, particularly as a factor in black Americans'
coming to terms with slavery and its legacy. The nominal 'editor' of Jane
Pittman's narrative begins by explaining: 'I had been trying to get Miss
Jane Pittman to tell me the story of her life for several years now, but
each time I asked her she told me there was no story to tell' (Ibid.: v).
Jane's protective companion, Mary Hodges, is initially more hostile:

> 'What you want know about Miss Jane for?' Mary said.

'I teach history', I said. 'I'm sure her life's story can help me explain things to my students'.

'What's wrong with them books you already got?' Mary said.

'Miss Jane is not in them', I said (Ibid.: v).

David Blight addresses this reluctance to tell with reference to the black editor Benjamin Tanner's lament in 1878 ('The very remembrance of our experience is hideous') and his decision to publish – and thereby endorse – Emma Wheeler Wilcox's poem, 'Keep Out of the Past' (1887):

> Keep out of the past! It is lonely
>> And barren and bleak to the view,
> Its fires have grown cold and its stories are old,
>> Turn, turn to the present, the new!
>>   (in Blight, 2001: 314)

Drawing on sociologist Kelly Miller's assessment of 'the crude physical discipline of slavery' as the 'starting point' or 'zero point' of black American history, Blight concludes that, through engaging with slavery, 'blacks risked reflection on their past' (Ibid.: 314).

While this is certainly the case, as Gurganus makes clear, part of the problem is the lack of a recoverable past upon which to reflect. Thus, while the history of slavery and emancipation is a collective story of triumph over adversity and injustice, it is also a story of the theft of information, as Castalia, the newly emancipated slave in Gurganus's novel, tells her former mistress: 'Maybe you biggest crime is: how you took me out the story of myself! You stole Castalia's true life-tale' (Gurganus, 1990: 604). The implication is that we will never know what the 'true life-tale' of black Americans would have been without the 250–year-long blight of slavery, and that single controlling factor challenges the representation of their history to a degree not faced by the white South after – in relative terms – only four years of war and twelve years of Reconstruction.

Of course, such an admittedly crude balancing of the white South's sixteen years of trauma against 250–plus years of black trauma (Northern and Southern) makes for an equally crude analysis of the nature of historical trauma and its cultural representation. It threatens to deny the reality of white Southern suffering during and after the war, which cannot be denied. Consequently, the white South's defeat has spawned its own cultural industry, indicating that the intensity of historical trauma cannot merely be measured in terms of years. The culture of Southern defeat exemplifies another fertile, if problematic, use of history as a 'starting point', offering politically charged scenarios of alternative history that run across the spectrum of cultural forms and practices.

'What If?'

We have already encountered the practical importance of programming the 'What if?' scenario into Civil War computer games (see Chapter 7). Cushman observes the same with regard to Civil War re-enacting, in which battles are sometimes staged without a mutually agreed outcome: 'For many reenactors the final phase of living history turns out to be revising history. No longer performers recreating what happened, living historians act out what might have happened. In this final phase, authenticity of one kind undoes authenticity of another' (Cushman, 1999: 65). On the re-enactment field, by far the largest number of 'What if?' scenarios 'tend to originate from the Southern point of view', reflecting 'the all-too-human desire to comprehend and control contingencies beyond comprehension and control' (Ibid.: 177).

As it is in computers and on the 'living history' battlefield, so it is in both fiction and non-fiction in which the great Southern 'What if?'s hinge on a crucial turning point. For William Faulkner, it is the disastrous Pickett's Charge at Gettysburg:

> For every Southern boy fourteen years old, not once but whenever he wants it, there is the instant when it's still not yet two oclock on that July afternoon in 1863, the brigades are in position behind the rail fence, the guns are laid and ready in the woods and the furled flags are already loosened to break out and Pickett himself with his long oiled ringlets and his hat in one hand probably and his sword in the other looking up the hill waiting for Longstreet to give the word and it's all in the balance, it hasn't happened yet, it hasn't even begun yet, it not only hasn't begun yet but there is still time for it not to begin ... (Faulkner, 1996: 194).

The greatest 'What if?' for many, however, revolves around Stonewall Jackson (see Chapter 3) and his death at Chancellorsville. Richard Gray notes the intellectual heights to which the fantasy of Jackson's survival has travelled, as he quotes the correspondence of two prominent Nashville Agrarians (see Chapter 2):

'I am already convinced', declared [Allen] Tate in May, 1927, 'that had Jackson been in chief command from the beginning we should be a separate nation and much better off than we are now: and that if Jackson hadn't been killed in 1863 the Battle of Gettysburg would have been won'. 'I quite agree', replied [Donald] Davidson, '… it is interesting to speculate on what could have happened if Jackson, not Lee, had been the supreme head. Also, I agree that we might have been a damn sight better off if Stonewall had lived to realise his ideas' (Gray, 1997: 130).

Whether black Americans would 'have been a damn sight better off' is a matter of debate. Nonetheless, the questions (and answers) proliferate over Jackson. Gary Gallagher asks, 'What if Jackson had commanded the Second Corps on the First Day at Gettysburg? … And what if Jackson had been in the Shenandoah Valley in 1864?' (Gallagher, 1998: 112). Douglas Lee Gibboney's novel, *Stonewall Jackson at Gettysburg* (1997) answers both questions by allowing Jackson to survive Chancellorsville and help Lee win at Gettysburg before heading south to confront Sherman: 'Had Jackson taken command when Sherman was still in the mountains of north Georgia, history would surely have seen a repeat of his 1862 campaign and the South would, today, be an independent nation' (Gibboney, 1997: 111). Gibboney does not allow Jackson to survive: he is finally killed by two Union soldiers after refusing to surrender – not, as in history, by his own men. This novel, along with Benjamin King's novel, *A Bullet for Stonewall* (1990), which asserts a Federal assassination plot, indicates a desire to rescue one of the white South's greatest icons from the clutches of history, which had him fall at the hands of his fellow Southerners.

On a broader canvas, three important texts – from MacKinlay Kantor, Harry Turtledove and Kevin Willmott respectively – explore the implications of what might have occurred if the South as a whole had been able to escape from history's clutches. The godfather of the Civil War 'What if?' industry is, by all accounts, Kantor, whose *If the South Had Won the Civil War* appeared as an extended speculative essay in the 22 November 1960 edition of *Look* magazine – part of the prodigious cultural output marking the Civil War's centenary. Kantor's alternative history begins with a simple accident: outside of Vicksburg, a little girl drops her cat. A dog pursues the cat, and the two animals dash under the feet of Ulysses Grant's horse. The horse rears; Grant is thrown off and killed. History's Union victories at Vicksburg are erased; the Confederates win at Gettysburg, while General Sherman is killed by a Southern sharpshooter. In defeat, Lincoln resigns the presidency and is imprisoned in Richmond, to be later released in 'a pronounced gesture of international amity' by the newly independent CSA (Kantor, 2001: 75). He returns to Illinois an outcast, to practise small-town law in obscurity. Cleveland, Ohio – renamed Columbia – becomes the new capital of the diminished USA, while Washington, DD ('District of Dixie'), becomes the new capital of the Confederate States of America. Robert E. Lee succeeds Jefferson Davis as president.

If that were all, Kantor's essay would be, at best, a playful (if historically informed) diversion. But its speculative power really begins when Kantor attempts to plot the future of the CSA. Kantor is convinced that the Southern states would have eventually emancipated their slaves under global pressure after 'clinging uncertainly to a system no longer justified by plutology or in the philosophy of their enlightened citizens' (Ibid.: 90). Thus, the CSA emancipates; but the new federal entity ruptures under the strains of its own founding principle of secession. Texas secedes from the CSA and reverts to the Lone Star Republic. When, in place of history's battleship *Maine*, the battleship *Mississippi* is sunk in Havana harbour on 15 February 1898, the CSA enters into war with Spain, defeats it, and gains Cuba as a new state. Woodrow Wilson, 'that great Virginian', becomes the eleventh president of the Confederacy, and as an avowed 'consolidationist' he dreams of reuniting the CSA, the USA and Texas (Ibid.: 97). All three entities join the First World War and the Second World War as allies and, faced with the 'somber threat of Communist domination', the people and leaders of the three separate nations conclude in 1960 that the 'reassembling of American power' is 'an almost religious necessity' (Ibid.: 110–11). Overall, Kantor proposes (in Harry Turtledove's words) that 'Americans would have stayed very much alike and maintained close ties to one another regardless of whether they chanced to live under the Stars and Stripes, the Stars and Bars, or the Lone Star Flag' (Turtledove, 2001: 9). It is a proposal wholly in keeping with the romantic reunionist sentiments of the Civil War centenary.

It was left to Turtledove to take some of the broad outlines from Kantor, who he names as a mentor, to perpetuate the story of a victorious, benign Confederacy that had fought for freedom rather than slavery, and had ultimately bowed to the global opinion that slavery had run its course. In Turtledove's novel, *The Guns of the South* (1992), Lee is again the successor to Jefferson Davis, and he defends his plan for gradual emancipation in terms identical to those that have long been voiced by Southern nationalists and neo-Confederates. When challenged by a disgruntled slaveowner, 'We might as well rejoin the United States as emancipate our slaves', Lee replies:

> 'I fear I cannot agree with you, sir ... We spent our blood to regain the privilege of settling our own affairs as we choose, rather than having such settlements enforced upon us by other sections of the US which chose a way different from ours and which enjoyed a numerical preponderance over us' (Turtledove, 1993: 531).

Turtledove's enjoyably bizarre twist is that the South wins the Civil War with the aid of time-travelling Afrikaners who have come from the year 2013 to tip the balance with 100,000 AK-47 rifles for Lee's forces. While this device explains the ultimate Confederate victory, it also implies something more problematic: there are racists, and then there are *racists*. Southern white supremacy is relatively mild when compared with that of the real villains of the piece, the Afrikaner reactionaries from post-Mandela South Africa who use the secessionist aims of the Confederacy for their own political purposes. Stumbling upon a cache of texts that the Afrikaners have brought with them, Lee learns of the future world's contempt for apartheid and discovers his allies' secret agenda:

> Lee was thinking hard. If mankind's opinion ... had decisively turned against these self-admitted Afrikaner outlaws a hundred fifty years ahead, then what better, more logical reason for their return to the Confederacy than an effort to build another nation that favored 'white power' to become South Africa's friend and collaborator in a changed future? (Ibid.: 464)

Lee's ultimate break with the Afrikaners comes with his realisation that they 'are as mad in support of whites in their times as John Brown was in support of blacks in ours' (Ibid.: 487). Lee's analogy is important in that it gets to the heart of African-American contempt for such Confederate apologist scenarios as these, which either imply or argue outright that, had white Southerners been left alone to deal with their 'peculiar institution', they would have delivered the death-blow themselves. Whether or not John Brown was himself clinically mad (see Chapter 3), Lee implies that it was his 'support of blacks' that was mad in his times – if so, it was a 'madness' that he shared with Frederick Douglass, the Grimké sisters, Charles Sumner, Wendell Phillips and many other equally determined abolitionists.

Confederate apologists have always had to acknowledge the indelible words of Alexander Stephens, the Confederacy's vice-president, who not only declared in 1861 that slavery was 'the immediate cause' of the Civil War, but who also argued before the world that the Confederacy's

> foundations are laid, its corner-stone rests, upon the great truth that the negro is not equal to the white man; that slavery, subordination to the superior race, is his natural and moral condition ... This, our new Government, is the first, in the history of the world, based upon this great physical, philosophical, and moral truth (in Cleveland, 1866: 721).

In light of such a 'foundational' statement and the history of Jim Crow in the post-Reconstruction South, progressive historians like Leon Litwack have engaged in their own speculation to counter the more benign 'What if?'s of Kantor, Turtledove and others: 'If the South had made good on its quest for independence, it would have perpetuated the enslavement of black men and women. The white South lost the war, not the black South' (Litwack, 1996: 138). Moreover, even if black Americans could suspend their scepticism over the likelihood of gradual emancipation in an independent CSA, their frustration with the implied counsel of patience – which, it must be said, invariably comes from a white perspective – is as palpable now as it was in the time of Douglass. Hence the historian Lerone Bennett's exasperation with the serenity with which gradualists have continued to propose 'how and why my ancestors could have been kept in slavery longer – for ten, fifty or even a hundred years longer' (Bennett, 2000: 40). Under such circumstances, it is understandable that most of the 'What if?' scenarios have not played well to black Americans.

Enter Kevin Willmott (see Chapters 4 and 5), the black film-maker from Kansas, whose film, *CSA: The Confederate States of America* (2003), was endorsed at the Sundance Festival by veteran black directors Melvin van Peebles and Spike Lee, the latter of whom scrambled to join as the film's executive producer (Simmons, 2004: n. p.). In his documentary parody of Burns's *The Civil War*, Willmott clearly sets out to combat the Confederate apologia that dominates the 'What if?' industy. *CSA* draws its inspiration from a particular episode in the Burns series, as Willmott explains: 'There's a section that talks about the South's actual plan had

Figure 12 'They Won': Kevin Willmott, Writer and Director of *CSA: The Confederate States of America*, 2005 (Matt Jacobson: courtesy of the photographer).

they won, called "The Tropical Empire". When I found out, I said, "Wow. I could make a film about how they carried out the plan"' (in Ibid.). This plan was not to emancipate gradually, but rather, as Marx feared (see Chapter 8), to conquer Mexico, Central America and South America for new slave territory.

Willmott's device is a documentary history of the victorious Confederacy made by the 'British Broadcasting Service' and controversially aired during a late-night slot on 'Channel 9, San Francisco: Confederate Television'. It is preceded by a warning: 'The following program is of foreign origin. The content does not reflect the views of this station and may be unsuitable for children and servants. Discretion is advised' (Willmott, 2003). The modern CSA in Willmott's scenario is a fascist empire maintaining slavery through terror, and reaching from the Canadian border to Tierra del Fuego. It has also conquered space: hence a portentous still photo of an Apollo 11 astronaut on the moon's surface, saluting a planted Confederate flag.

The CSA's history as an independent nation begins with Lee's victory at Gettysburg, aided by British and French forces defending not slavery per se but rather the 'freedom of private property'. It continues with the escape and capture of Abraham Lincoln in blackface, the annexation of the defeated US, the enforced reintroduction of slavery in the North upon pain of punitive taxation, and the flight of all abolitionists to Canada. Latin America is progressively conquered after the CSA's victory in the Spanish–Confederate War of 1898; the renewal of the slave trade in the 1930s lifts the CSA out of the Great Depression, and Nazi Germany rises to become an ally in white supremacy. Wholesome 'antebellum values' characterise the Confederate 1950s, but national tranquillity is threatened by militant abolitionism from Canada, which takes the place of the Soviet Union as the Red Menace. The heavily fortified CSA–Canada border becomes the 'Cotton Curtain' that substitutes for history's Berlin Wall. The Republican president, John F. Kennedy, is assassinated for his tentative steps toward abolition, and slave rebellions erupt in Watts and Newark. In a subplot, the 2002 Democratic presidential candidate, a scion of a slaveholding dynasty, is ruined by revelations of his African blood in an echo of the Clinton—Lewinsky scandal: 'My great-granddaddy did *not* have sexual relations with that woman!' (Ibid.).

In terms of its format, *CSA* is a masterful parody of *The Civil War*, utilising carefully doctored still photographs and archival footage, voice-over narration and interviews with faux historians closely modelled on Shelby Foote and Barbara J. Fields, Burns's two main commentators. In between the documentary segments a series of commercials advertise Confederate Life Insurance ('For over 100 years, protecting a people and their property'), opportunities in the Confederate Air Force, sitcom reruns (*Leave It to Beulah*, with Hattie McDaniel), reality cop-shows ('*Runaway!* Tonight at 10.30!'), lifestyle programmes (*Better Homes and Plantations*) and the Slave Shopping Network (Ibid.). Overall, Willmott's objective is two-fold: to challenge the Confederate-friendly legion of 'What if?' speculators, and to remind people to take Alexander Stephens at his word. As Willmott pleaded at Sundance: 'I hope we can admit as a nation that the war was fought over slavery. Not states' rights. Slavery' (Butler, 2004: A8).

Thus, the Civil War has spawned a corpus of powerful and provocative 'What if?' scenarios depicting the broad sweep of alternative nationhood, informed as much by race as by sectionalism. The Civil War has also led to the profound depiction of contemporary individuals for whom the visitation of total war and conquest becomes as much a metaphor for personal as for national trauma. Two further subjects – the Mississippi novelist and short-story writer, Barry Hannah, and the North Carolina film-maker, Ross McElwee – deserve our attention as, in conversation with Gurganus and others, their works invoke Southern defeat as a possible route to personal catharsis and healing.

'Appomattox, Appomattox, Appomattox, Baby'

At one point in *Oldest Living Confederate Widow Tells All*, Lucy Marsden contemplates the group of Vietnam veterans who habitually gather in the shopping mall near her rest home: 'The Rebs and the South Asian vets, they both lost. Makes your being home-and-hurting mean something different. You win, you're forgiven more. Lose, means you've lost, both in your own head and in others' (Gurganus, 1990: 207). In his study, *Vietnam and the Southern Imagination* (1992), Owen Gilman explores how the Vietnam War 'has been fitted into the larger history that is always present for southerners', a past into which they seem 'programmed to gaze' (Gilman, 1992: 6, 7–8).

In particular, Gilman focuses on Barry Hannah for his capacity to 'confront imaginatively the violence linked to America's doomed foray into combat in Southeast Asia' (Gilman, 1992: 79). Hannah is important because, while he is not a Vietnam veteran, he identifies and utilises the traumatic currents that wracked the American nation and its citizens during the war and which have not disappeared in the wake of defeat. While Hannah at times brings Civil War references into Vietnam combat settings, he more forcefully allows Vietnam to intrude on his treatment of the Civil War. Hence the scenario he repeats in two separate stories in *Airships* (1978), in which a jaded Confederate soldier acts on his impulse to kill his commander and hero, Jeb Stuart, for the marauding violence he has demanded of his men during raids into the North, reflecting the increasingly common Vietnam War practice by which US soldiers killed or 'fragged' their own officers. In 'Dragged Fighting from His Tomb', the narrator screams at Stuart, 'You shit! What are we doing killing people in Pennsylvania?', earning the reply: 'Showing them that we can, Captain Howard!' (Hannah, 1991: 54). In this story, the narrator actually kills Stuart, while in 'Knowing He Was Not My Kind Yet I Followed', a different narrator only goes so far as to threaten Stuart with the same fate, having succumbed to the mental and physical exhaustion that marks such drug-fuelled Vietnam narratives as Michael Herr's

Dispatches and Francis Ford Coppola's *Apocalypse Now*: 'We're too far from home. We are not defending our beloved Dixie anymore. We're just bandits and maniacal. The gleam in the men's eyes tells this. Everyone is getting crazier on the craziness of being simply too far from home for decent return' (Ibid.: 140).

Hannah most fully develops his Civil War–Vietnam mélange in the novella, *Ray* (1980), in which a psychologically wounded doctor, formerly a combat fighter pilot, also dreams of Civil War battles in which he serves under Jeb Stuart: 'Oh, help me! I am losing myself in two centuries and two wars' (Ibid.: 234). Ray's conflation of these two wars also merges a public, historical trauma with a personal and private one, as he reflects upon his troubled marriage, his sexual impotence and his lost hours in a local drinking den called 'Lee's Tomb':

> Sabers up! Get your horses in line! They have as many as we do and it will be a stiff one. Hit them, hit them! Give them such a sting as they will never forget. Ready? *Avant!* Avant, avant, avant! Kill them!
>
> Horses gleaming with sweat everywhere, Miniés flying by you in the wind.
>
> Sometimes there is no answer from your wife, even when you're sweet as pie. Sometimes there is no answer from the world (Ibid.: 238–9).

Importantly, and in spite of the degree of his psychological trauma, Ray eventually arrives at peace and reconciliation as he slots his memories of both Vietnam and the Civil War in with the small victories he is able to achieve at last as a doctor, a husband and a bedfellow. Implicitly, he illustrates the process of drawing up an armistice like that described by Gurganus's Confederate widow, who concludes: 'Left on its own, Memory tends to make – not war – but many little treaties' (Gurganus, 1990: 210).

In Lucy Marsden's case, this realisation comes fully upon her at the close of the book, as, flying above the Georgia landscape during her first airplane ride, she notices a bright, fertile swath of green. A fellow passenger explains its origins:

> 'Sherman's path', Bill says. 'Still shows from way up here, imagine. Ma'am, see how it changes at that river crossing? Going in at one spot, then wading out with the horses and torches downstream, there? Stretches clear to Atlanta, which he burned ... Yes, ma'am, the whole

burned part grew back greener … Maybe charcoal helps trees come up stronger?' (Ibid.: 717)

While neither Hannah nor Gurganus explicitly connect Sherman's march to the Vietnam War, the connection is, in some ways, unavoidable. It is, admittedly, a complicated and ironic connection because it compares the victorious Union marauders with the defeated Americans in Vietnam. However, on the road to their own defeat in Saigon the US forces relied on the scorched-earth policy of napalm, carpet-bombing, Agent Orange and village massacres – a historical fact that places extra weight on the observation of Rita Mae Brown's Geneva Chatfield (see Chapter 6): 'We all live in the dark shadow of Sherman' (Brown, 1987: 412).

The film-maker Ross McElwee has also lived in Sherman's 'dark shadow'. In his highly idiosyncratic documentary, *Sherman's March* (1991), an unnamed Southern woman observes: 'Sherman was merciless … I'm sure we did the same thing in Vietnam.' However, McElwee's film, as he explains, was not originally intended to comment on anything other than 'the lingering effects of Sherman's march on the South'. In the final product, devastation remains the key focus, but – as the film's subtitle indicates – it is no longer strictly about the historical legacy of Sherman's march. What McElwee offers is 'A Meditation on the Possibility of Romantic Love in the South during an Era of Nuclear Weapons Proliferation' (McElwee, 1991).

Like Gurganus and Hannah, McElwee utilises Civil War history as a source for intensely personal introspection. Following the route of Sherman's march, McElwee lays bare his own romantic failures as he meets and disastrously loses a series of potential lovers along the way. These failures, and the continued loneliness that they promise, dovetail into McElwee's terror of thermonuclear war, based on his having witnessed a hydrogen bomb test at the age of twelve. As he says, when his love life is hopeful, his nightmares of nuclear holocaust 'gather dust in their silos'; when not, 'they take to the skies night after night'. The route of Sherman's campaign, which 'marked the first time in modern history that total warfare had been waged against a primarily civilian population', is home to a cast of burned-out characters, besides McElwee: an isolationist community of paranoid bachelors who have taken to the woods and built fall-out shelters; a small-time actress hopelessly fixated on meeting and seducing Burt Reynolds; a woman who places all her hopes in the 'total Reconstruction' of cosmetic surgery. These potentially discarded individuals are all metaphorical, if not actual, descendants of the 60,000 who died in two hours at Peachtree Creek, outside of Atlanta, for 'a piece of land the size of a Little League baseball field' (Ibid.).

Crucially, McElwee makes it clear that the devastation of the South is not yet over. He encounters an old girlfriend at an anti-nuclear protest at a South Carolina plutonium processing site; she is 'angry over the fact that most of the nation's nuclear waste happens to be dumped in South Carolina, primarily by Northerners'. With the state overrun by nuclear reactors, she and her defeated colleagues gather, after ten years of fruitless campaigning, around a monument 'for survivors of nuclear war, explaining in twelve languages how to reconstruct civilisation' – an experience, obviously, to which both the white and black South can relate (Ibid.).

One of McElwee's narrative strategies is to construct himself consciously as a loser who wears romantic defeat on his sleeve and does not succeed in moving beyond it until, at the end of the film, he escapes to the North, where he finds a partner. His engagement with Sherman's march thus contrasts starkly with that of Gurganus, whose Lucy Marsden, looking down from the airplane, concludes:

> Fresh green is teaching me something. This burn rambles clear from Virginia past our hometown to Atlanta. What a beautiful map of a scar! Educational – a bitter, optimistic green. I recognise it. Up under my ribs, a sweet unlatching starts, a tallying. I stare down at that tint changed by hurt. Recovery has upgraded everything that blossomed after. I know scorched-earth policy. And I know about continuing, child. But I never knew that keeping on could, from this high, just *look* so pretty (Gurganus, 1990: 717).

Confronting the scar on the back of the white South – the 'upgraded' path of Sherman's march – enables Lucy, finally, to look down on her world and say 'I am still here' and 'The war is over' (Ibid.: 718). As she reflects upon her late husband, the bitter Confederate veteran mentally imprisoned in his Civil War battles, she recalls 'cooing the only word that ever helped: "Appomattox, Appomattox, Appomattox, baby"' (Ibid.: 6).

That final word may be uttered in a variety of voices. It may be a neutral expression of historical fact. It may be, as Lucy Marsden utters it, a comforting utterance signifying the end of a painful struggle. It may be a stern vindication from an unsympathetic black Southerner who was asked by Tony Horwitz in the late 1990s 'how he felt about people still celebrating the Confederacy': 'I got one word for those folks – Appomattox. The game's up, you lost. Get over it' (Horwitz, 1998: 43). To neo-Confederates, of course, the word is poison, for which the only antidote is energetic cultural agitation.

Consequently, as we have seen throughout this book, the culture war being waged by neo-Confederates and their progressive adversaries shows no sign of abating. If anything, it proliferates over a territory that continues to expand beyond the boundaries of the textual to the lived, beyond the real to the virtual, and beyond the national to the transnational. In the wider realm of culture, there is – as yet – no Appomattox.

Sources and Further Reading

I have made a point of accessing primary material from online sources where possible, and restricting my usage to reputable sites such as the University of North Carolina's 'Documenting the American South', the University of Virginia's 'American Studies Hypertexts', the University of Indiana's 'Wright American Fiction', Cornell University's 'Making of America' and Project Gutenberg.

AARC (2004) Webpage for the African-American Resource Center, Tulsa City-County Library. http://www.tulsalibrary.org/aarc/month.htm.

Aaron, Daniel (1973) *The Unwritten War: American Writers and the Civil War*. New York: Alfred A. Knopf.

ACWGC (2004) Webpage for American Civil War Game Club. http://www.wargame.ch/wc/acw/ACWmainpage.htm.

ACWS (2004) Webpage for American Civil War Society, Ltd, UK. http://www.acws.co.uk.

Aitken, Roy E., as told to Al P. Nelson (1965) *The Birth of a Nation Story*. Middleburg, VA: William W. Denlinger.

Alcott, Louisa May (1996) *Little Women* (Book 1). Project Gutenberg etext: http://www.gutenberg.org/etext/514. First pub. 1868.

Alemán, Jesse (2003) 'Authenticity, Autobiography, and Identity: *The Woman in Battle* as a Civil War Narrative', in Velazquez, Loreta Janeta (2003) *The Woman in Battle: The Civil War Narrative of Loreta Velazquez, Cuban Woman and Confederate Soldier*. Madison: University of Wisconsin Press.

Anderson, Maxwell (1939) *Key Largo*. Washington, DC: Anderson House.

Andress, Michael (2004) Review of HP Simulations *Campaign Corinth* for *The Wargamer*. http://www.wargamer.com/reviews/campaign_corinth_ preview. asp.

Anon. (1862) 'Brady's Photographs: The Dead of Antietam'. *New York Times*, 20 October: 5.

Anon. (1882) *Minstrel Songs, Old and New*. Boston: Oliver Ditson and Co.

Anon. (2004) 'Farnsley, Charles Rowland Peaslee', *Biographical Directory of the United States Congress, 1774–Present*. Online edition: http://bioguide. congress. gov/scripts/biodisplay.pl?index=F000023.

Armour, Robert A. (1981) 'History Written in Jagged Lightning: Realistic South vs. Romantic South in *The Birth of a Nation*', in French, Warren (ed.) (1981), *The South and Film*. Jackson: University Press of Mississippi: 14–21.

Asbury, Herbert (2002) *The Gangs of New York*. London: Arrow Books. First pub. 1927.

Askins, Allison and Joseph S. Stroud (2000) '"The Flag Is Coming Down", 46,000 Cry at King Day Rally', *The State* (Columbia, SC), 18 January, A1, A9–10.

Avalon Hill (2004) Product description for Avalon Hill's *Battle Cry* board game. http://www.wizards.com.

BBC (2003) 'Last Yankee War Widow Dies'. BBC News World Edition, 20 January, http://news.bbc.co.uk/2/hi/americas/2677095.stm.

Bakhtin, Mikhail (1984) *Rabelais and His World*. Translated by Helene Iswolsky. Bloomington: Indiana University Press.

Banks, Russell (1998) *Cloudsplitter*. London: Secker and Warburg.

Basler, Roy, et al. (eds) (1953–55) *The Collected Works of Abraham Lincoln*. 9 vols, 2 suppl. vols (1974, 1990). New Brunswick, NJ: Rutgers University Press. Abraham Lincoln Association/University of Michigan online version: http://www.hti.umich.edu/l/lincoln/.

Baudrillard, Jean (1983) *Simulations*. Translated by Paul Foss, et al. New York: Semiotext(e).

Benét, Stephen Vincent (1990) *John Brown's Body*. Chicago: Elephant Paperbacks. First pub. 1928.

Bennet, Lerone, Jr (2000) *Forced into Glory: Abraham Lincoln's White Dream*. Chicago: Johnson Publishing Company.

Berry, Ian, et al. (eds) (2003) *Kara Walker: Narratives of a Negress*. Cambridge, MA: MIT Press.

Blackett, R. J. M. (1999) 'Cracks in the Antislavery Wall: Frederick Douglass's Second Visit to England (1859–1860) and the Coming of the Civil War', in Rice, Alan J. and Martin Crawford (eds) (1999) *Liberating Sojourn: Frederick Douglass and Transatlantic Reform*. Athens, GA: University of Georgia Press: 187–206.

Blackett, R. J. M. (2001) *Divided Hearts: Britain and the American Civil War*. Baton Rouge: Louisiana State University Press.

Blanton, DeAnne and Lauren Cook (2002) *They Fought Like Demons: Women Soldiers in the American Civil War*. Baton Rouge: Louisiana State University Press.

Blassingame, John (1975) 'Using the Testimony of Ex-Slaves: Approaches and Problems'. *Journal of Southern History*, 41, no. 4 (November): 473–92.

Blight, David (2001) *Race and Reunion: The Civil War in American Memory*. Cambridge, MA: Harvard University Press.

Blomqvist, Bosse (2004) Personal letter to author, 7 November.

Bogart, Paul (dir.) (1971) *Skin Game*. Hollywood: Warner Brothers/Cherokee.

Bogle, Donald (1994) *Toms, Coons, Mulattoes, Mammies, and Bucks: An Interpretive History of Blacks in American Films*. Oxford: Roundhouse. First pub. 1973.

Boritt, Gabor S. (1996) 'Lincoln and Gettysburg: The Hero and the Heroic Place', in Toplin, Robert Brent (ed.) (1996) *Ken Burns's* The Civil War: *Historians Respond*. New York: Oxford University Press: 81–100.

Boritt, Gabor S. (ed.) (2001) *The Lincoln Enigma: The Changing Faces of an American Icon*. Oxford and New York: Oxford University Press/OUP USA.

Boritt, Gabor S. (2001a) 'Did He Dream of a Lily-White America?', in Boritt, G. S. (ed.) (2001) *The Lincoln Enigma: The Changing Faces of an American Icon*. Oxford and New York: Oxford University Press/OUP USA: 1–19.

Bradshaw, Wesley (Charles Wesley Alexander) (1862) *Pauline of the Potomac; or, General McClellan's Spy*. Philadelphia: Barclay. University of Indiana 'Wright American Fiction' etext: http://www.letrs.indiana.edu/cgi/t/text/text-idx?c=wright2;idno=wright2–0048.

Brogan, Hugh (1990) *The Penguin History of the United States of America*. London: Penguin. First pub. 1985.

Brown, Rita Mae (1987) *High Hearts*. New York: Bantam. First pub. 1986.

Brown, William Wells (1853) *Clotel; or, the President's Daughter: A Narrative of Slave Life in the United States*. London: Partridge and Oakley. University of North Carolina, 'Documenting the American South' etext: http://docsouth.unc.edu/southlit/brown/menu.html.

Bruce, Lenny (1975) *The Essential Lenny Bruce*, ed. John Cohen. St Albans: Panther. First pub. 1972.

Burlingame, Michael (1994) *The Inner World of Abraham Lincoln*. Urbana: University of Illinois Press.

Burns, Ken (dir.) (1990) *The Civil War* (PBS television documentary). Five episodes. Florentine Films.

Burns, Ken (1996) 'Four O'Clock in the Morning Courage', in Toplin, Robert Brent (ed.) (1996) *Ken Burns's* The Civil War: *Historians Respond*. New York: Oxford University Press: 153–83.

Butler, Judith (1993) *Bodies that Matter: On the Discursive Limits of 'Sex'*. New York: Routledge.

Butler, Robert W. (2004) 'Buzz Building for Filmmaker' [on Kevin Willmott]. *Kansas City Star*, 11 April, A1, A8.

Campbell, Edward D. C., Jr (1983) *The Celluloid South: Hollywood and the Southern Myth*. Knoxville: University of Tennessee Press.

Capra, Frank (dir.) (1939) *Mr. Smith Goes to Washington*. Columbia Pictures.

Caruthers, William A. (1968) *The Cavaliers of Virginia; or, the Recluse of Jamestone*. Ridgewood, NJ: Gregg Press. First pub. 1835.

Caruthers, William A. (1968a) *The Kentuckian in New York; or, the Adventures of Three Southerns*. Ridgewood, NJ: Gregg Press. First pub. 1834.

Cash, Wilbur J. (1991) *The Mind of the South*. New York: Vintage Books. First pub. 1941.

Cashin, Joan E. (ed.) (2002) *The War Was You and Me: Civilians in the American Civil War*. Princeton: Princeton University Press.

Cawardine, Richard J. (2004) 'Lincoln through British Eyes'. *Wall Street Journal*, 14 April: n. p. Online version at: http://www.opinionjournal.com/la/?id=110004949.

CC (2004) Creed, Children of the Confederacy. CC homepage: http://www.hqudc.org/CofC/creed.html.

Chandler, James (1994) 'The Historical Novel Goes to Hollywood: Scott, Griffith, and Film Epic Today' (first pub. 1990), in Lang, Robert (ed.) (1994) *The Birth of a Nation*. New Brunswick, NJ: Rutgers University Press: 225–49.

Chesnut, Mary (1905) *A Diary from Dixie*. New York: D. Appleton and Co. University of North Carolina, 'Documenting the American South' etext: http://docsouth.unc.edu/chesnut/menu.html.

Ching, Barbara (2004) 'Country Music', in Gray, Richard, and Owen Robinson (eds) (2004) *A Companion to the Literature and Culture of the American South*. Oxford: Blackwell: 203–20.

Cleveland, Henry (1866) *Alexander H. Stephens in Public and Private: With Letters and Speeches Before, During, and Since the War*. Philadelphia: National Publishing Co.

Clifford, James, and George E. Marcus (eds) (1986) *Writing Culture: The Poetics and Politics of Ethnography*. Berkeley, CA: University of California Press.

Clines, Francis X. (2001) 'Museums of Civil War Are Torn by Debate', *New York Times*, 25 November, A20.

Clinton, Catherine (1995) '*Gone with the Wind*', in Carnes, Mark C., et al. (eds) (1995) *Past Imperfect: History According to the Movies*. New York: Henry Holt and Co.: 132–5.

Clinton, Catherine (1996) 'Noble Women as Well', in Toplin, Robert Brent (ed.) (1996) *Ken Burns's* The Civil War*: Historians Respond*. New York: Oxford University Press: 61–80.

CNN (2004) 'Widow of a Civil War Veteran Dies'. 15 June 15. http://edition.cnn.com/2004/US/South/05/31/obit.martin.ap/.

Cobb, Jim (2004) Review of HP Simulations *Campaign Gettysburg* for *The Wargamer*. http://www.wargamer.com/reviews/campaign_gettysburg/

Collier, Peter (2003) 'Committed Storyteller [Ronald F. Maxwell]'. *Washington Times*, 22 February, D1.

Collins, Bruce (1981) *The Origins of America's Civil War*. London: Edward Arnold.

Cooper, James Fenimore (1997) *The Spy: A Tale of the Neutral Ground*. London: Penguin. First pub. 1821.

Copland, Aaron (1987) *Lincoln Portrait and Other Works* (audio CD). Cleveland: Telarc International. First perf. 1942.

Coski, John M. (2005) *The Confederate Battle Flag: America's Most Embattled Emblem*. Cambridge, MA: Harvard University Press.

Coulter, Ann (2003) *Slander: Liberal Lies about the American Right*. New York: Three Rivers Press.

Crane, Stephen (1895) *The Red Badge of Courage*. New York: D. Appleton and Co. University of Virginia etext: http://etext.lib.virginia.edu/toc/modeng/public/CraRedb.html.

Craven, Avery (1957) *The Coming of the Civil War*. Chicago: University of Chicago Press. First pub. 1942.

Cromwell, John (dir.) (1940) *Abe Lincoln in Illinois* (British title: *Spirit of the People*). RKO Studios.

Cullen, Jim (1995) *The Civil War in Popular Culture*. Washington, DC: Smithsonian Institution Press.

Curtiz, Michael (dir.) (1940) *Santa Fe Trail*. Warner Brothers Studios.

Cushman, Stephen (1999). *Bloody Promenade: Reflections on a Civil War Battle*. Charlottesville: University Press of Virginia.

Daniels, Charlie (1990) 'The South's Gonna Do It Again', on Charlie Daniels Band, *Fire on the Mountain* (audio CD). First recorded 1975.

Danky, James and Maureen Hady (1999) *African-American Newspapers and Periodicals: A National Bibliography*. Cambridge, MA: Harvard University Press.

Dann, Martin (ed.) (1971) *The Black Press, 1827–1890: The Quest for National Identity*. New York: Putnam.

Daugherty, Herschel (dir.) (1969) *Star Trek*, Episode 77: 'The Savage Curtain'. NBC Television. First aired March 7.

Davis, Michael (1971) *The Image of Lincoln in the South*. Knoxville: University of Tennessee Press.

Dick, Philip K. (1997) *We Can Build You*. London: HarperCollins. First pub. 1972.

DiLorenzo, Thomas J. (2003) *The Real Lincoln*. New York: Three Rivers Press.

'Dion' (1853) 'Our Literature'. *Frederick Douglass' Paper*, 23 September. Accessible Archives etext: http://www.accessible.com.

Dixon, Thomas (1902) *The Leopard's Spots: A Romance of the White Man's Burden, 1865–1900*. New York: Doubleday, Page and Co. University of North Carolina, 'Documenting the American South' etext: http://docsouth.unc.edu/dixonleopard/menu.html.

Dixon, Thomas (1905) *The Clansman: An Historical Romance of the Ku Klux Klan*. New York: Doubleday, Page and Co. University of North Carolina,

'Documenting the American South' etext: http://docsouth.unc.edu/dixonclan/menu.html.

Donald, David (1961) 'Getting Right with Lincoln', in Donald, David (1961) *Lincoln Reconsidered*. New York: Alfred A. Knopf: 3–18. First pub. 1956.

Donnelly, Thomas (2003) 'Planning for War Against Iraq and for Its Aftermath: What Would Lincoln Do?', *National Security Outlook*, 1 January. American Enterprise Institute for Public Policy Research website: http://www.aei.org.

Dos Passos, John (1967) *Adventures of a Young Man*. Boston: Houghton Mifflin. First pub. 1938.

Douglass, Frederick (1845) *Narrative of the Life of Frederick Douglass, an American Slave*. Boston: Anti-Slavery Office. University of North Carolina, 'Documenting the American South' etext: http://docsouth.unc.edu/douglass/douglass.html.

Douglass, Frederick (1853) *The Heroic Slave*. From *Autographs for Freedom*, ed. Julia Griffiths. Boston: John P. Jewett and Co. University of North Carolina, 'Documenting the American South' etext: http://docsouth.unc.edu/neh/douglass1853/menu.html.

Douglass, Frederick (1892) *Life and Times of Frederick Douglass, Written by Himself*. Boston: De Wolfe and Fiske Co. University of North Carolina, 'Documenting the American South' etext: http://docsouth.unc.edu/neh/dougl92/menu.html.

Du Bois, W. E. B. (1903) *The Souls of Black Folk: Essays and Sketches*. Chicago: A. C. McClurg and Co. University of North Carolina, 'Documenting the American South' etext: http://docsouth.unc.edu/church/duboissouls/menu.html.

Du Bois, W. E. B. (2001) *John Brown*. New York: Modern Library. First pub. 1909.

Dyer, Richard (1996) 'Into the Light: The Whiteness of the South in *The Birth of a Nation*', in King, Richard and Helen Taylor (eds) (1996) *Dixie Debates: Perspectives on Southern Cultures*. London: Pluto Press: 165–76.

Earle, Steve (1999) 'Dixieland', on Steve Earle and the Del McCoury Band, *The Mountain* (audio CD). E-Squared Artimis.

Eastman, Mary Henderson (1852) *Aunt Phillis's Cabin; or, Southern Life as It Is*. Philadelphia: Lippincott, Grambo and Co. University of Virginia, American Studies hypertext: http://www.iath.virginia.edu/utc/proslav/eastmanhp.html.

Eby, Cecil (1969) *Between the Bullet and the Lie: American Volunteers in the Spanish Civil War*. New York: Holt, Rhinehart and Winston.

Edgerton, Gary R. (2001) 'Mediating *Thomas Jefferson*: Ken Burns as Popular Historian', in Edgerton, Gary R. and Peter C. Rollins (eds) (2001) *Television Histories: Shaping Collective Memory in the Media Age*. Lexington: University Press of Kentucky: 169–92.

Edgeville, Edward (1865) *Castine*. Raleigh, NC: W. B. Smith. University of Indiana

'Wright American Fiction' etext: http://www.letrs.indiana.edu/cgi/t/text/text-idx?c=wright2;idno=wright2-0835.

Editors, *Cahiers du Cinéma* (1970) 'John Ford's *Young Mr. Lincoln*', in Nichols, Bill (ed.) (1976) *Movies and Methods*. Vol. 1. Berkeley: University of California Press: 493–529.

Edmonds, Sarah Emma (1999) *Memoirs of a Soldier, Nurse and Spy: A Woman's Adventures in the Union Army*, ed. Elizabeth D. Leonard. De Kalb: Northern Illinois University Press. First pub. 1864.

Ellison, Ralph (1967) *Shadow and Act*. London: Secker and Warburg. First pub. 1964.

Fahs, Alice (2001) *The Imagined Civil War: Popular Literature of the North and South, 1861–1865*. Chapel Hill: University of North Carolina Press.

Faulkner, William (1996) *Intruder in the Dust*. London: Vintage. First pub. 1948.

Faust, Drew Gilpin (1988) *The Creation of Confederate Nationalism: Ideology and Identity in the Civil War South*. Baton Rouge: Louisiana State University Press.

Fields, Annie Adams (ed.) (1898) *Life and Letters of Harriet Beecher Stowe*. Boston: Houghton, Mifflin. First pub. 1897.

Firestone, David (2001) 'The New South: Old Times There Are Not Forgotten', *New York Times*, 28 January, B4.

Foner, Eric (ed.) (1950–55) *The Life and Writings of Frederick Douglass*. 4 vols. New York: International Publishers.

Foner, Eric (1970) *Free Soil, Free Labor, Free Men: The Ideology of the Republican Party before the Civil War*. New York: Oxford University Press.

Foner, Eric (2003) 'Divinely Ordained', *London Review of Books*, 23 October, 12–14.

Ford, John (dir.) (1939) *Young Mr. Lincoln*. Twentieth-Century Fox.

Ford, John (dir.) (1964) *Cheyenne Autumn*. Warner Brothers/Ford-Smith.

Fort, Bruce (1998) 'Reading the Narratives'. *American Slave Narratives: An Online Anthology*. University of Virginia, American Studies hypertexts: http://xroads.virginia.edu/~hyper/wpa/wpahome.html.

Foster, Gaines M. (1987) *Ghosts of the Confederacy: Defeat, the Lost Cause, and the Emergence of the New South*. New York: Oxford University Press.

Foster, Harve (dir.) (1946) *Song of the South*. Walt Disney Productions.

Foster, Stephen Collins (1848) 'Away Down South', in *Songs of the Sable Harmonists*. Cincinnati: Peters, Field and Co. Library of Congress, 'Music for the Nation: American Sheet Music' (online 'American Memory' project): http://memory.loc.gov.

Franklin, H. Bruce (2001) *Vietnam and Other American Fantasies*. Amherst: University of Massachusetts Press.

Fraser, George MacDonald (1999) *Flashman and the Angel of the Lord*. London: HarperCollins. First pub. 1994.

Frassanito, William A. (1975) *Gettysburg: A Journey in Time*. New York: Charles Scribner's Sons.

Frassanito, William A. (1978) *Antietam: The Photographic Legacy of America's Bloodiest Day*. New York: Charles Scribner's Sons.

Frassanito, William A. (1994) 'The Guns at Gettysburg', in Davis, William C. and Bell I. Wiley (eds) (1994) *The Photographic History of the Civil War*. 2 vols. New York: Black Dog and Leventhal Publishers. Vol. I: 1271–1339.

Frazier, Charles (1997) *Cold Mountain*. London: Hodder and Stoughton.

Gage, Frances D. (1881) 'Reminiscences of Sojourner Truth', in Stanton, Elizabeth Cady, et al. (eds) (1881–1922) *History of Woman Suffrage*. 6 vols. Rochester, NY: Fowler and Wells. Vol. I: 115–17.

Gaines, Ernest J. (1972) *The Autobiography of Miss Jane Pittman*. New York: Bantam Books. First pub. 1971.

Gallagher, Gary W. (1998) *Lee and His Generals in War and Memory*. Baton Rouge: Louisiana State University Press.

Garrison, Wendell Phillips (1885) *William Lloyd Garrison, 1805–1879: The Story of His Life, Told by His Children*. Vol. I. New York: Century Company.

Gaston, Paul M. (1970) *The New South Creed: A Study in Southern Mythmaking*. New York: Alfred A. Knopf.

Gates, Henry Louis, Jr (ed.) (1987) *The Classic Slave Narratives*. New York: Mentor Books.

Gavin, Patrick (2003) 'What Would Lincoln Do?', *Counterpunch*, 22 December. Online version at http://www.counterpunch.org.

Geertz, Clifford (1993) *Local Knowledge*. London: Fontana. First pub. 1983.

Geldud, Harry M. (ed.) (1971) *Focus on D. W. Griffith*. Englewood Cliffs, NJ: Prentice-Hall.

Gellhorn, Martha (1959) *The Face of War*. New York: Simon and Schuster.

Gibboney, Douglas Lee (1997) *Stonewall Jackson at Gettysburg*. Fredericksburg, VA: Sergeant Kirkland's Museum.

Gilman, Owen W. (1992) *Vietnam and the Southern Imagination*. Jackson: University Press of Mississippi.

Gilmore, Paul (1997) '"De Genewine Artekil": William Wells Brown, Blackface Minstrelsy and Abolitionism'. *American Literature*, 69, no. 4 (December): 743–80.

Graham, Allison (2001) *Framing the South: Hollywood, Television, and Race during the Civil Rights Struggle*. Baltimore: Johns Hopkins University Press.

Gray, Richard (1997) *Writing the South: Ideas of an American Region*. Baton Rouge: Louisiana State University Press. First pub. 1986.

Gray, Richard (2004) 'Writing Southern Cultures', in Gray, Richard and Owen Robinson (eds) (2004) *A Companion to the Literature and Culture of the American South*. Oxford: Blackwell: 3–26.

Grayson, William J. (1907) *Selected poems by William J. Grayson, selected and comp. by Mrs. William H. Armstrong (his daughter)*. New York: Neale

Publishing Co. University of Michigan, 'Making of America' Digital Books Project: http://www.hti.umich.edu/m/moagrp/.

Greaney, Dan (2000) 'Bart to the Future'. *The Simpsons*. Fox Television. First aired 19 March.

Griffith, D.W. (dir.) (1915) *The Birth of a Nation*. Epoch Studios.

Guelzo, Allen C. (2001) 'Apple of God in a Picture of Silver: The Constitution and Liberty', in Boritt, G. S. (ed.) (2001) *The Lincoln Enigma: The Changing Faces of an American Icon*. Oxford and New York: Oxford University Press/ OUP USA: 86–107.

Guetersloh, Herman (2000) 'The Old South', *Free Times* (Columbia, SC), 30 August–5 September, 10, 12.

Gurganus, Allan (1990) *Oldest Living Confederate Widow Tells All*. London: Faber and Faber. First pub. 1989.

Guttman, Alan (1962) *The Wound in the Heart: America and the Spanish Civil War*. New York: Free Press of Glencoe.

Hale, Sarah Josepha (1852) *Northwood; Or, Life North and South Showing the True Character of Both*. New York: H. Long and Brother. First pub. 1827.

Hall, Richard (1993) *Patriots in Disguise: Women Warriors of the Civil War*. New York: Paragon House.

Hall, Rolf (2004) 'Rolf Hall's Scenarios for Corinth': http://www.brettschulte. net/rolfhall.htm.

Hall, Stuart (1980) 'Cultural Studies: Two Paradigms'. *Media Culture and Society*, 2, no. 1 (January): 57–72.

Hamilton, Cynthia S. (1999) 'Frederick Douglass and the Gender Politics of Reform', in Rice, Alan J. and Martin Crawford (eds) (1999) *Liberating Sojourn: Frederick Douglass and Transatlantic Reform*. Athens, GA: University of Georgia Press: 73–92.

Hamilton, Rich (2004) Webpage for Scenario Design Center: http://www. hist-sdc.com.

Hannah, Barry (1991) *Airships/Ray*. London: Vintage. First pub. 1978/1980.

Hardack, Richard (1999) 'The Slavery of Romanism: The Casting Out of the Irish in the Work of Frederick Douglass', in Rice, Alan J. and Martin Crawford (eds) (1999) *Liberating Sojourn: Frederick Douglass and Transatlantic Reform*. Athens, GA: University of Georgia Press: 115–40.

Harris, Joel Chandler (2000) *Uncle Remus: His Songs and Sayings*. Project Gutenberg etext: http://www.gutenberg.org/etext/2306. First pub. 1880.

Harris, Kenneth A. (2002) 'Flag on Capitol Grounds Torched', *The State* (Columbia, SC), 18 April, A1, A7.

Hart, James D. (1963) *The Popular Book: A History of America's Literary Taste*. Berkeley: University of California Press. First pub. 1950.

Hemingway, Ernest (1967) *By-Line: Selected Articles and Dispatches of Four Decades*, ed. William White. New York: Charles Scribner's Sons.

Hemingway, Ernest (1968) *The Fifth Column*. London: Jonathan Cape. First pub. 1939.

Hemingway, Ernest (1978) *For Whom the Bell Tolls*. London: Jonathan Cape. First pub. 1941.

Henson, Josiah (1849) *The Life of Josiah Henson, Formerly a Slave*. Boston: A. D. Phelps. University of North Carolina, 'Documenting the American South' etext: http://docsouth.unc.edu/neh/henson49/menu.html.

Henson, Josiah (1876) *Uncle Tom's Story of His Life: An Autobiography of the Rev. Josiah Henson (Mrs. Harriet Beecher Stowe's 'Uncle Tom')*. London: Christian Age Office. University of North Carolina, 'Documenting the American South' etext: http://docsouth.unc.edu/neh/henson/menu.html.

Hiatt, Mary P. (1993) *Style and the 'Scribbling Women': An Empirical Analysis of Nineteenth-Century American Fiction*. Westport, CT: Greenwood Press.

Hicks, Brian (2000) 'An Old Flag Raises New Passions as Southerners Fight Over Its Meaning', *Post and Courier* (Charleston, SC), 12 March, at http://www.charleston.net/pub/news/flag/dixie0312.htm.

Hicks, Brian (2000a) 'Echoes of Civil War, Civil Rights Past Linger in Alabama Capital', *Post and Courier* (Charleston, SC), 13 March, at http://www.charleston.net/pub/news/flag/flagtwo0313.htm.

Hirsch, Stephen A. (1978) 'Uncle Tomitudes: The Popular Response to *Uncle Tom's Cabin*', in Joel Myerson (ed.) (1978) *Studies in the American Renaissance*. Boston: Twayne: 303–30.

Hitt, Jack (2001) 'Blood and Sauce', *The State* (Columbia, SC), 30 August, D1, D5.

Holmes, Oliver Wendell (1863) 'Doings of the Sunbeam'. *Atlantic Monthly*, 7, no. 69 (July): 11–12.

Hook, Andrew (2004) 'Fugitives and Agrarians', in Gray, Richard and Owen Robinson (eds) (2004) *A Companion to the Literature and Culture of the American South*. Oxford: Blackwell: 420–35.

Horwitz, Tony (1998) *Confederates in the Attic: Dispatches from the Unfinished Civil War*. New York: Vintage Books.

Houghton Mifflin (2004) 'Information About Suntrust Bank v Houghton Mifflin Company' [concerning lawsuit over Alice Randall's *The Wind Done Gone*]: http://www.houghtonmifflinbooks.com/features/randall_url/.

Hughes, Langston (1977) *Langston Hughes in the Hispanic World*, ed. Edward J. Mullen. Hamden, CT: Archon Books.

Hughes, Langston (1996) *The Collected Poems of Langston Hughes*, ed. Arnold Rampersad and David Roessel. New York: Alfred A. Knopf.

Humez, Jean M. (2003) *Harriet Tubman: The Life and the Life Stories*. Madison, WI: University of Wisconsin Press.

Huston, John (1951) *The Red Badge of Courage*. Metro-Goldwyn-Mayer.

Hutcheon, Linda (2000) *A Theory of Parody: The Teachings of Twentieth-Century Art Forms*. Urbana: University of Illinois Press. First pub. 1985.

Ignatiev, Noel (1995) *How the Irish Became White*. London: Routledge.

Jackson, Nancy (1997) *Photographers: History and Culture through the Camera*. New York: Facts on File, Inc.

Jacobs, Harriet Ann ("Linda Brent") (1861) *Incidents in the Life of a Slave Girl*. Boston: Published for the Author. University of North Carolina, 'Documenting the American South' etext: http://docsouth.unc.edu/jacobs/jacobs.html.

Jacobson, Doranne (1996) *The Civil War in Art: A Visual Odyssey*. New York: Todri Book Publishers.

Jenkins, Henry and Kurt Squire (2002) 'The Art of Contested Spaces', in King, Lucien (ed.) (2002) *Game On: The History and Culture of Videogames*. London: Laurence King Publishing, Ltd: 64–75.

Jones, Alfred Haworth (1974) *Roosevelt's Image Brokers: Poets, Playwrights, and the Use of the Lincoln Symbol*. Port Washington, NY: National University Publications/Kennikat Press.

Joyner, Charles (1996) 'African and European Roots of Southern Culture: The "Central Theme" Revisited', in King, Richard and Helen Taylor (eds) (1996) *Dixie Debates: Perspectives on Southern Cultures*. London: Pluto Press: 12–30.

Kantor, MacKinlay (2001) *If the South Had Won the Civil War*. New York: Forge Books. First pub. 1960.

Keckley, Elizabeth (1868) *Behind the Scenes, Or, Thirty Years a Slave, and Four Years in the White House*. New York: G. W. Carleton and Co. University of North Carolina, 'Documenting the American South' etext: http://docsouth.unc.edu/keckley/menu.html.

Kennedy, James Ronald and Walter Donald Kennedy (2001) *The South Was Right!* Gretna, LA: Pelican Publishing. First pub. 1991.

Kennedy, John Pendleton (1986) *Swallow Barn; or, a Sojourn in the Old Dominion*. Baton Rouge: Louisiana State University Press. First pub. 1832.

King, Benjamin (1990) *A Bullet for Stonewall: A Novel*. Gretna, LA: Pelican Publishing.

King, Ed, et al. (1997) 'Sweet Home Alabama', on Lynyrd Skynyrd, *Second Helping*. (audio CD). First released 1974.

King, Martin Luther (1990) *A Testament of Hope: The Essential Writings and Speeches of Martin Luther King, Jr*, ed. James M. Washington. New York: HarperCollins.

King, Richard (1980) *A Southern Renaissance: The Cultural Awakening of the American South, 1930–1955*. New York: Oxford University Press.

Kipling, Rudyard (1902) *Just So Stories*. Project Gutenberg etext: http://www.gutenberg.org/etext/2781.

Kirby, Jack Temple (1978) *Media-Made Dixie: The South in the American Imagination*. Baton Rouge: Louisiana State University Press.

Klement, Frank L. (1999) *Lincoln's Critics: The Copperheads of the North*. Shippensburg, PA: White Mane Books.

Knight, Lucian Lamar (1923) *Stone Mountain: or the Lay of the Gray Minstrel*. Atlanta: Johnson-Dallis Co.

Lang, Robert (1994) '*The Birth of a Nation:* History, Ideology, Narrative Form', in Lang, Robert (ed.) (1994) *The Birth of a Nation*. New Brunswick, NJ: Rutgers University Press: 3–24.

LCW (2004) Webpage for Alberta Martin, the 'Last Confederate Widow'. http://www.lastconfederatewidow.com.

League of the South (1998) 'The Death of Michael Westerman'. DixieNet homepage: http://www.dixienet.org/spatriot/vol2no1/westrman.html.

League of the South (2004) *The Grey Book: Blueprint for Southern Independence*. College Station, TX: Traveller Press.

League of the South (2004a) Official homepage: http://www.dixienet.org.

Lederman, Douglas (2001) 'Old Times Not Forgotten: A Battle Over Symbols', in Eitzen, D. Stanley (2001) *Sport in Contemporary Society*. New York: Worth Publishers: 109–33. First pub. 1993.

Lee, Ang (dir.) (1999) *Ride with the Devil*. Universal Studios.

Leonard, Elizabeth D. (2001) *All the Daring of a Soldier: Women of the Civil War Armies*. New York: Penguin. First pub. 1999.

Lewis, Lloyd (1941) *Myths After Lincoln*. New York: Readers Club. First pub. 1929.

Library of Congress (2005) *Bill Mauldin: Beyond Willie and Joe: An Online Tribute Drawn from the Collections of the Library of Congress*: http://www.loc.gov/rr/print/swann/maudlin.

Lieberman, Jethro K. (1987) *The Enduring Constitution*. New York: Harper and Row.

Litwack, Leon F. (1961) *North of Slavery: The Negro in the Free States, 1790–1860*. Chicago: University of Chicago Press.

Litwack, Leon F. (1995) '*The Birth of a Nation*', in Carnes, Mark C., et al. (eds) (1995) *Past Imperfect: History According to the Movies*. New York: Henry Holt and Co.: 136–41.

Litwack, Leon F. (1996) 'Telling the Story: The Historian, the Filmmaker, and the Civil War', in Toplin, Robert Brent (ed.) (1996) *Ken Burns's* The Civil War*: Historians Respond*. New York: Oxford University Press: 119–40.

Logan, Joshua (dir.) (1956) *Bus Stop*. Twentieth-Century Fox.

Lorant, Stefan (1969). *Lincoln: A Picture Story of His Life*. New York: Bonanza Books.

Lott, Eric (1993) *Love and Theft: Blackface Minstrelsy and the American Working Class*. New York: Oxford University Press.

Malone, Bill C. (1979) *Southern Music, American Music*. Lexington: University Press of Kentucky.

Marcus, Greil (1991) *Mystery Train: Images of America in Rock 'n' Roll Music*. London: Penguin. First pub. 1975.

Marius, Richard (ed.) (1994) *The Columbia Book of Civil War Poetry*. New York: Columbia University Press.

Marx, Karl and Frederick Engels (1984) *Collected Works*, Vol. 19. London: Lawrence and Wishart.

Marx, Karl and Frederick Engels (1985) *Collected Works*, Vol. 20. London: Lawrence and Wishart.

Massey, Mary Elizabeth (1994) *Women in the Civil War*. Lincoln, NE: University of Nebraska Press. First pub. 1966 as *Bonnet Brigades: American Women and the Civil War*.

Maxwell, Ronald F. (dir.) (1993) *Gettysburg*. Warner Brothers/Turner Pictures.

Maxwell, Ronald F. (dir.) (2003) *Gods and Generals*. Warner Brothers/Turner Pictures.

May, Lary (1983) *Screening Out the Past: The Birth of Mass Culture and the Motion Picture Industry*. Chicago: University of Chicago Press. First pub. 1980.

McCutcheon, John (2003) 'The Abraham Lincoln Brigade' on Joe Weed and Heather Rose Bridger (prod.) (2003) *Spain in My Heart: Songs of the Spanish Civil War* (audio CD). Appleseed Recordings.

McElwee, Ross (dir.) (1991) *Sherman's March*. First Run Features.

McMillan, Ann (1999) *Angel Trumpet*. New York: Viking Penguin.

McMillan, Ann (1998) *Dead March*. New York: Viking Penguin.

McMillan, Ann (2001) *Civil Blood*. New York: Viking Penguin.

McMillan, Ann (2003) *Chickahominy Fever*. New York: Viking Penguin

McPherson, James M. (1988) *Battle Cry of Freedom: The Civil War Era*. New York: Oxford University Press.

McWhiney, Grady (1988) *Cracker Culture: Celtic Ways in the Old South*. Tuscaloosa: University of Alabama Press.

Melville, Herman (1984) *Pierre, Israel Potter, The Confidence-Man, Tales, and Billy Budd*. New York: Literary Classics of the United States, Inc.

Melville, Herman (2000) *Battle Pieces: The Civil War Poems of Herman Melville*. Edison, NJ: Castle Books. First pub. 1866. Accessible as a Project Gutenberg etext: http://www.gutenberg.org/etext/12384.

Meredith, Roy (1951) *Mr. Lincoln's Contemporaries: An Album of Portraits by Mathew B. Brady*. New York: Charles Scribner's Sons.

Meredith, Roy (1976) *The World of Mathew Brady*. Los Angeles: Brooke House Publishers. First pub. 1970.

Meyer, George (1991) 'Mr Lisa Goes to Washington'. *The Simpsons*. Fox Television. First aired 26 September.

Middleton, Lee (1993) *Hearts of Fire: Soldier Women of the Civil War*. Coolville, OH: Alberta Taylor Civil War Books.

Miller, Kirby (1985) *Emigrants and Exiles: Ireland and the Irish Exodus to North America*. New York: Oxford University Press.

Minghella, Anthony (dir.) (2003) *Cold Mountain*. Miramax Films.

Mitchell, Margaret (1993) *Gone with the Wind*. New York: Warner Books. First pub. 1936.

Moore, Madeline (1862) *The Lady Lieutenant*. Philadelphia: Barclay. University of Indiana 'Wright American Fiction' etext: http://www.letrs.indiana.edu/cgi/t/text/text-idx?c=wright2;idno=wright2–1499.

Morris, Errol (2003) *The Fog of War: Eleven Lessons of Robert S. McNamara*. Sony Pictures Classics.

Morris, Jan (1999) *Lincoln: A Foreigner's Quest*. London: Viking.

Morrison, Toni (1988) *Beloved*. London: Picador. First pub. 1987.

Morse, Minna (1999) 'The Changing Face of Stone Mountain'. *Smithsonian*, 29, no. 10 (January): 56–69.

Murray, Mary (1994) *The Law of the Father: Feminism and Patriarchy*. London: Routledge.

Neely, Mark E., Jr (1995) 'The Young Lincoln: Two Films', in Carnes, Mark C., et al. (eds) (1995) *Past Imperfect: History According to the Movies*. New York: Henry Holt and Co.: 124–7.

Newbury, Mickey (1971) 'An American Trilogy', on Elvis Presley, *Elvis as Recorded at Madison Square Garden* (1992) (audio CD). First released 1972.

Newman, Kim (1990) *Wild West Movies*. London: Bloomsbury.

Nolan, Alan T. (1998) 'Considering *Lee Considered*: Robert E. Lee and the Lost Cause', in Simon, John Y. and Michael E. Stevens (eds) (1998) *New Perspectives on the Civil War*. Madison, WI: Madison House: 25–48.

Nora, Pierre (ed.) (1999) *Rethinking France: Les Lieux de Mémoire, Volume I: The State*. Translated by Mary Seidman Trouille, et al. Chicago: University of Chicago Press. First pub. 1984.

Northup, Solomon (1853) *Twelve Years a Slave*. Auburn, NY: Derby and Miller. University of North Carolina, 'Documenting the American South' etext: http://docsouth.unc.edu/northup/northup.html.

O'Brien, Michael (2004) *Conjectures of Order: Intellectual Life and the American South*. 2 vols. Chapel Hill: University of North Carolina Press.

Otis, Eliza A. W. (2001) *Architects of Our Fortunes: The Journal of Eliza A. W. Otis, 1860–1863, with Letter and Civil War Journal of Harrison Gray Otis*, ed. Ann Gorman Condon. San Marino, CA: Huntington Library Press.

Page, John W. (1853) *Uncle Robin, in His Cabin in Virginia, and Tom without One in Boston*. Richmond, VA: John W. Randolph. University of Virginia, American Studies hypertext: http://etext.lib.virginia.edu/toc/modeng/public/PagUncl.html.

Painter, Nell Irvin (1997) *Sojourner Truth: A Life, A Symbol*. New York: W. W. Norton.

Parks, Suzan-Lori (1995) *The America Play and Other Works*. New York: Theatre Communications Group.

Parks, Suzan-Lori (2002) *Topdog/Underdog*. New York: Theatre Communications Group.

Pattee, Fred L. (1940) *The Feminine Fifties*. New York: Appleton-Century Co.

Paulding, James Kirke (2004) *The Puritan and His Daughter*. Milton Keynes: Lightning Source UK, Ltd. First pub. 1849.

Paulding, James Kirke (2004a) *Westward Ho!* Milton Keynes: Lightning Source UK, Ltd. First pub. 1832.

Pearce, Celia (2002) 'Story as Play Space: Narrative in Games', in King, Lucien (ed.) (2002) *Game On: The History and Culture of Videogames*. London: Laurence King Publishing, Ltd: 112–19.

Pearce, Diana (1978) 'The Feminization of Poverty: Women, Work and Welfare'. *Urban and Social Change Review*, 11: 28–36.

Pesce, Mark (2002) 'Head Games: The Future of Play', in King, Lucien (ed.) (2002) *Game On: The History and Culture of Videogames*. London: Laurence King Publishing, Ltd: 130–7.

Peterson, Merrill D. (1994) *Lincoln in American Memory*. New York: Oxford University Press.

Pettinger, Alasdair (1999) 'Send Back the Money: Douglass and the Free Church of Scotland', in Rice, Alan J. and Martin Crawford (eds) (1999) *Liberating Sojourn: Frederick Douglass and Transatlantic Reform*. Athens, GA: University of Georgia Press: 31–55.

Phillips, Donald T. (1993) *Lincoln on Leadership: Executive Strategies for Tough Times*. New York: Warner Books.

Pickard, Kate E. R. (1856) *The Kidnapped and the Ransomed. Being the Personal Recollections of Peter Still and His Wife 'Vina', After Forty Years of Slavery*. Syracuse, NY: William T. Hamilton. University of North Carolina, 'Documenting the American South' etext: http://docsouth.unc.edu/pickard/pickard.html.

Poe, Edgar Allan (1993) *Tales of Mystery and Imagination*. London: Everyman/J. M. Dent.

Pratt, Linda Ray (1979) 'Elvis, or the Ironies of a Southern Identity', in Tharpe, Jac L. (ed.) (1979) *Elvis: Images and Fancies*. Jackson: University Press of Mississippi: 40–51.

Railton, Stephen (2004) '*Uncle Tom's Cabin* and American Culture: A Multi-Media Archive'. University of Virginia, Institute for Advanced Technology in the Humanities: http://iath.virginia.edu/utc.

Randall, Alice (2001) *The Wind Done Gone*. New York: Houghton Mifflin.

Randolph, Sarah Nicholas (1876) *The Life of General Thomas J. Jackson*. Philadelphia: J. B. Lippincott and Co.

Ray, Frederic E. (1994) 'The Photographers of the War', in Davis, William C. and Bell I. Wiley (eds) (1994) *The Photographic History of the Civil War*. 2 vols. New York: Black Dog and Leventhal Publishers. Vol. I: 409–60.

Reed, Ishmael (1998) *Flight to Canada*. New York. Scribner/Simon and Schuster. First pub. 1976.

Rhodes, Jane (1998) *Mary Ann Shadd Cary: The Black Press and Protest in the Nineteenth Century*. Bloomington: Indiana University Press.

Rice, Alan J. and Martin Crawford (eds) (1999) *Liberating Sojourn: Frederick Douglass and Transatlantic Reform*. Athens, GA: University of Georgia Press.

Richards, Jeffrey H. (ed.) (1997) *Early American Drama*. London: Penguin.

Roberts, Andrew (1999) *Salisbury: Victorian Titan*. London: Phoenix.

Roberts, Diane (1996) 'Living Southern in *Southern Living*', in King, Richard and Helen Taylor (eds) (1996) *Dixie Debates: Perspectives on Southern Cultures*. London: Pluto Press: 85–98.

Robertson, James I., Jr (1997) *Stonewall Jackson: The Man, the Soldier, the Legend*. New York: Macmillan.

Robertson, James I., Jr (1998) 'Stonewall Jackson: A "Pious, Blue-Eyed Killer?"', in Simon, John Y. and Michael E. Stevens (eds) (1998) *New Perspectives on the Civil War*. Madison, WI: Madison House: 69–92.

Robertson, Robbie (1969) 'The Night They Drove Old Dixie Down', on The Band, *The Band*. Capitol Records.

Ross, Lillian (1952) *Picture*. London: Non-Fiction Book Club.

Rosten, Norman (1940) *Return Again, Traveler*. New Haven: Yale University Press.

Rourke, Constance (1931) *American Humor: A Study of the National Character*. New York: Harcourt, Brace and World.

Russwurm, John and Samuel Cornish (1827) 'To Our Patrons', *Freedom's Journal*. 16 March, 1. Online version at Wisconsin Historical Society: http://www. wisconsinhistory.org/libraryarchives/aanp/freedom/.

Sacks, Howard L. and Judith Rose Sacks (1993) *Way Up North in Dixie: A Black Family's Claim to the Confederate Anthem*. Washington, DC: Smithsonian Institution Press.

Sandburg, Carl (1982) *Abraham Lincoln: The Prairie Years and the War Years*. New York: Harvest/Harcourt. First pub. 1926 and 1939.

Sawyer, David Jonathan (1995) *My Great-Grandfather Was Stonewall Jackson: The Story of a Negro Boy Growing Up in the Segregated South*. Baltimore: Jonathan Publishing Co.

Schulte, Brett (2002) Interview with *Campaign Corinth* games designer Drew Wagenhoffer. 28 November. ACWCDC webpage: http://www.brettschulte. net/drewwagenhoffer.htm.

Schulte, Brett (2004) Webpage for the American Civil War Campaigns Design Center (ACWCDC). http://www.brettschulte.net/hps_acw.htm.

Schulte, Brett (2004a) Interview with *Campaign Gettysburg* games designer Doug Strickler. 3 August. ACWCDC webpage: http://www.brettschulte.net/ dougstrickler.htm

Scorsese, Martin (dir.) (2002) *Gangs of New York*. Hollywood: Miramax Films.

Scott, Anne Firor (1970) *The Southern Lady: From Pedestal to Politics, 1830–1930*. Chicago: University of Chicago Press.

SCV (2004) Sons of Confederate Veterans homepage: http://www.scv.org/.

Sejour, Victor (2000) *The Fortune-Teller*. Translated by Norman R. Shapiro. Urbana: University of Illinois Press. First pub. in French, 1859.

Sejour, Victor (2000a) *The Jew of Seville*. Translated by Norman R. Shapiro. Urbana: University of Illinois Press. First pub. in French, 1944.

Shaara, Jeff (2002) *Gods and Generals*. New York: Ballantine Books. First pub. 1996.

Shaara, Michael (1996) *The Killer Angels*. New York: Ballantine Books. First pub. 1974.

Sherman, David (2004) Rebel Yell brand website, David Sherman Corporation: http://www.rebelyellwhiskey.com/reflect/heritage.html.

Sherwood, Robert E. (1966) *Abe Lincoln in Illinois*. New York: Dramatists Play Service. First performed 1938.

Silber, Nina (1992) 'Intemperate Men, Spiteful Women, and Jefferson Davis', in Clinton, Catherine and Nina Silber (eds) (1992) *Divided Houses: Gender and the Civil War*. New York: Oxford University Press: 283–305.

Silber, Nina (1993) *The Romance of Reunion: Northerners and the South, 1865–1900*. Chapel Hill: University of North Carolina Press.

Silverman, Joan L. (1981) '*The Birth of a Nation*: Prohibition Propaganda'. *Southern Quarterly*, 19 (Spring–Summer): 23–30.

Simmons, Russ (2004) 'Kevin Willmott: The Sundance Kid'. *eKC Online* (February), at http://www.kcactive.com.

Smith, Mark M. (2001) *Listening to Nineteenth-Century America*. Chapel Hill: University of North Carolina Press.

Snead, J. A. (1988) 'Images of Blacks in Black Independent Films: A Brief Survey', in Cham, M. and C. Andrade-Watkins (eds) (1988) *Blackframes: Critical Perspectives on Black Independent Cinema*. Cambridge, MA: MIT Press: 16–25.

Sondheim, Stephen and John Weidman (1991) *Assassins*. New York: Theatre Communications Group.

Stanton, Elizabeth Cady, et al. (eds) (1881–1922) *History of Woman Suffrage*. 6 vols. Rochester, NY: Fowler and Wells.

Starling, Marion Wilson (1988) *The Slave Narrative: Its Place in American History*. Washington, DC: Howard University Press. First pub. 1981.

Steinem, Gloria (1987) *Marilyn*. London: Victor Gollancz, Ltd.

Stewart, John L. (1965) *The Burden of Time: The Fugitives and Agrarians*. Princeton: Princeton University Press.

Stone, Oliver (dir.) (1995) *Nixon*. Entertainment/Illusion/Cynergi.

Stoneley, Peter (2004) 'Mark Twain', in Gray, Richard and Owen Robinson (eds) (2004) *A Companion to the Literature and Culture of the American South.* Oxford: Blackwell: 388–402.

Stott, William (1973) *Documentary Expression and Thirties America.* New York: Oxford University Press.

Stowe, Harriet Beecher (1852) *Uncle Tom's Cabin; or, Life among the Lowly.* Boston: John P. Jewett and Co. University of Virginia, American Studies hypertext: http://etext.lib.virginia.edu/toc/modeng/public/StoCabi.html.

Stowe, Harriet Beecher (1853) *The Key to Uncle Tom's Cabin.* London: Clarke, Beeton and Co. University of Virginia, American Studies hypertext: http://etext.lib.virginia.edu/toc/modeng/public/StoKeyu.html.

Taliaferro, John (2002) *Great White Fathers: The Story of the Obsessive Quest to Create Mount Rushmore.* New York: PublicAffairs.

Tanner, Robert G. (1994) 'Jackson in the Shenandoah', in Davis, William C. and Bell I. Wiley (eds) *The Photographic History of the Civil War*, Vol. 1. New York: Black Dog and Leventhal Publishers: 772–97.

Tate, Allen (1928) *Stonewall Jackson: The Good Soldier.* New York: Minton, Balch and Co.

Tate, Allen (1936) 'To the Lacedemonians', in Tate, Allen (1989) *Collected Poems, 1919–1976.* Baton Rouge: Louisiana State University Press: 85–8.

Taylor, Helen (1989) *Scarlett's Women: Gone with the Wind and Its Female Fans.* London: Virago.

Taylor, Helen (2001) *Circling Dixie: Contemporary Southern Culture through a Transatlantic Lens.* New Brunswick, NJ: Rutgers University Press.

Taylor, William R. (1963) *Cavalier and Yankee: The Old South and American National Character.* London: W. H. Allen. First pub. 1961.

Templeton, [Maria] Alazar (1984) 'John Ericsson Day in Sweden'. *Cheesebox,* 3:1 (June), 9.

Thomas, Christopher A. (2002) *The Lincoln Memorial and American Life.* Princeton: Princeton University Press.

Thomsen, Brian and Martin H. Greenberg (eds) (2002) *Alternate Gettysburgs.* New York: Berkeley Books.

Thoreau, Henry David (1860) 'After the Death of John Brown', in James Redpath (ed.), *Echoes of Harper's Ferry.* Boston: Thayer and Eldridge: 439–55. Thoreau Institute, Walden Woods Project etext: http://www.walden.org/Institute/thoreau/writings/essays/After%20the%20death%0of%20John%20Brown.htm.

Thoreau, Henry David (1860a) 'A Plea for Captain John Brown', in James Redpath (ed.), *Echoes of Harper's Ferry.* Boston: Thayer and Eldridge: 17–42. Thoreau Institute, Walden Woods Project etext: http://www.walden.org/Institute/thoreau/writings/essays/Plea.htm.

Tisa, John (1985) *Recalling the Good Fight: An Autobiography of the Spanish Civil War.* South Hadley, MA: Bergin and Garvey Publishers.

Toll, Robert C. (1974) *Blacking Up: The Minstrel Show in Nineteenth-Century America*. New York: Oxford University Press.

Toplin, Robert Brent (ed.) (1996) *Ken Burns's* The Civil War*: Historians Respond*. New York: Oxford University Press.

Townsend, Charles (1996) 'Negro Minstrels', in Bean, Annmarie, et al. (eds) (1996) *Inside the Minstrel Mask: Readings in Nineteenth-Century Blackface Minstrelsy*. Hanover, NH: Wesleyan University Press: 121–5.

Trachtenberg, Alan (1989) *Reading American Photographs: Images as History, Mathew Brady to Walker Evans*. New York: Hill and Wang.

Tratner, Michael (2003) 'Movies and Mass Politics'. *Criticism*, 45: 1 (Winter), 53–73.

Trollope, Frances (1949) *Domestic Manners of the Americans*. New York: Alfred A. Knopf. First pub. 1832.

Tucker, George (1970) *The Valley of the Shenandoah, or the Memoirs of the Graysons*. Chapel Hill: University of North Carolina Press. First pub. 1824.

Tucker, Nathaniel Beverley (1836) *George Balcombe*. 2 vols. New York: Harper and Brothers.

Tucker, Nathaniel Beverley (1971) *The Partisan Leader*. Chapel Hill: University of North Carolina Press. First pub. 1836.

Turner, Darwin T. (1981) 'Daddy Joel Harris and His Old-Time Darkies', in Bickley, R. Bruce, Jr (1981) *Critical Essays on Joel Chandler Harris*. Boston: G. K. Hall and Co.: 112–30.

Turtledove, Harry (1993) *The Guns of the South*. New York: Ballantine Books. First pub. 1992.

Turtledove, Harry (2001) 'Introduction', in Kantor, Mackinlay (2001) *If the South Had Won the Civil War*. New York: Forge Books: 5–10.

Twain, Mark (1883) *Life on the Mississippi*. Boston: James R. Osgood and Co. University of North Carolina, 'Documenting the American South' etext: http://docsouth.unc.edu/twainlife/twain.html.

'Twelve Southerners' (1977) *I'll Take My Stand: The South and the Agrarian Tradition*. Baton Rouge: Louisiana State University Press. First pub. 1930.

UDC (2004) United Daughters of the Confederacy. Official homepage: http://www.hqudc.org/.

United States War Department (1880–1901) *The War of the Rebellion: A Compilation of the Official Records of the Union and Confederate Armies*. Washington, DC: Government Printing Office. Cornell University 'Making of America' etext: http://cdl.library.cornell.edu/moa/browse.monographs/waro.html.

Van Henten, Jan Willem (2002) *Martyrdom and Noble Death*. London: Routledge.

Velazquez, Loreta Janeta (2003) *The Woman in Battle: The Civil War Narrative of Loreta Velazquez, Cuban Woman and Confederate Soldier*. Madison: University of Wisconsin Press. First pub. 1876.

Vidal, Gore (1984) *Lincoln: A Novel*. New York: Ballantine Books.

Vonnegut, Kurt (1997) *Timequake*. London: Jonathan Cape.

Walker, David (1830) *An Appeal in Four Articles*. Boston: David Walker. University of North Carolina, 'Documenting the American South' etext: http://docsouth.unc.edu/nc/walker/walker.html.

Walker, Kara (1998) 'The Debate Continues: Kara Walker's Response'. *International Review of African-American Art*, 15, no. 2: 44–50.

Walton, John K. (2004) 'The Transatlantic Seaside from the 1880s to the 1930s', in Campbell, Neil, Jude Davies and George McKay (eds) (2004) *Issues in Americanisation and Culture*. Edinburgh: Edinburgh University Press: 111–25.

Warren, Charles Marquis (dir.) (1954) *Seven Angry Men*. Allied Artists.

Warren, Robert Penn (1929) *John Brown: The Making of a Martyr*. New York: Payson and Clarke, Ltd.

Washington, Booker T. (1901) *Up from Slavery: An Autobiography*. Garden City, NY: Doubleday and Co. University of North Carolina, 'Documenting the American South' etext: http://docsouth.unc.edu/washington/washing.html.

Watson, J. R. and Timothy Dudley-Smith (eds) (2002) *An Annotated Anthology of Hymns*. Oxford: Oxford University Press.

Wells, H. G. (2004) *Little Wars*. Project Gutenberg etext: http://onlinebooks.library.upenn.edu/webbin/gutbook/lookup?num=3691. First pub. 1913.

Wells, Paul (1996) 'The Last Rebel: Southern Rock and Nostalgic Continuities', in King, Richard and Helen Taylor (eds) (1996) *Dixie Debates: Perspectives on Southern Cultures*. London: Pluto Press: 115–29.

Welter, Barbara (1966) 'The Cult of True Womanhood: 1820–1860'. *American Quarterly*, 18: 151–74.

Wetherby, W. J. (1989) *Conversations with Marilyn*. London: Sphere. First pub. 1976.

Williams, Frank J. (1994) 'Lincolniana in 1993'. *Journal of the Abraham Lincoln Association*, vol. 15, no. 2 (Summer): 45–92. Online version at: http://jala.press.uiuc.edu/15.2/williams.html.

Williams, Hank Jr (1990) 'If the South Woulda Won', on Hank Williams Jr, *Wild Streak* (audio CD). First released 1988.

Williamson, Mrs Mary L. (1899) *The Life of Thomas J. Jackson ('Stonewall'), In Easy Words for the Young*. Richmond, VA: B. F. Johnson Publishing Co.

Willmott, Kevin (dir.) (2003) *CSA: The Confederate States of America*. Hodcarrier Films.

Wills, Garry (1992) *Lincoln at Gettysburg: The Words that Remade America*. New York: Touchstone.

Wilson, Edmund (1966) *Patriotic Gore: Studies in the Literature of the American Civil War*. New York: Oxford University Press. First pub. 1962.

Wilson, Harriet (1859) *Our Nig; Or, Sketches from the Life of a Free Black*. Boston: George C. Rand and Avery. University of Virginia, hypertext: http://etext.virginia.edu/toc/modeng/public/WilOurn.html.

Wolf, Mark J. P. (2001) 'Narrative in the Video Game', in Wolf, Mark J. P. (ed.) (2001) *The Medium of the Video Game*. Austin: University of Texas Press: 103–09.

Wolff, Milton (2001) *Another Hill: An Autobiographical Novel*. Urbana: University of Illinois Press. First pub. 1994.

Wood, Marcus (2000) *Blind Memory: Visual Representations of Slavery in England and America, 1780–1865*. Manchester: Manchester University Press.

Woodward, C. Vann (ed.) (1981) *Mary Chesnut's Civil War*. New Haven: Yale University Press.

Woodward, C. Vann and Elisabeth Muhlenfeld (eds) (1984) *The Private Mary Chesnut: The Unpublished Civil War Diaries*. New York: Oxford University Press.

Woodward, C. Vann (1996) 'Help from Historians', in Toplin, Robert Brent (ed.) (1996) *Ken Burns's* The Civil War: *Historians Respond*. New York: Oxford University Press: 3–16.

Young, Elizabeth (1999) *Disarming the Nation: Women's Writing and the American Civil War*. Chicago: University of Chicago Press.

Young, Neil (1990) 'Southern Man', on Neil Young, *After the Gold Rush* (audio CD). First released 1970.

Zeller, Bob (1997) *The Civil War in Depth: History in 3–D*. San Francisco: Chronicle Books.

Zwick, Edward (dir.) (1989) *Glory*. Columbia TriStar Pictures.

Zwick, Jim (2005) 'Abraham Lincoln in Political Cartoons', in Zwick, Jim (ed.), *Political Cartoons and Cartoonists*. Online version at: http://www.boondocksnet.com/gallery/cartoons/cw/index_abe.html.

Index

Page numbers in **bold** type indicate illustrations.

The British Association for American Studies (BAAS)

The British Association for American Studies was founded in 1955 to promote the study of the United States of America. It welcomes applications for membership from anyone interested in the history, society, government and politics, economics, geography, literature, creative arts, culture and thought of the USA.

The Association publishes a newsletter twice yearly, holds an annual national conference, supports regional branches and provides other membership services, including preferential subscription rates to the *Journal of American Studies*.

Membership enquiries may be addressed to the BAAS Secretary. For contact details visit our website: www.baas.ac.uk.